20/20: A Clear Vision for America

Bill Muckler

DEDICATION

I respectfully dedicate "20/20" to the Founding Fathers of this great republic of the United States of America, and to all who have defended it with honor, especially those who gave all. — Bill Muckler

CHAPTERS

CHARACTERS

Process Director: Tom Rostal
Senior Consultants: Genie Moore, Ron Shock, Dave West

Cover and Art By: Vlad Gheneli
© Copyright 2014 by Paradigm Publishing LLC
ISBN Number: 978-0-9964724-0-1

PREFACE

In reading "20/20," the reader feels a call to action. Each of us should adopt the enthusiasm of the Vision of these four colleagues. What an America we could have again if we would begin to change or restore the pillars of our nation.

Before action, however, we need reflection. Here is what our United States of America could be, what it should be. The contents of this book contain the sovereign nation that Jefferson and Madison envisaged. "20/20" becomes the appropriate name for this work.

If only every high school senior were to read and reflect on these ideas as he or she prepared for their solemn responsibility of casting ballots to determine the future course of our nation.

"The founding fathers were not only brilliant; they were system builders and systematic thinkers. They came up with comprehensive plans and visions."
— Ron Chernow, American writer, journalist, historian, and biographer.

INTRODUCTION

The United States is at a crisis point. Dysfunction in Washington is rampant. The economy is crumbling. The country is on the wrong course. Solutions are scarce and appear unwanted by politicians.

This book, "20/20: A Clear Vision for America" brings rock-solid solutions to make our nation prosperous again, explains how to reinstate our Constitution, and how to give our children and grandchildren a bright future.

The "20/20" book tells what is wrong with modern America. It guides us down a path that few tread, to reveal how this great nation lost its way, and then provides practical, "Founding Father" solutions to problems that our dysfunctional federal government has imposed on "We the People."

Twenty chapters explore each issue in depth and then provide sound solutions to prove how a small and limited federal government can balance the budget while it pays down the national debt.

For example, the "20/20" Plan identifies the value of eliminating more than one hundred burdensome taxes, explores the gains realized when all Americans contribute to the economy. It shows that productivity gains from substantive job training and real jobs for all, and demonstrates the benefit of educational vouchers for all children including home schooling.

This book radiates the optimism of take-home pay increased by as much as 40 percent and the joy of higher wages that eliminate poverty. The pioneering spirit of the people is rejuvenated by the revival of the space program. The nation is electrified with a common purpose in a period of new exploration.

The "20/20" Plan creates a safe, secure nation. The military is sustained and strengthened. Armed forces personnel receive a 20 percent increase in pay and benefits. The Veterans Administration is streamlined and accessible.

The United States resigns from the United Nations and establishes a new organization free of corruption, built on the ideals of freedom. Foreign aid is eliminated and countries calling for help receive training and tools instead of dollars.

> Social Security recipients receive a 20 percent tax-free increase of up to $4,000 per year.
>
> Health care is privatized and affordable to all.
>
> Locked-down borders restore the lawful immigration process.
>
> The United States becomes energy independent.
>
> Confidence in Internet freedom is restored.
>
> Domestic spying is abolished.
>
> Current illicit drugs are re-legalized and subject to taxation.
>
> Non-violent prisoners are paroled and enrolled in established work programs.
>
> Civility is restored.
>
> Political Correctness is revoked.
>
> Term limits are imposed on Congress.
>
> The States affirm their rightful jurisdiction and authority.

The "20/20" Plan is the escape plan for all Americans; the escape from oppressive government tyranny. It makes the United States a unified nation. It urges citizens to learn the importance of love and respect for country, their Constitution and one another.

The "20/20" Plan teaches all citizens how critical each individual is to the success of this nation, and how vitally important it is to preserve a strong United States.

Where We Are

"Society in every state is a blessing, but government even in its best state is but a necessary evil; in its worst state an intolerable one; for when we suffer, or are exposed to the same miseries by a government, which we might expect in a country without government, our calamity is heightened by reflecting that we furnish the means by which we suffer..."

— Thomas Paine, Common Sense

The setting is a large industrial plant that has entered into a contract with a consulting firm specializing in the assessment and analysis of business operations in all types of businesses and organizations. The consultants develop and design substantial improvement solutions utilizing proven principles and techniques to train management and supervision. They implement those solutions in the structure of results oriented work management processes.

They have successfully implemented work management processes employing principles and techniques such as Cost-Benefit Analysis, Root Cause Analysis, Base Data Statistical Analysis and other processes along with good, plain, common sense. Their new assignment is to design and implement a work management process.

The project schedule is for one year. The four person consulting team typically travels and meets at the nearest airport in the client's area on Sunday, spends the entire week living in a hotel, driving a rental car to the client's facility daily, and then traveling home on Friday afternoon to see the family, run errands, take care of the home and refresh. The time is late Tuesday afternoon. The team has just wrapped up the work activities of a long day.

TUESDAY AFTERNOON. WEEK 1.

The team was sitting in a small conference room the plant manager had arranged for their use for the duration of their project. It serves as the consultants' office and temporary headquarters. The consultants commandeered a large, wooden table, crisscrossed with power cables and covered in papers and reports with laptops arranged around the table.

"You guys about ready to go?" Tom Rostal asked the team from the head of the table.

"What time is it?" Dave West inquired from Tom's left. "Ten after five," replied Genie Moore from the other end of the conference room table. "I can be ready at five thirty. Got a few loose ends to wrap up," said Ron Shock from Tom's right.

"Okay. Let's finish everything and leave at 5:30. Be sure all of our materials are put away and the table is clear," Tom Rostal said coolly. "That should get us back to our hotel around 6 o'clock." Tom is the leader of the team and has been a consultant for over 30 years. He has prior management and supervisory experience and his wisdom and wide-ranging knowledge is well respected. His expertise is directing the implementation of work management processes and operating systems for all types of public and private institutions.

The team members recognize Tom as a true leader and professional. The other three consultants possess varying amounts and types of experience. They have worked together on numerous assignments and have developed a sense of mutual respect and camaraderie. The four consulting team members left their makeshift office located in their client's facility and started for the parking lot.

It was the first week of April and the sun was shining low in the west. Dave opened the trunk with the remote as they approached their rental car. Everyone put their laptops and briefcases in the trunk. Tom asked, "Dave, are you driving?"

"Sure," said Dave as Tom got in the front seat. The Process Director always exercised his right to ride shotgun. As the others got in Tom asked, "is anyone having problems they would like to discuss?"

As they pulled out of the parking lot Genie replied, "my area is on schedule. I'm receiving good cooperation from all the supervisors and staff. The Implementation Action Team is having a very difficult time thinking outside the box. They are just too used to things the way they have always been. They do not fully understand the concept of paradigm paralysis, and they have not developed a true sense of urgency. They haven't realized there can be a better work life ahead of them."

Paradigm
par•a•digm: a theory or a group of ideas about how something should be done, made, or thought about

"That's typical," Tom replied. "Our client has a long history of success. Most of the folks working here equate that with doing a good job. They have been doing things the same way for so long they have convinced themselves 'their way is the only way.' It prevents them from thinking outside of the box. They never had to consider there might be another way, or a better way, to manage their resources. We've been blessed with the opportunity to experience many diverse work environments. We attend many work management process conferences and seminars and we watch many training films including the pitfalls of paradigm paralysis and the positive results of busting paradigms.

"The greatest barrier to a paradigm shift is the reality of paradigm paralysis; the inability or refusal to see beyond current models of thinking. This is the difficulty of thinking outside the box, the belief that contrasting solutions will make things better. Historic examples include rejection of the quartz clock, Galileo's theory of a heliocentric universe, the discovery of electrostatic photography and xerography and scores of others.

"We revel in past client's successes when they made significant changes resulting in improved profitability, increased productivity, superior safety rates and near perfect product quality. This client has not experienced the true joy of genuine success."

"Of course this won't happen if they can't get past their paradigm paralysis," Dave said. "However, it helps a lot when we give them examples such as the Swiss Watch Story or others like the Story of Galileo. I expect they can relate to the Swiss Watch Makers. They were fine craftsmen and well known for doing excellent work." Dave reflected on his past. He did not come from the best of neighborhoods but was fortunate to have excellent teachers who inspired him to take his education seriously. He was a good athlete in school and had a burning desire to excel and help others succeed.

"But it wasn't enough to save their industry," Genie interjected. "In 1968, the Swiss dominated the watchmaking industry producing 65 percent of the watches in the world combined with realizing 80 percent of the profits, however just ten years later their market share took a nose dive to 10 percent. At one time, more than 65,000 Swiss watchmakers were producing the finest timepieces in the world. They were blindsided.

"The quartz digital watch was introduced at one of their conferences. What happened? Several companies not prominent in watchmaking envisioned this new type of watch. These interlopers were not confined by the old technology. The outsiders visualized new opportunities. The Swiss could not fathom that a device could be a timepiece without gears, springs, jewels and tiny parts. That just was not their paradigm.

"Seiko and Texas Instruments, as outsiders, were two companies that saw a great opportunity in this new technology, because they could think outside of the box. They took over the market the Swiss once dominated. The rest is history. Now, almost everyone wears a digital watch. Who were the inventors of this innovative technology?

"Swiss researchers invented the electronic (Quartz) watch and Swiss executives rejected their own innovation. The Swiss were convinced electronics were not the future of watch making. They did not even protect their own invention with a copyright.

"The Swiss watch industry is just one of many examples of the companies and the industries that missed great opportunities by their failure of being unable to think outside the box," Ron interjected. "The American and Japanese electronics industries were not locked into a complacent mindset, so they took over the Swiss market and their jobs. The Swiss did not have the foresight to understand they needed to change the way they looked at things. That changed their entire future. How's that for a segue into Galileo's difficulties with the authorities in the early 17th century?

"Not that far back. About 400 years ago people thought the earth was the center of the solar system."

"Galileo Galilei was an Italian philosopher, physicist, mathematician, engineer and astronomer," Dave stated. "He played a major role in the scientific revolution of his era. He made major improvements to the telescope and his astronomical observations supported Copernicanism, those who believed the earth revolved around the sun and not the other way around. They called it heliocentrism. The scientists and the church did not have the foresight to look past their own paradigms. They held fast to the belief that this extreme theory was against current theological teachings. The Roman Inquisition of 1615 investigated Galileo and concluded heliocentrism was false and contrary to scripture. This placed works advocating the Copernican system on the index of banned books and forbade Galileo from advocating heliocentrism. As we now know, Galileo's theories were right, but that would not save him in 1615. He was imprisoned. A tough reward for discovering a way to see the world in a new and different way."

As they approached their hotel, Tom turned on the car radio to listen to the six o'clock news. The report once again focused on unemployment, the economy, the national debt, the deficit, immigration and innumerable bad news stories. "The news gets worse every day, "Tom said. "Many experts agree that China is on its way to becoming the world's dominant economic and political force. High taxes, a move towards socialized medicine, enormous expenditures aimed at preventing global warming prove no one knows how to solve the problems in Washington. The USA is becoming increasingly European in its translation of democracy. The federal government gets bigger as they continue to hike up taxes and spend more and more borrowed money."

"The more they spend, the worse it gets," Dave interrupted. "Congress is coerced by lobbyists to pass pet projects that have no long-term, comprehensive plan in place. They operate as if they are playing Whac-a-Mole. They attempt to solve one problem and more pop up. They are clueless when it comes to understanding how everything in government is interrelated. Everyone in government has their own special boondoggle. They pull them off by arm twisting fellow politicians to support their deal on a 'you scratch my back, I'll scratch your back' basis.

"While this may get some things done, it rarely gets the right things done. The Boston Tunnel is a typical example of government ineptness. Nicknamed the 'Big Dig' it is the poster child of government corruption. Big government doing what it does best. Overruns and missed schedules. The result is roads, buildings and airports that don't serve the general public, or building bridges to nowhere."

"The government solution to a problem is usually as bad as the problem and very often makes it worse." — Milton Friedman

"Listening to the news," Ron jumped in, "I'm sure there are thousands of wasted projects costing billions of dollars that weaken our once strong country. These wasted dollars are a drain on the economy plus they weaken this republic in every way." Ron had a garage band during high school and then attended the US Naval Academy. He served as a commissioned officer in the United States Marine Corps.

Upon retirement, the consulting firm recruited him. Disciplined with a strong sense of duty with a side that lives up to his name, he has a knack for shocking people with the stark truth and is never afraid to say what is on his mind. Ron is one of those unique characters who know how to work hard but has unusual tastes that run from hard rock to sci-fi to dark humor. On the bright side, he adores his wife and four kids.

"The federal government itself does not know how many departments and agencies it has. They do not even have a method to calculate how many agencies there are because they are physically located in many different places and the records are maintained in countless places with varied formats. It surely is many thousands. Does anyone know if any, or all, add value and strength to benefit the prosperity of the United States?"

"The madness runs deeper than any of us can imagine," Genie said. "The political rabbit hole runs deep and has so many tunnels leading nowhere that we all end up chasing our tails. Someone has to unravel the threads and find the bottom of the seemingly bottomless pit. Whether we who are not so young will live to see it I don't know."

Genie lost her husband in the Gulf War and never remarried. A tall statuesque blonde, Genie was a gifted student who later earned her MBA. She possesses an exceptionally analytical mind and has the ability to remember information and data on just about every subject. She assumed the unofficial role of mentor for Dave and treats him like a son although one would never know it from the way she continually questions him. She is also the computer guru of the team. "But we must try to make a difference," Genie continued. "That is what matters. The politicians thrive on power and control but what they are accomplishing is crippling the future of this republic."

Dave spoke up from the driver's seat, "Genie, you are absolutely right about that. They never analyze the entire process, or system. They try to solve everything by bits and pieces. Their decision making process depends on how the politicians think they can keep their offices and/or their constituents happy and voting for them.

"I doubt if any one of them ever had the experience of designing and implementing an entire cohesive process. Nevertheless, that is just what is needed to lead the entire federal government to a position of economic and cultural success and prosperity."

"We can accomplish that by applying our tried and true successful principles and techniques on how to operate organizations, toward how to operate the government." Tom challenged, "anyone up for kicking that around during our travel time?"

"That's an interesting thought. We usually talk about politics, movies and sports during our trips to the work site and back," Genie mused. "Why not? I know we can do it."

Dave replied from behind the wheel, "I like it. I will do whatever it takes to come up with a solution to make the government smaller and less intrusive. The federal government is too big and my experience is that most of the issues it meddles in are the same issues the individual states are working on. I've worked in plants where the people were thoroughly frustrated because the Federal and State EPAs were on location at the same time with both forcing opposing regulations on the plant.

"Let me tell you how it will be
There's one for you, nineteen for me
'Cause I'm the taxman, yeah, I'm the taxman
Should five per cent appear too small
Be thankful I don't take it all
'Cause I'm the taxman, yeah I'm the taxman
If you drive a car, I'll tax the street,
If you try to sit, I'll tax your seat.
If you get too cold, I'll tax the heat,
If you take a walk, I'll tax your feet.
Don't ask me what I want it for
If you don't want to pay some more
'Cause I'm the taxman, yeah, I'm the taxman
*   Now my advice for those who die*
Declare the pennies on your eyes
'Cause I'm the taxman, yeah, I'm the taxman
And you're working for no one but me."

— Written by George Harrison.

The redundancy is staggering and it takes forever to get things done. There is no sense of urgency in Washington, while the people suffer from 'inside the beltway' indifferences. It is impossible for our cities, counties and states to be governed effectively from Washington. Local government, by the people, is superior to big government by and for politicians fueled by lobbyists."

"If we tackle the tax issues, count me in," Ron almost shouted from the back seat. "I still remember a Beatles song from their 1966 Revolver Album about taxes and the politicians' pursuit of more taxes. I'll sing it for you. The 'Taxman' lyrics go like this:

After a vigorous golf clap, Tom smiled and said, "It looks like we're all agreed. Let's do what we do best. We'll look at how the country got into this condition; develop a clear vision to approach the issues; and then design a comprehensive process for the United States of America to deliver superior government services to the citizens at a minimal cost." Tom further stated, "let's think about this tonight and brainstorm it on the way to work tomorrow."

As Dave pulled into the hotel parking lot, the four were thinking about researching the important issues of the day while also getting their project work planned for the next day. They all knew that getting the government and its relentless taxation off the backs of citizens would provide higher wages for Americans and a brighter future for the children. This is paramount. If America stays on its current course, the youth of the country face a bleak future and an insurmountable debt. Although no one wanted to say it, the United States of America is on the brink of bankruptcy and disaster. America is dying before their eyes. The four were not obsessed with doom and gloom. None of the four are alarmists; just realists who do not want to witness the demise of their country.

The country's future lies with the youth of the country. The youth are possessed with great potential. The country has to provide a great environment for them to achieve that potential. The opportunity is there. The citizens must act now.

CHAPTER ONE | *Where We Are Summary*

1. Paradigm Paralysis prevents us from thinking "outside the box."

2. The US has become a victim of Paradigm Paralysis.

3. It is difficult for citizens to bust their paradigms.

4. Foolhardy politicians control and divide citizens to maintain their power.

5. Many citizens have become apathetic regarding government and politics.

6. Too many people accept things the way they are.

7. Many are conditioned to rely on the federal government for care from cradle to grave.

8. Many citizens think they have no voice. Their vote does not count.

9. The irresponsible, dysfunctional federal government has become the norm.

10. Many have forgotten that a small, limited federal government equates to liberty.

11. Outsiders are not confined to old ideas. They visualize new opportunities.

12. Freedom loving citizens are branded as extremists.

13. Many citizens are convinced the federal government cannot solve problems.

14. The burdensome government-imposed taxes are crippling this nation.

15. The federal government has become too large to be effective.

16. The federal government has redundant, counter-productive control over the states.

17. Elected officials have neither a sense of urgency nor an incentive to solve governmental problems. They perceive problems as devices to gain more power and votes.

18. The country must provide a great environment for children to achieve their potential.

CHAPTER TWO

How We Got Here

"I predict future happiness for Americans, if they can prevent the government from wasting the labors of the people under the pretense of taking care of them." — Thomas Jefferson

WEDNESDAY MORNING. WEEK 1.

The next morning the four met in the hotel lobby after breakfast. There was heightened enthusiasm that promised an exciting drive to the plant. As the team got into the car, the seating arrangements were the same as the day before. No one wanted to break the momentum as Tom said, "judging from the conversation at breakfast I can sense everyone wants to talk about America this morning instead of sports or entertainment."

"Let's start at the beginning," Genie opened the brainstorming. "Let's set the stage right from the start. We need to review the ideals and visions of our Founding Fathers. We cannot cover more than 240 years of history, but it will serve us well if we refresh ourselves with the original concepts of liberty, freedom and government by the people, for the people and of the people. Any one of us can research the history and details of the course of the United States of America. Let's just do it in our own words.

"The United States of America is a country that evolved from, or revolted out of, a group of British colonies. The 1770's were a decade of oppressive tax burdens levied by England that escalated to a point where the colonists felt they no longer had control over their destiny and were losing their freedom. British soldiers quartered themselves in the colonists' homes. And as everyone knows, the British Government and British Military ruled the colonies with a brutal hand."

"It was a period when a group of about 100 exceptional men and women, one of the most outstanding collection of people who ever lived on this planet, came together with a bold vision to form a new way of life in their brand-new land. They were mostly all gathered in one area, the Atlantic seaboard of North America. They came together with common goals and a common purpose," said Ron from the back seat. "The one issue they all rallied around was 'taxation without representation' which is exactly what we are facing today. The taxation issue is clearly the stranglehold the federal government holds over all of us in this present time some 240 years later."

"On July 4, 1776, 'The unanimous Declaration of the thirteen united States of American Independence' was written by Thomas Jefferson and ratified by the signing of 56 brave men. Jefferson expressed the convictions held in the minds and hearts of the American colonists. The political philosophy of the 'Declaration' was not new; its ideals of individual liberty were previously expressed by John Locke and again by the Continental Congress. Jefferson summarized this philosophy in 'self-evident truths' and put forth a list of grievances against King George III of England to justify, before the world, the breaking of ties between the colonies and the mother country." Dave further affirmed, "shots had already been fired, and battles waged when it became apparent a war would be fought to gain independence from the British rule of King George III."

"The Revolutionary War was fought to gain freedom from oppression and to form a new government of self-rule." Tom proclaimed, "Our Founding Fathers were very clear on how the states would form a union of states.

"A Constitution was written beginning with the words 'We the People' and contained 7 Articles. Ten Amendments, known as the 'Bill of Rights,' were written later.' The Tenth Amendment specifically limits the powers of the federal government to those delegated to it by the Constitution. Seventeen additional amendments have been ratified. Included in those are the Sixteenth Amendment which Permits Congress to levy an income tax without apportioning it among the states or basing it on the United States Census; and the Seventeenth Amendment, which establishes the direct election of United States Senators by popular vote. The sixteenth and seventeenth amendments are deep roots of the systemic problems the republic faces today as they embolden the two houses of Congress to levy taxation as if they are entrenched feudal lords.

"Alexander Hamilton, James Madison and John Jay penned a series of 85 articles and essays called The Federalist Papers to promote the ratification of the Constitution of the United States. In Federalist paper No. 1, Hamilton wrote: 'It has been frequently remarked, that it seems to have been reserved to the people of this country, by their conduct and example, to decide the important question, whether societies of men are really capable or not, of establishing good government from reflection and choice, or whether they are forever destined to depend, for their political constitutions, on accident and force.'

"This brilliant statement is just as true today as it was in the 1787. We often hear people say, 'we get the government we deserve,' or some variation of that. Politicians in Washington have too much control over issues we face. Citizens have delegated power to them because they do not want to be involved and they surely do not want to be bothered. It is just plain easier to let someone else do the work and then assume the attitude of 'it is what it is,' pay extra taxes, not be involved or bothered and be the unwitting victims of inflation."

"For us to design and implement solutions for what needs to be achieved a majority of citizens will have to want it," Genie stated. "Do the citizens want the convoluted policies of today, or are they inspired to 'reboot' the system, add some new apps and beneficial files, and re-implement the Founding Fathers vision using current technology as it pertains to present conditions?

"The Congress and Executive branches are jointly responsible for creating a budget and they haven't done their job in years. We keep hearing about continuing resolutions (CRs) and earmarks to keep the country's obligations funded. Amendments, having nothing in common with the original measure, are attached to coerce members to vote for the entire bill. This is a total waste of our good money. We need a budget and more importantly a balanced budget. Our federal government has the power to print money and they do just that to pay the bills, while at the same time increasing the national debt. Then they vote to raise the debt ceiling. Is not that the same type of thinking a person would use to solve their personal financial problems that include huge credit card debt by then asking the credit card company to raise their 'credit limit?'

"We have more than $18 trillion in debt today and the national debt is increasing at a record pace to a point where it will certainly exceed $20 trillion before we know it. Simple math tells us we will then pay upwards of $1 trillion dollars in interest when the debt reaches that unsustainable level. The debt-to-GDP ratio is ballooning to a point of obscenity. A low ratio of a country's government national debt and its gross domestic product (GDP) is imperative for a stable economy. A low debt-to-GDP ratio indicates an economy producing and selling goods and services sufficient to pay back debt without incurring further debt."

"No one knows for certain," Dave said from behind the wheel of the red hybrid, "because no one is analyzing it, but the federal government will soon be required to pay 20-30 percent of annual revenue to service the interest on the national debt. These interest payments add no value to the country, and in truth take valuable resources away from what the country desperately needs to build a robust economy. Approximately one-third of the national debt is owned by foreign countries, China and Japan to name a few, some of whom are not friendly toward us."

Dave then quoted from a statement composed at the time our Constitution was authored. "There is a parallel to what Alexander Tyler, a Scottish history professor at the University of Edinburgh, supposedly said in 1887 about the fall of the Athenian Republic (democracy) more than 2,000 years prior:

"A democracy is always temporary in nature; it simply cannot exist as a permanent form of government. A democracy will continue to exist up until the time that voters discover that they can vote themselves generous gifts from the public treasury. From that moment on, the majority always votes for the candidates who promise the most benefits from the public treasury, with the result that every democracy will finally collapse over loose fiscal policy, (which is) always followed by a dictatorship."

"The average age of the world's greatest civilizations from the beginning of history, has been about 200 years. During those 200 years, these nations always progressed through the following sequence:

"The USA is on course to repeat the below cycle. As a representative republic we have certain advantages empowering us to stop this process. We can 'reboot.' We can elect the right people to lead the federal government to change the present course. The massive national debt must be gradually reduced and eventually eliminated otherwise our economy will collapse from extensive interest payments. The government needs to be less intrusive, less overreaching and more cost effective by returning redundant bureaucracies back to the states."

"From bondage to spiritual faith;
From spiritual faith to great courage;
From courage to liberty;
From liberty to abundance;
From abundance to complacency;
From complacency to apathy;
From apathy to dependence;
From dependence back into bondage."

Everyone was thinking about the future of the nation and contemplating which phase of the cycle of democracy the USA was in. Do the citizens of this republic truly have the foresight to bust their personal paradigms and break the cycle? Just then, they arrived at the main gate and changed their focus to work as they entered the plant.

WEDNESDAY AFTERNOON. WEEK 1.

The drive back to the hotel started with everyone ready to put the long day in the rear view mirror. They could not wait to get started with their new discussions.

"We have become slaves to the existing tax code," Ron bluntly warned from the back seat. "Businesses make decisions based on how taxes affect their operation. People purchase houses to receive mortgage deductions. They foolishly want to pocket a tax refund of their own money. They rely on their yearly tax refund. They donate to charities to get deductions. We track our travel expenses to receive tax deductions. Citizens waste time working around the tax code to find loopholes. The Founding Fathers did not envision this. There is nothing like this in the Federalist Papers.

"Too many people are involved with, and way too many manhours are spent each year on tax preparation, and how to work within the existing tax code," Ron went on. "According to the National Taxpayers Union, U.S. taxpayers spend more than 7.6 billion hours complying with federal tax requirements. That is the equivalent of 3,800,000 people working 2,000 hours per year just on tax work. Imagine what our society would look like if all that time was spent on more economically profitable activities; adding value to our country and culture; doing community service work; instead of spending 'wasted days and wasted nights' searching for receipts and filling in mystifying IRS forms. This equates to 3,800,000 people times $51,000 per year. Our country is spending over a trillion dollars per year doing valueless tax work.

"Meanwhile, annual median household income fell slightly to $51,017 in 2012, down from $51,100 in 2011. This is a change the Census Bureau does not consider statistically significant. Nevertheless, it is significant. We are travelling on the bridge to nowhere while our income remains stagnant. Much of this effort is manipulative as companies and individuals attempt to find the loopholes and the best ways to 'beat the system.' This time and effort is not 'value added.' Tax preparation does not add value to goods or services. Time, effort and dollars are completely wasted on efforts to raise revenue for the government."

"On top of that the federal government spends an excessive amount of taxpayer dollars to review, audit and police tax preparation and collection," Genie added. "There has to be a simpler, more efficient way than paying $2.45 of every $100.00 dollars collected. That is a disproportionate price to pay to provide the funds the government needs to keep us safe and provide the services required by the Constitution." "Where did you get that number?" Tom asked. "The IRS must have a huge bureaucracy to have costs that are that high. That's paying a tax on a tax."

"The IRS employs more people than the CIA and FBI combined. The latest total reported is 114,000 employees. That's an enormous work force to fund just to collect taxes and anger citizens." Genie replied. "The many federal government websites contain this information. It is not easy to find and most of the statistics are lagging. I am afraid the cost of collecting taxes is just another example of a federal government grown out of control. These high costs cripple the economy because this money belongs to the taxpayers who could instead spend it on goods and services to build the economy and create jobs."

"Another issue that drains the economy and adds no value is the inability to inspire our citizens to be law abiding," Dave said. "I grew up with far too many people now incarcerated in prisons and jails. The war on drugs is a losing battle."

"We spend more time on political correctness than civility and helping and supporting our families, friends and neighbors," Ron pronounced. "Civility has become a lost art. Our colleges offer courses on lurid themes from masturbation to prostitution, even as campus sexual-harassment suits over hurtful language are at an all-time high."

"Our lives are not as private as they once were," Genie expressed. "We don't know if our government is spying on us and we can't be sure they are not. Each political party puts a different spin on it so we will never know whom to believe. The federal government has become so bloated that no one believes it is efficient, or effective. As it continually expands, it loses the ability to govern adequately. It is so far removed from the local scene where people live that politicians are oblivious as to what it takes to earn enough money to fill the grocery cart and gas tank each week."

"Prices on everything are up. Basic products are becoming much more expensive to purchase. Unemployment is high and millions of workers only have part time jobs," Tom proclaimed. "Inflation is killing the economy while the politicians manipulate the Consumer Price Index (CPI) to make us believe they have control over inflation. They do not and the middle class is suffering because of it. The average annual income for citizens is not keeping up with the price of goods. Fifty years ago, gas was $0.199 per gallon. $4.00 per gallon at the pump is common today. This is an increase of up to 20 times. The difference in filling a gas tank, then and now, with 15 gallons of gas is $57.00. Think about that. 15 gallons times $0.20 is $3.00. 15 gallons times $4.00 is $60.00. Politicians do not care because they are mostly concerned with their re-election.

"Incomes are only 5 to 10 times higher than they were fifty years ago. Prices are twenty times higher. Wages remain stagnant while our purchasing power decreases.

"A few examples of basic items to give us some perspective are," Ron declared, "10 pounds of potatoes were purchased for $0.39 cents in the 1960s. Now they are $1.29 per pound, or $12.90 for ten pounds, an increase of more than 30. Cheese was about $0.39 per pound 50 years ago. Today it varies from $5.00 to $10.00 per pound for popular brands and types. An increase of about 15. A can of popular brand soup was $0.89 for six cans. Today it is $1.75 per can, or $10.50 for six cans. More than 10 times the cost. Meat, bread, milk and other staples have experienced similar increases. Consumers must pay these inflated prices with stagnant paychecks further depleted by increased taxes, including higher retail taxes and higher costs of regulations.

"Rent for a nice 2 bedroom apartment in the 1960's was about $150.00 to $200.00 per month depending on location. Now, rent is typically $1,500 to $2,000.00 per month for a similar apartment. Wages have not kept up with rent. Our standard of living has improved because we have more innovative conditions, products and services, but we pay a much higher percentage of our stagnant incomes for this standard of living."

"We have entered an age of high technology, and that brought us a new kind of criminal," Genie warned. "We now have 'hackers' who take advantage of others who are less skilled or talented in the usage of this new technology. Corporations plant viruses and pop-ups on our computers and then offer to erase them if we buy their security devices. They have frightened us into thinking they are helping us.

"Some have found ways to infect our computers with 'ransom ware' that encrypt our files until we pay a ransom to remove it. All these are costly and time-consuming. They make us weaker instead of stronger.

"Others are stealing the identity of citizens. This wreaks havoc on their lives. Stealing a person's identity is so vile an act it is too onerous to describe.

"Our federal government is now mandating our method of health care payment instead of how to improve our health care. The VA has problems taking care of our veterans and no one knows how to design solutions or implement improvements."

"More than 500 people were murdered in Chicago last year," Dave said. "Other cities are experiencing similar high rates. Some look like war zones. The Founding Fathers did not envision this type of activity when they founded this republic. There are so many examples we could spend months citing just the worst cases."

The conversation was so compelling Tom forgot to turn on the car radio to listen to the evening news before Dave pulled into the hotel parking lot. Tom remarked as they opened the car doors and climbed out, "this has been enlightening. Let's continue our research tonight and discuss this again tomorrow morning."

THURSDAY MORNING. WEEK 1.

The journey to discover solutions resumed on the ride to work. They continued to study the issues and perform root cause analysis on the basic problems of government.

"The Social Security System is in serious trouble and facing forced extinction," Tom advised from the front seat. "Benefit payments exceed revenues, as the deficit escalates. Workers retiring today have paid more into the system than they will ever receive. Future retirees will collect less and less and finally nothing when Social Security self-destructs. A $20 trillion national debt will unquestionably bankrupt it. Proposed solutions to increase the Social Security payroll tax and raise the retirement age will devastate future retirees.

"Employers got involved in health insurance when President Franklin Roosevelt imposed wage controls during World War II. This prevented employers from increasing rates. They resorted to offering non-wage benefits to attract employees since they could not compete with one another by offering attractive salaries. This started the trend toward employees wanting more and more benefits. In reality, employees themselves pay for those benefits. Employees should receive their full wages instead of a corrupt intermediary taking their unearned cut. Another sad example of lost freedom."

"In 1953, the IRS ruled that employer-provided health insurance would not be taxed as wage compensation," Ron barked. "As such, employees pay taxes only on their wages, even while receiving thousands of dollars' worth of health benefits. This ruling forced employers to either pass these expenses on to their consumers or limit wage increases. This affected all workers as they now pay higher prices for goods and services but receive no additional funds in their paychecks. Taxes cripple the economy.

Tax his land,
Tax his bed,
Tax the table
At which he's fed.

Tax his tractor,
Tax his mule,
Teach him taxes
Are the rule.

Tax his cow,
Tax his goat,
Tax his pants,
Tax his coat.

Tax his ties,
Tax his shirt,
Tax his work,
Tax his dirt.

Tax his tobacco,
Tax his drink,
Tax him if he
Tries to think.

Tax his cigars,
Tax his beers,
If he cries, then
Tax his tears.

Tax his car,
Tax his gas,
Find other ways
To tax his ass.

Tax all he has
Then let him know
That you won't be done
Till he has no dough.

When he screams and hollers,
Then tax him some more,
Tax him till
He's good and sore.

Then tax his coffin,
Tax his grave,
Tax the sod in
Which he's laid.

Put these words upon his
tomb, "Taxes drove me to my
doom..."

When he's gone,
Do not relax,
It's time to apply
The inheritance tax.

"Today, 58.4 percent of non-elderly Americans get health insurance through their employers. This results in overconsumption, because it hides the actual cost of care from consumers. On the other hand, losing a job eventually means losing health insurance. Those with preexisting conditions have great difficulty in purchasing new insurance. More unintended consequences from foolhardy shortsighted politicians. This is a poem sent to me by a friend. We receive dozens of these every day by email. We all know many are not worth reading. I thought this "poem" was amusing at first . . . then I realized the shocking truth of it," Ron quipped as he recited it for the group:

"Still think this poem is funny?" Ron demanded. "Few of these taxes existed 100 years ago, when the USA was the most prosperous country the world ever knew. Now we have an overburdening tax code and our nation is less and less prosperous.

"The national debt was less than $3 billion one hundred years ago. America had the largest middle class in the world. Dad worked so Mom could stay home to raise the kids. What in the hell happened? Can you spell politicians?" Ron growled. As the drive to the plant was ending, the team began a general discussion on taxation. They wondered how to persuade the public that deducting mortgage payments and receiving tax refunds was a government plan to confiscate a portion of their hard-earned paycheck with the promise they could get some of it back in the form of windfall profits. Enlightenment is right in front of our eyes as Ron finished singing Bob Dylan's anthem,

"Blowin' in the Wind."
"The answer, my friend, is
blowin' in the wind, The
answer is blowin' in the
wind."

15

1. Taxation without representation is as crucial an issue today just as it was in 1770.

2. The colonists sensed they no longer had control over their own destiny.

3. The colonists lost their freedom just as the citizens of today have.

4. The Revolutionary War was fought to gain freedom from oppression and to form a new government of "self-rule." We must regain "self-rule."

5. The citizens of the USA are in great peril of losing their liberty.

6. The states formed the United States of America. Not the opposite.

7. The Constitution begins with the words "We the People."

8. Politicians have become career public servants who serve themselves.

9. Special interest lobbyists set the agenda in Washington.

10. Citizens have become slaves to a tax code.

11. Taxation is clearly the stranglehold the federal government holds over us.

12. The 16th and 17th Amendments contribute to big government problems.

13. Federalist Paper Number 1 states "whether societies of men are really capable or not, of establishing good government from reflection and choice, or whether they are forever destined to depend, for their political constitutions, on accident and force."

14. US citizens must challenge themselves to break free from the oppressive rule of federal government just as our founders did from King George III.

15. The Revolutionary War was fought to form a new government of self-rule.

16. The US is at the tipping point of citizens voting themselves largesse.

17. The US is fast approaching the phase of "From dependence back into bondage."

18. It is simple math. We cannot afford to pay interest on the national debt.

19. The country needs a balanced budget.

20. We the people "must reboot the system" to clear out the convoluted policies of today. Add some beneficial new apps and files, and implement the vision of the Founding Fathers using the technology of today.

"I am in favor of cutting taxes under any circumstances and for any excuse, for any reason, whenever it's possible." – Milton Friedman

---

CHAPTER TWO | *How We Got Here; Taxation Summary*

1. US citizens are slaves to the existing tax code.

2. U.S. taxpayers spend 7.6 billion hours complying with tax requirements.

3. Median household income fell to $51,017 a year in 2012, from $51,100.

4. Taxpayers pay $2.45 for the IRS to collect $100.00 tax dollars. (2.45%)

5. More time is misused on political correctness than practicing civility.

6. We now know our government is spying on us.

7. Politicians are clueless of the struggle to earn sufficient wages to fill the grocery cart and gas tank.

8. Prices are increasing daily as politicians manipulate the CPI.

9. The price of household goods have increased 20 times in the last 50 years.

10. American income has only increased 10 times in the last 50 years.

11. New technologies have created new brands of high tech criminals.

12. Identity theft wreaks havoc on the lives of victims.

13. The government mandates our health care payment method, not health care enhancement.

14. The VA is unable to care of our military veterans. Politicians are clueless on how to solve the problem nor knowledgeable enough to design methods to implement improvements.

15. Murder is rampant in some American cities that now resemble war zones.

16. The Social Security program is in serious trouble with no viable solution.

17. Employers can no longer afford to pay for health insurance for their employees.

18. More than 100 taxes are on the books today that never existed 100 years ago.

19. The USA had the largest middle class in the world, now the USA has the largest tax code in the world.

20. The citizens have turned the government over to the politicians who are rapidly destroying the republic. It is time to "reboot" and "restore."

CHAPTER THREE

The 20/20 Vision

"It's not tyranny we desire; it's a just, limited, federal government." — Alexander Hamilton

THURSDAY AFTERNOON. WEEK 1.

As the team buckled in for the ride back to the hotel, Tom said. "We discussed matters that weaken our republic, concerns of issues not going as well as they should and those preventing us from being a strong viable country. Now, we need to focus on how to restore the USA, once the greatest republic the planet has ever known. How to mend the USA and maintain it once again as the greatest country that ever existed. If we are not a strong country, we cannot help our own citizens, much less be strong enough to help others in need. We need to formulate a clear vision.

"When a client engages us, our first priority is to assess the culture of the organization. Then we offer a vision and formulate a plan. We then lead our client's people to define and sustain a successful team to implement necessary changes. Each organization is only as strong as each individual member. Therefore, a strong, solid organization must have stalwart people fully involved and fully contributing to the success of the organization. All must have 'skin in the game.'

"We need to state our principles, or precepts, and our vision to guide us on this journey," Tom asserted. "These principles must be in place for America to offer prosperity for all. The country must provide a positive environment for the bright youth to achieve their full potential. Our vision must be a 'Clear 20/20 Vision for America.'"

THE 20/20 VISION PRINCIPLES

The United States has a population of approximately 320 million residents. An estimated 30 to 40 million foreign nationals reside in the country. Every one of these more than 300 million people play a role in the future of the United States. They play these roles in a constant and perpetual manner. Every one of these 300 million plus people must add value to their country in order for the country to continually succeed and be prosperous. When more of these 300 million plus people adds value to the country, the country becomes more successful.

The 20/20 Vision provides an environment of success for all 300 million plus people to add value, especially for those who are not yet doing so.

All people are equally valuable. Their roles, although varied, distinct and different, are equally important roles. People can be positive, neutral or negative forces on the success of the republic. They are in three groups.

They are people whom:

1. Contribute to the success of the nation in many diverse ways and add value. These people carry the entire burden of the nation. These are citizens who:

Have jobs where they make things, service things, provide services, care for people, protect people and/or perform value added duties or undertakings.

Are attending schools, academies or other learning or training facilities in order to become productive citizens who will add value to the future success of the USA.

Are young and will become future students who will add value to the future success of the USA. Currently they add joy and comfort to all.

Are senior citizens who added value in the past and who are now retired and still adding value with their wisdom, experience and good will.

Are unable to produce, or serve, through no fault of their own but still bring joy, wonder and enlightenment to all.

2. Merely exist. They do no harm, but add no value. They are a burden on the people who add value. They do not move the nation forward. They typically have no use for society and have no interest to fit in and help others.

3. Take from others, harm others, consume and may be destructive. They subtract value from society and the economy. They place a continual burden on the people who add value. They are high maintenance people who drag people who add value down. They do not work. They may be criminals who often harm other citizens and/or their property.

Organizations, by definition, have more than one member. Each member, no matter the number, has an important role to play in the success, or failure, of the organization. Contributing members add value and ensure prosperity and future well-being. An unsuccessful organization fails and ceases to exist. Therefore, all members must contribute and add value to the organization in order for it to thrive, succeed and sustain itself. Each entity, organization or country must have continuity. There cannot be gaps in which performance starts and stops. There cannot be years of revenue loss, reckless spending, inadequate training and poor planning.

Example: A typical organization, or company, has an organization chart. All members, or staff/employees, are included on that chart. They occupy various levels and play various roles to make up the whole. There are officers, directors, managers, supervisors, members, associates and/or employees at many levels and skills who perform the duties, tasks and activities required for the entity to function. Each member is equally important, and must perform ably, or the entity does not need them on the roster. The entity cannot function well unless all are engaged in effective and productive performance of their duties. The entity cannot survive and fulfill its mission unless each member does their part and plays their role. Those who do not perform drag the organization down and destroy it in one way or manner.

Example: The United States of America is a very large organization with many member citizens. In order for the USA to thrive and perpetuate itself, all citizens must be contributing members. Each citizen must play a positive role. Presently, many people do not play a positive role. The USA is currently on a backward slide. We must reverse this trend in order for our children and grandchildren to have meaningful futures. Our children have great potential – we must provide them with a great country to fulfill their great potential.

Example: Military ground organizations contain units of various types and sizes. An infantry unit might be composed of squads, platoons, companies, battalions, regiments and divisions. Each larger unit is dependent on the smaller units that make up the whole. Each unit adds value to the overall mission or purpose. If one unit fails, or does not perform, the entire larger unit cannot function and eventually fails its mission. A squad has members and leaders. When one or more squad member is wounded, missing or killed, the entire unit is in jeopardy. That in turn jeopardizes the safety and success of the platoon, company and so on.

Example: Likewise, the United States is in jeopardy when its citizens are weakened, harmed or not able to perform for one reason or another. Every citizen, city, county, and state must be engaged in positive, productive activities and behaviors that add value to the country. Non-engaged, non-productive, destructive citizens take value away from the country. This weakens the nation and requires value-adding citizens to carry their own burden plus the extra weight of others. The United States cannot tolerate criminal activity, laziness, incompetence, disloyalty or treason. The nation must unite as a nation of laws.

Example: Military air organizations contain units of various types and sizes. An air unit might be composed of squadrons, groups and wings. Like ground units, each higher unit depends on the smaller units that make up the whole. Each unit adds value to the whole. A typical squadron has a commanding officer and staff to lead, administer and plan. The pilots are an important component of the squadron just as are the personnel who maintain and arm the aircraft. Without mechanics, electronics and avionics technicians, armament and fueling personnel the aircraft cannot fly. All are equally important in the success of the overall purpose and mission of the squadron. Without all roles, the air wing cannot function as designed.

Example: This same concept applies to the United States. A country is only strong, effective and successful when all citizens contribute and add value with their efforts and skills. A nation of highly educated, well-trained and knowledgeable citizens with solid, positive core beliefs and a true moral compass of the purpose and well-being of the country add value to the lives of all citizens. The United States must strive to give purpose and a moral compass to all its citizens and receive value from all citizens.

Example: American citizens have nurtured this country since 1776. Some served in leadership roles as the Founding Fathers and others. Many served as farmers, mill workers, manufacturers, artisans, craftsmen, smiths, shopkeepers, bakers, bricklayers, printers, weavers, and so forth. All were equally important in the origin of this new republic.

Many also served in the Continental Army, Navy and Marine Corps. Some served a short time and some served for the entire duration of the Revolutionary War. All were equally important because the continental military forces could not have survived without continuity. Armed forces cannot disband and reconstitute themselves without continuous staffing and training. All have served, and the nation owes them a debt that can never be paid. We would not have the freedom and liberty we now enjoy without our armed forces.

Each veteran played an equal role in the security, and safety, of our nation whether on active duty during peacetime or time of conflict. The military is in a continuous state of readiness. Every veteran served to make that happen. A veteran who served in peacetime, for just a few years, is equally as important as one who served many years during time of conflict. It was not their choice that it was peacetime, or wartime, they still carried the flag for the next veteran.

A chain is the perfect analogy. Visualize a thick heavy golden chain with more than 300 million links stretching from sea to shining sea. Imagine each citizen is a link in this 300 million plus link chain. Each link holds this nation together, making it strong.

In the private sector, and as well as the public sector, each link, or member, in the chain must be a polished, bright, strong link. Everyone has a role to play in the success of his or her organization. Each individual is equally important even though each has a different role to play. Everyone must be involved and pull their own weight. A chain that must be constantly repaired and strengthened eventually fails.

320 MILLION LINKS. ONE CHAIN. ONE NATION.

The Armed Forces is like a chain with about 1.8 million active duty and reserve links. Each member from lowest rank to four-star rank is a link in that chain. Every link is equally important and each link must be reliable. Weak links do not perform well. Broken links cause failure and jeopardize the mission.

The same applies to the citizens of the United States. All productive, positive citizens who add value are equally important no matter how many years they lived or where they lived or the nature of their occupation or career. Each has an important role in the perpetuation of the country. Citizens who add value are the strong links. Young citizens, those in school and in training are links being strengthened. Other links are strong because of the service they once gave us or the joy they now bring us. Each citizen symbolizes a link in the chain that personifies the United States. The stronger this 300 million-link chain, the stronger the country.

Weak links make the chain weaker and weaken our republic. Weak links are high maintenance and a huge drain on the economy. Destructive links harm not only the country, but other citizens as well. Each time a crime is committed against a citizen or business, that criminal act weakens that specific link in the chain and in turn weakens the nation. Each citizen must be involved and doing their part to make the country resilient and be a positive force who contributes to the benefit of the country. Each must have 'skin in the game' and work to become as sturdy and strong as possible. Each citizen link has a role to play and that link must be involved and sustain its own weight. All links are equally important and strong or it will not work the way it should and the United States will eventually fail.

Another analogy for this high tech age of electronics and computers is stuff clogs up the system. Computers eventually become digital junk drawers. To unclog the clutter, one has to reboot, defrag or run disk clean-up to erase corrupted files on the computer. Keep the operating system. It works. The same can be said for the United States of America. Visualize our land as a computer hard drive and our Constitution/Republic as a superior operating system. Clear out the political confusion and clutter of excessive regulations and federal government junk and start afresh. Keep the Constitution. It works well.

"The government has ignored the many citizens who never had a real opportunity," Dave asserted. "The 20/20 Plan gives them an opportunity for a better life. It eliminates the poverty level. The United States has too much potential to accept poverty of its citizens. Our citizens should never taste the bitterness of poverty.

"Some people, mostly politicians, lobbyists and media pundits say this is impossible. We have a government that began taxing productive workers about 100 years ago. That act is as immoral as it is irresponsible. We have a government that helped establish a private cartel of banks to manipulate our currency. That is inflationary, and irresponsible. We have a government that eradicated the right of the individual states to elect their own Senators. That is foolhardy. We are sheep slowly but surely led to believe that what is pervasive is sane, and what is sane is pervasive.

"To effect such a dramatic change in culture, many things must happen. Our citizens must discover that government is best when its power is checked and most beneficial when it is small, and on a local level. The federal government has to get out of the lives of the citizens and allow the states, counties and municipalities to govern."

"So getting back to my original comments," Tom interjected, "we must design a process to engage every citizen, to not only contribute, but participate. For example, people volunteering to do community service and charitable work. There are an infinite number ways citizens can help, and the country needs them all. The vision is the 20/20 Plan for Prosperity.

During the rest of the ride back to the hotel, the entire team reiterated how everyone needs to participate to restore the country. The discussion centered on major points that would shape their vision. The objective is to inspire people who do not recognize that when something is broken, there is always a way to repair it.

It always takes a good plan, hard work and determination. People locked into "paradigm paralysis by analysis" find it difficult to recognize positive changes are necessary. They are the ones we so often hear say: "it is what it is," or "if it isn't broke, don't fix it;" or "it's not my problem;" or "I don't want to get involved."

In every case, it takes a leader with vision. It takes a person with passion to inspire and motivate those who cannot see, or refuse to see. It takes a leader to influence those who accept everything the way it is; a leader to motivate those who never dreamed something could be better; to instill passion to want to help others; and to embolden those who do not think they can make a difference.

Another point involves areas of a more technical nature. Everyone should have at least a basic understanding of math and science. The Pareto Principle also known as the 80–20 rule, states for many events, 80 percent of the effects come from 20 percent of the causes. This is a common rule business problem solvers utilize.

> 80 percent of retail sales come from 20 percent of the inventory items.
>
> 80 percent of a company's profits come from 20 percent of its customers.
>
> 80 percent of complaints come from 20 percent of its customers.
>
> 80 percent of the employees cause 20 percent of the problems.
>
> The Pareto Principle is utilized to show the distribution of income and wealth among populations and other societal phenomena.
>
> 80 percent of wealth is owned by 20 percent of the population.
>
> 80 percent of taxes are paid by 20 percent of the taxpayers.
>
> 80 percent of crime is caused by 20 percent of the population.
>
> 80 percent of the illegal drugs are used by 20% of the population.

For example:
Concepts such as the Pareto Principle, and others, are important for citizens to know and understand when electing officials and voting on bills. Being well-informed leads to making intelligent decisions.

Root Cause Analysis is a problem solving technique. The issues in the US are recognized. Unfortunately, they are never fully examined to determine the deep-rooted causes. Surface solutions are oftentimes utilized to fix the symptom, never the cause. Band-Aids are typically applied instead of drilling down until the true cause is identified.

The conversation on the drive back to the hotel concluded with some back and forth concerning freedom and liberty. The team worried that the federal government appears to be pushing the citizens toward a socialistic government style instead of allowing citizens to choose their own destiny. Is it the duty of the federal government to control all aspects of the daily lives of the people? That should prompt a lot of debate. Does Congress really listen to the people and do they vote for what is best for all people? Have politicians become so callous they truly believe they know what is best for us and that it is their sworn duty to protect us from ourselves?

This prompted Ron to interrupt the silence, "do any of you know how to catch a wild pig?" The other three-team members looked at Ron as if he had stepped into the Twilight Zone. "I'll take that as a no. This story has been around and it is applicable.

"A chemistry professor at a large college had some exchange students in the class. One day while the class was in a lab session the Professor noticed one young man (exchange student) who kept rubbing his back, and stretching as if his back hurt. The professor asked the young man what was wrong. The student said he had a bullet lodged in his back. He was wounded while fighting the communists who were trying to overthrow his native country's government and install a communist government.

"In the midst of his story he looked at the professor and asked a strange question. 'Do you know how to catch wild pigs?' The professor thought it was a joke and asked for the punch line. The young man said this was no joke. 'You catch wild pigs by finding a suitable place in the woods and then put corn on the ground. The pigs find it and begin to come every day to eat the free corn. When they are used to coming every day, you put a fence down one side of the place where they come. When they get used to the fence, they begin to eat the corn again and you put up another side of the fence. They get used to that and start to eat again.

"You continue until you have all four sides of the fence up with a gate in the last side. The pigs, who are used to the free corn, start to come through the gate to eat. You slam the gate on them and catch the whole herd. Suddenly the wild pigs have lost their freedom. They run around and around inside the fence, but they are undeniably trapped.

"Soon they go back to eating the free corn. They are so used to it that they have forgotten how to forage in the woods for themselves, so they accept captivity."

"The young man then told the professor that is exactly what is happening in America. The government keeps pushing us toward socialism by spreading the free corn in the form of programs such as supplemental income, tax credits for unearned income, corporate subsidies, dairy subsidies, payments not to plant crops, welfare, medicine, drugs, etc. Therefore, we continue to lose our freedom, just a little at a time.

"That is a very captivating parable. The federal government has built four sides of our fence. They are now erecting the gate. We need to awaken and be on guard since we are gradually being sucked into the trap of total dependency on government corn. We are losing our sense of responsibility for our own lives, and even worse, our very spark of life."

"Yes, I agree," Genie chimed in, "but can we let the wild pigs run completely untamed? What I mean is, if I understand the analogy correctly, doesn't a nation need laws and regulations to serve and protect the people from unscrupulous acts?"

"Absolutely," Ron answered.

"Our dilemma is in our political system. The politicians keep running back and forth between taming the wild pigs and allowing them to run free. If we equate the wild pig analogy to freedom and liberty, our people can run free. Freedom inspires creativity, inventiveness, entrepreneurialism, and so forth." Tom further stated, "the country benefits from the free flow of thought and energy to stimulate new innovation."

"The real question is how does the nation find balance?" Ron stated. "None of us relishes the current financial crisis. We are all dismayed when we see elected officials fighting over how high to raise the national debt so they can spend more money. They know how to cause problems, but not how to resolve them."

"But when there is an unbounded flow of energy there is the danger of chaos, which then has to be balanced to correct itself," Genie countered. "It boils down to what we said earlier. The republic needs a leader who understands the need for balance and stops with the rhetoric of political counterparts making one side wrong and the other right. None of us care which side we are on. The time for true leadership in America is now. Leadership that connects with the people and provides us with balance. The country needs leadership, but that leadership must have a vision of America. Vision, wisdom and the capacity to govern utilizing a thorough, comprehensive process."

"Another question requiring an immediate answer," Tom interjected. "How soon will the federal government slam the gate shut? There's no such thing as a free lunch!"

Another long day at work came to a close as the four team members climbed out of the rental car, picked up their briefcases and walked across the parking lot to the hotel lobby all the way thinking about how soon the gate will be slammed shut. They could feel the gate closing. Nevertheless, they were undaunted. They had a clear vision for America.

"If your answer to every failure of the federal government is more government, you are like an alcoholic trying to drink yourself into sobriety." - Paraphrased from Will Spencer.

FRIDAY MORNING. WEEK 1.

The team met for breakfast in the hotel lobby. The enthusiasm was still there. The team got into the car, sitting in the same seats as the day before. No one wanted to break the momentum. Tom said, "I presume everyone wants to talk about 'America' this morning instead of sports, music and entertainment.

"Our vision for this great nation must be clear and it must be effective. We should entitle it '20/20: A Clear Vision for America.' This is our vision to develop and document the '20/20 Plan' to incorporate the wisdom of The Founding Fathers, to frame solutions to build a bridge to the future."

Everyone agreed. Dave said, "in order to accomplish this, we'll have to 'reboot' what is in place now, and 'reset' it back to a functional point. The politicians have everything so scrambled up that a complete reversal in thinking is required by everyone to shed their 'paradigm paralyses' in order to accept change."

"This is a tremendous country populated with remarkable people," Tom replied. "They will support a vision that makes sense and strengthens the chain. They understand when the computer is jumbled up with useless cookies and stuff, they click 'shut down' and then 'reboot' for a fresh start. This is what America needs today; a fresh start. The country needs to eliminate the debt and regulations that have frozen the system. If not, the bureaucratic viruses will be too complex for our children to clear up, reboot and overcome. They will have an insurmountable debt too huge to overcome to live a self-fulfilling life.

"Give me the green light to submit an overview or list of the important issues to address in order to 'reboot' or 'reset' the landscape of how we are governed and the culture we live in. As we all well know, identifying only one problem at a time and implementing a solution for that problem is not the answer. That solution never remains implemented. It must be a comprehensive approach of implementation of all solutions, in all problem areas, to be effective and lasting. Piecemeal solutions are not sufficient. After we settle on our list of issues, we can create the solutions.

"I made a list of some points. I will try to keep them brief and concise. They are in no specific order, but they are all equally important and interrelated. It is essential to implement these solutions now. The gate is closing.

This is our call to action:

1. Capitalism is the foundation of the success of the United States of America. The nation cannot fund its services and provide security without revenue. A vibrant growing economy must be in place to achieve our goals and common purpose.

2. The nation's debt to gross domestic product has become unsustainable. The ratio was 43 percent in the mid-sixties. Current slow growth of the economy, along with burgeoning debt, continues to raise that ratio to a point where it will reach 100 percent in the very near future. That spells impending disaster. Domestic and foreign investment will stimulate the economy by eliminating all Capital Gains Taxes and Corporate Taxes. Urgent steps must be implemented to build a sound economy. Business leaders and entrepreneurs need confidence to grow and prosper.

3. Budgeting Revenue and Expenditures. Expenditures of the collected revenues is based on agreed upon line item percentages determined jointly by the Congress and the Executive Branch. The Congress will then prepare the budget in accordance with agreed upon percentages, which never exceed 100% of revenue. Expenditures are based on percentages of fiscal year revenue. Reduction of the national debt and interest payments on the national debt is a fixed budget item. Reserves are set aside for shortfalls.

4. Employment. Install active training programs to provide fundamental basic training and on-the-job training utilizing an intern process.

5. Security and Safety. Maintain the Armed Forces as presently organized. A stable military will be funded, staffed and equipped at optimum force levels. Mission accomplishment is a top priority.

6. Veterans Administration. Place the VA under the Department of Defense which will provide health care, health related services and other veterans services. All Honorably Discharged veterans will be eligible for all VA services.

7. Health Care. Social Security recipients are granted full health care. User-friendly processes are instituted for seniors 66 years of age and above.

8. Social Security and Medicare. The current Social Security System is phased out over a gradual time-period. All citizens, 66 years of age and older, who have contributed to Social Security, and/or their eligible family members, continue to be fully enrolled and maintained in the Social Security System. Social Security contributors between ages 50 and 66 may volunteer to remain in, or opt out of the system and be refunded 100 percent of their total contributions. They will enter the IRA and IHA Programs in Chapter 8. Social Security contributors under 50 years of age are refunded 100 percent of their total social security contributions. They will enter the IRA and IHA Programs in Chapter 8.

9. Health insurance is available for all citizens. Customized health insurance can be purchased through private insurance companies. Policies will be accessible across state lines with coverages and premiums structured similar to automobile or homeowners insurance. All citizens have the option to self-insure or partially self-insure.

10. The USA will decrease its dependence on foreign energy, except for energy sources from Canada and Mexico, to become an exporter of excess energy products. Federal land

will be made available. Permits will be granted and expedited for all qualified entities involved in the exploration, production and distribution of domestic energy. Mining permitting will be significantly expedited. The USA will focus on mining and processing rare earth metals, and other minerals required for industry and defense with emphasis on developing safe and economical nuclear energy. Energy production and distribution restrictions and regulations are rolled back 20 years. New nuclear power plants will be permitted according to safe, reasonable standards. Coal Fired Generating Station regulations will be examined and adjusted to allow the stations to operate within those guidelines. The energy distribution grid and pipelines and other energy distribution methods are brought to state of the art standards. An emphasis is placed on hydro, natural gas, wind, solar and other methods of power production.

11. Transportation efforts to develop new bio fuels is emphasized in order to promote more efficient transportation methods for goods and materials. Regulations are examined and adjusted to allow private enterprise to produce and develop new transportation methods and resources.

12. The USA will maintain its' present embassies and consulates. The US will respond with deadly force to protect each embassy. The US will demonstrate to the world that terrorism will not prevail. The USA will terminate its membership in the United Nations and request it to relocate outside of the USA. The USA will invite selected nations, with similar forms of government and similar ideals, to create and form a new functional world organization that supports and protects its members. NATO and former SEATO members might be likely prospective members.

13. Our military presence will be limited to our new partners. Military protection and assistance will be provided to countries that share our principles and ideals.

14. Education will be the responsibility of the parents. Vouchers are issued for all students enrolled in grades 1 through 12 to attend the school of their choice.

15. A country without borders is not a country. All borders and shores will be totally locked down to illegal trespassers.

16. All foreign nationals residing in the USA will have an option to enroll in a pathway to citizenship queue; be enrolled into a worker only queue; be placed into an education only queue; or be permitted to exit the USA. Established regulations will be established to ensure each queue meets prescribed standards.

17. The failed 'War on Drugs' will cease. Illicit drugs will be re-legalized and taxed at special rates. No one under 21 years of age is permitted to purchase, or use drugs of any kind or type except prescription drugs prescribed by physicians.

18. Current laws pertaining to the sale and use of alcohol-based products will remain the same with the exception they will be taxed at a uniform rate and will only be legal for purchase and use by those 21 years and older.

19. The 2nd Amendment is protected as written in the Constitution.

20. All prisoners convicted of violent crimes or crimes committed with weapons will serve their respective sentences. All other prisoners will qualify to enter a parole process, to gradually release all prisoners to be enrolled into productive work release programs.

21. The judicial structure will be studied and adjusted at all federal levels. Tort Reform will be implemented. Malpractice lawsuits will be fully examined and frivolous lawsuits scrutinized.

22. Term limits for elected officials and appointed federal officials will be instituted. The current system needs to be 'reset' as the true intent of public service has become "career oriented" instead of "service oriented."

23. The Congress must provide more oversight for all government activities. The Congress needs to function on a constitutional basis instead of an ideological basis. The Congress and the President will prepare annual balanced budgets.

24. Communications and the internet must be free and secure. The transmission of information and data is vital to the well-being of the country. Fiber-optic communication systems revolutionized the telecommunications industry. They will play a major role in the Information Age. New networks must be built.

25. Political correctness has become a self-serving, destructive monster that must be abolished. It is currently destroying the republic.

26. All redundant agencies duplicated by state agencies will be reviewed, assessed, reduced and/or eliminated.

27. Operation of the Federal Government will be streamlined to operate in a structured, cost effective manner. Elimination of waste and redundancy become a top priority. The federal government must change its culture to serve the states, and its citizens, not the other way around.

Dave wheeled into the plant parking lot a little early. Before they climbed out to retrieve their laptops and gear Tom cautioned, "We have a big day ahead of us. Genie is facilitating an important Implementation Action Team Meeting and Dave is training front line supervision on confrontation skills. Ron and I have a Progress Meeting with the plant staff. We have an intense day ahead of us. I am confident you will all perform superbly. I believe our new endeavor has raised our overall performance level. Good job everyone. We now start creating solutions.

"Bright futures do not just happen. They are the result of implementing well thought visions." — Bill Muckler

CHAPTER THREE | *The 20/20 Vision Summary*

1. Strong, sound organizations require strong people who are involved, and who contribute to the success of the organization.

2. Everyone has a role to play. Everyone is equally important.

3. The country is like a chain; each citizen is a link in that chain.

4. The USA must be like a stout chain with more than 300 million sturdy, golden links.

5. The 20/20 Plan provides opportunity for better conditions. It eliminates the poverty level.

6. US citizens should never taste the bitterness of poverty.

7. Many citizens are currently disinterested in the operation of the government.

8. The nation is now in the "dependency" phase.

9. Each person has a role to play in the success of the nation.

10. All individuals must add value, no matter their role, to this country.

11. Congress established a private cartel of banks to manipulate our currency.

12. The country needs to 'reboot' itself from jumbled restrictions.

13. There are many issues facing the nation. All are interrelated.

14. All issues must be resolved to be strong and prosperous.

15. Implementation of a total, comprehensive process is the only answer.

16. Government is best when it is limited, small and local.

17. The US has become a nation of subdued, captured wild pigs.

18. Capitalism is the foundation of the success of the United States of America.

19. The 20/20 Plan reviews and assesses all government agencies.

20. The 20/20 Plan eliminates waste and redundant agencies.

CHAPTER FOUR

The Economy

"Economy has frequently nothing whatever to do with the amount of money being spent, but with the wisdom used in spending it." - Henry Ford

FRIDAY AFTERNOON. WEEK 1.

Upon wrapping up their meetings and submitting their weekly reports that afternoon, everyone knew there was a lot of work to do for their client, and their newly acquired client: the USA. Neither would be an easy task. Gladly, it was Friday and the thought of going home to see families and refresh was welcome relief after a hard week at work. Some intense conversation during their travel time to the airport lay ahead.

The team had a typical Friday writing reports and conducting progress meetings with various managers and departments. A lot of effort was put into the plans and schedules for next week for both the client and the consultants. As the getaway time was approaching, Tom asked if anyone needed help, and would everyone be ready to leave for the airport on time. While the car was leaving the parking lot Tom declared, "As we said yesterday, we need to clearly state the problems and then design and create solutions plus an Implementation Plan for our 20/20 Vision. The culture of the country needs sweeping changes. It cannot be achieved piecemeal. The Whac-A-Mole mentality justified the excessive deficit spending that put the USA in this current catastrophic situation of a national debt sure to surpass $20 trillion by the next election."

Ron spoke up, "We can't discuss, or write, everything at once so we'll have to start somewhere. I say we work on solving the problems with the economy. Then move right into working on tax problems. That will get the ball rolling to solve the rest of the problems. When we solve the tax problem, we can start putting people back to work."

"Hold on a minute there big guy," Genie interrupted, "you're on the right track, but don't we have to have a budget first? We have to budget how much revenue is required to cover the country's obligations."

"You're right Genie," Ron answered. "We will also need to have a discussion on currency. I picked up something from the 'National Center for Constitutional Studies' that frames the issue. It gives insight on the gold standard and bailouts, etc.

"Congress shall have the power 'to coin money, regulate the value thereof, and of foreign coin, and fix the standard of weights and measures.'" (Article I, section 8, clause 5.)

"Why do politicians ignore the Founders wisdom? Requiring money to have a gold and silver standard is a protection for the people. It maintains a check on profligate spending by politicians. If politicians want to create a welfare or bailout program that costs, say $100 billion, and if our currency were still redeemable in gold and silver, they would have to come up with $100 billion of precious metal in order to generate the money needed. However if our currency has no redeemable value, all they need to do is to crank up the printing presses and print the money. As it pours out into the hands of the people, the people think they are really getting something so they will remember the generous politician at the next election. Except what they are indeed getting is devalued fiat money, but the people don't immediately know the difference. It is one of the oldest banking tricks around. It is stealing the value of the people's money."

The team arrived at the airport and turned in the red rental car. As they headed for their departure gates all wished each other safe trip and a good weekend. Everyone, especially Dave, was excited and eager to give the 20/20 Vision more thought.

MONDAY MORNING. WEEK 2.

Monday morning was greeted with much enthusiasm. The team was not only excited to go to work and help with all the plans and schedules they prepared Friday, but they were percolating with excitement to start designing and developing the new, clear vision for the country they loved. The 20/20 Plan would dominate the conversation during every opportunity they had away from work.

"I've thought a lot about this over the weekend," Dave exclaimed. Genie asked, "how about at the airport and your long flight home? Get your naps in?" Dave, being the junior member on the team was used to some teasing and smiled. "Actually, I got out my laptop at the airport gate and started making some notes. When I boarded, I decided to leave the laptop out and continue research on our 20/20 Vision."

"Next thing you're going to tell us is you finally got an upgrade," Genie teased. "You got it. Finally got an upgrade to first class. Seat 3D. Sure made working with the laptop easier. After that, the thought occurred to me that what we are doing is giving the entire population an upgrade. A citizen's upgrade to a better standard of living. To keeping more of their own hard-earned money. To prosperity and a sunnier life. An upgrade of their liberty and freedom."

"Awesome," Genie said stunned. "You've certainly found the passion and enthusiasm we should have all of the time. I'm impressed, and excited too."

"Let me share some of the economic issues the country is facing today," Ron opined. "According to polls, The Federal Reserve, Corporate Taxes, Housing Market, National Debt, Tax Reform, Trade, The Internet and Spying are the issues many are most concerned with. "The real issue is that everything in the country is related either directly, or indirectly, to the economy. America is most successful and sound when the economy is vibrant and growing; when people have well-paying jobs; and when they can make purchases and businesses can flourish. Right now, there is not a lot of confidence in the economy. The economy is growing marginally and at a snail's pace.

"The problem is the federal government is too involved in the economy. The Federal Reserve prints money and controls interest rates and the monetary process. Corporate taxes burden businesses and regulations stifle new growth. The Capital Gains Tax hinders investments in the economy and penalizes investors who most often are people who have their money in retirement funds.

"The 20/20 Vision gives business leaders and entrepreneurs' confidence to grow the economy and prosper. Rolling back regulations 20 years on the restrictions the government has placed on businesses is a great start. Elimination of Corporate Taxes will unleash an economy never designed to be shackled in the first place.

"Rescinding the corporate income tax will be a significant benefit to all American workers. Most people do not realize the token amount of revenue collected from the corporate income tax. $288 billion was collected in 2013, which was about seven percent of total tax revenues, or about 2 percent of the Gross Domestic Product (GDP). This tax burden forces American corporations to operate overseas, and thus keep their profits abroad to avoid paying these high taxes, rather than reinvesting them back into the United States. "Companies will have no incentive to operate overseas if the corporate tax is eliminated. When the corporate tax obligation is totally eliminated the Gross Domestic Product will skyrocket; real wages will increase significantly; and capital stock will increase dramatically. That will have a massive growth impact on the economy.

"It is common thinking that only businesses bear the brunt of corporate taxes. Nevertheless, in reality, it is the American economy, and ultimately each individual American who is punished by these taxes. The incentive for businesses to move and invest overseas is negated by eliminating the corporate tax. Workers also gain through significantly higher paying jobs. The United States has the highest corporate tax rate on the planet at about 40 percent when federal and state taxes are included. These taxes hurt American workers and the economy at large. According to a Congressional Budget Office study, workers bear 70 percent of the corporate tax burden. The Organization for Economic Cooperation and Development has identified the corporate tax as the most harmful tax for economic growth. Multinational corporations will flock to the United States to avoid corporate taxes.

"The federal government makes poor decisions when they hand out free money to banks and businesses that make bad decisions. Bailouts compound the problem. Politicians advocate bailouts for political reasons. Either they do not care, or they just do not understand the disastrous effects of propping up failed businesses.

"Rewarding bad decisions by giving a second, or third, chance doesn't make sense. Giving banks and businesses a safety net promotes continued bad practices. There is no penalty for failure or continuing to make faulty business decisions. No one learns from mistakes made because bad businesses are bailed out for making poor decisions.

"Another serious issue, and an even bigger controversy, is the Federal Reserve System. It is not a federal agency of the US government. It has no reserves and it is not a system. A group of international bankers privately owns the 'Fed.' They are a private banking cartel who Congress has given the total monopoly to 'create' money for the U.S. government. Their sole purpose is to turn a profit at the expense of unsuspecting citizens in the republic. In other words, they use their power to manipulate currency for their own gain and the taxpayer's loss.

They utilize two methods to accomplish this:

1. They manipulate interest rates to create "boom-bust" cycles which work to the advantage of the Federal Reserve and its banks, as they know exactly when our economy will boom, and when it will bust.

2. They increase the money supply by "creating" money. The United States government granted that authority to the 'Fed' when the Federal Reserve Act of 1913 was signed into law. The Fed doesn't use their capacity to fix economic problems. They use their influence to manipulate the economy to their advantage. That is clearly a conflict of interest. They are responsible for every inflationary period, every economic recession and every depression that has occurred during their entire unconstitutional existence.

"Our currency has lost almost all value. The dollar today is worth only four tarnished pennies down from one hundred when the Federal Reserve was created in 1913. The Fed profits from each financial bailout our government approves. These bailouts all ultimately fail and harm our economy even more. The more money the Fed creates, the more our national debt and inflation increase. Both conditions are cataclysmic.

"The Consumer Price Index (CPI) Annual Average has increased from 9.9% in 1913 when the Federal Reserve Act was first signed into law to 233% in 2013. Consumers pay much more for goods and services than their income has increased. Prices go up while wages stay the same or fail to keep up with the CPI. Everyone loses but the 'Fed.'

"I'd like to share how the younger generation views the course the federal government is on," Dave interjected. "I found some interesting information on the internet concerning millennials which is close in age to where I come from. This is from the National Center for Policy Analysis (NCPA) and other studies.

"Millennials distrust political parties and are largely socially liberal but fiscally centrist, according to the latest Reason-Rupe survey. Young Americans are largely unaligned with traditional political parties. Millennials support for a government that provides more services declines when the costs of such services become clear.

"When millennials make more money, they become more responsible. The poll reports 54 percent favor "larger government with more services," while 43 percent favor "smaller government with fewer services." However after introducing tax rates into the mix, 57 percent favor smaller government. Similarly, of those millennials whose parents pay their health insurance, 57 percent favor increasing health insurance premiums to provide the uninsured with health coverage. Fifty-nine percent of millennials who pay for their own health insurance oppose paying more in premiums, while just thirty-nine percent favor paying higher premiums.

"Of those making less than $20,000 annually, 53 percent support income redistribution, while 39 percent oppose it. Among those making $40,000 or more, only 42 percent support income redistribution while 54 percent oppose it. The survey found mixed support for government action:

Seven in 10 millennials support government guarantees for housing, health insurance and income, yet only 32 percent reported that they preferred a government-managed economy, compared to 64 percent who supported a free market over a state-managed market. Sixty-four percent of millennials have a positive view of competition and profit. More than half reported that they would like to start their own businesses.

While just 42 percent of millennials believed that government was inefficient and wasteful in 2009, 66 percent reported thinking so today. Sixty-three percent said that regulators favor special interests over the public.

"Significantly, only 16 percent of those surveyed could accurately define socialism, yet 42 percent reported preferring socialism to capitalism. The survey also indicated that young American adults believe in personal responsibility and other free-market values. When asked to explain success, respondents listed hard work, ambition, and self-discipline as the top three explanations for wealth. The most common reasons for poverty were poor life choices, lack of job opportunities, and lack of work ethic. According to the report, six in ten want to live in a society that distributes wealth based on achievement, even at the expense of unequal outcomes. Source: "Millennials: The Politically Unclaimed Generation," Reason-Rupe 2014 Millennial Survey, July 10, 2014.

"While this shows some confusion, I think it clearly states that people from the younger generation prefer personal responsibility and free market values over a life of little achievement with no clear vision of the future," Dave continued. "And I guarantee we don't like being taxed for everything we do especially when we don't know where the tax money goes or if it is spent wisely or judiciously. Young Americans are trapped as the gate is being slammed shut."

The discussion on the economy concluded as the team arrived at the plant to start the new week. It was becoming apparent the four fully understood economic issues and they had a firm grasp on reality.

MONDAY AFTERNOON, WEEK 2.

A robust discussion was certain to take place as the four-team members started their ride to their home away from home. The economy always generated a lively debate. They were also going to weigh in on the controversial Federal Reserve System. Ron kicked things off with some basic background about the Fed.

"The Federal Reserve Act was enacted on December 23, 1913, as an Act of Congress that created and set up the Federal Reserve System. The Fed is a central banking system granted the legal authority to issue Federal Reserve Notes, commonly known as the U.S. Dollar and the Federal Reserve Bank Notes as legal tender. The Act was signed into law by President Woodrow Wilson."

"There are a lot of pros and cons about the 'Fed,' its establishment and usefulness in the US," Tom interjected. "The nation used to be on the gold standard. After many years, America ended the gold standard in 1933, when President Franklin Roosevelt banned private ownership of the metal. President Richard Nixon severed the tie to gold in 1971. What we have left is a system of 'fiat money' which means the dollar is backed by the good faith of the government rather than gold. Some economists state reverting to gold could do more harm than good. The gold standard brought about some long-run price stability, but it also led to short-run volatility. The management of money is easier with fiat currency. There may not be enough gold to back the dollar. Gold and silver plus other precious metals could be the answer."

"The American people need to learn more about the Federal Reserve and their policies," Dave said. "The Fed is exempt from paying income tax on their profits. They cannot be audited and do not answer to the President or the Congress. The President appoints the Board of Governors but has no control over their activities. Congress has no control over their activities either. They hardly ever agree to appear before Congress.

"The Federal Income Tax Law was enacted in the same year as the Federal Reserve Act. Prior to 1914, the U.S prospered and the government paid its' bills without revenue from income tax." Ron interrupted, "Excellent point Dave," Ron continued. "Individual income taxes accounted for 45 percent of all federal tax revenue in 2012. Social Security and Medicare payroll taxes (which are also a tax on income) brought in 35 percent. Corporate income tax and all other tax sources made up the remaining 20 percent.

"Prior to ratification of the 16th (income tax) Amendment in February 1913, the federal government managed its few constitutional responsibilities without an income tax. During peacetime tariffs made up most or all of the revenue collected. Congress could afford to run the federal government on tariffs alone because federal needs did not include welfare programs, agricultural subsidies, or social insurance programs like Social Security or Medicare. The government paid off its entire national debt once without the existence of an Internal Revenue Service. President Andrew Jackson boasted in his veto of the Maysville Road Bill in 1830 that God had blessed the nation with no taxes, except tariffs, and no national debt.

"The advent of the income tax prompted some congressmen to note this tax was designed not principally for revenue — the U.S. government had always had plenty of money from tariffs — but to manipulate the American people and their choices in the market. Some said the chief purpose was social, not financial. It was said the individual citizen would be called on to lay bare the innermost recesses of his soul in affidavits, and with the aid of the Federal inspector who will supervise his books and papers and business secrets. He may be made to be good, according the notions of virtue at the moment prevailing in Washington."

"100% of the income taxes Americans pay is used to pay off the national debt, which the 'Fed' creates. The purpose is to manage the nation's money supply and achieve the task of full employment and stable prices while they are fighting inflation, or deflation. These goals can be at cross purposes," Tom declared from the shotgun seat.

"How would the U.S. economy function if the Federal Reserve was eliminated?" Genie asked. "Something has to take its place, doesn't it?

"The same way it did prior to 1913. Very well indeed. Global markets would need economic direction from the U.S. The Fed manages the world's leading currency, the dollar. Elimination of the 'Fed' could put those markets into chaos about who's managing U.S. interest rates and the American economy," Ron said.

"If the 'Fed' were eliminated and the nation did not return to the gold standard, couldn't the Treasury Department be responsible for the amount of money being injected into the economy?" Genie asked.

"Congress would then resume their lawful responsibility for the regulation of the value of the nation's currency. That is in the Constitution. The citizens then could vote on who controls the US currency and therefore the US economy," Dave retorted.

"The Treasury Secretary is appointed by the President but must be approved by the Senate. That could cause some interesting political debates. But the greater good of the country is more important than political battles," Tom answered emphatically.

"The 'Fed' has legal independence from the White House and Congress," Ron replied. "If decisions are made by the Treasury Department, that economic autonomy could be in question. The political parties' economic policy battles could be brutal.

"Whatever replaces the 'Fed' should be independent. There would need to be an agency in the government that replaces what the Fed does while also being completely free of political interference. The political influence of the 'Fed' has grown over the years. Critics of the 'Fed' have grown as well. It is almost impossible to limit the power of the 'Fed.' Whatever replaces the 'Fed' must be more transparent in its actions and policies."

"Transparency is certainly needed," Dave interjected. "Many people have creative ideas about how to regulate the value of the currency. This quote is intriguing:

The central bank is an institution of the most deadly hostility existing against the Principles and form of our Constitution. I am an Enemy to all banks discounting bills or notes for anything but Coin. If the American People allow private banks to control the issuance of their currency, first by inflation and then by deflation, the banks and corporations that will grow up around them will deprive the People of all their Property until their Children will wake up homeless on the continent their Fathers conquered. "

— Texas Congressman Wright Patman, in 1933

Pattman appears to have been the first to say Thomas Jefferson said this. If Thomas Jefferson had seen the Federal Reserve System of today, he surely would have said something similar to this.

"This may be the most controversial issue among economists," Tom said. "The only thing we know for sure is what is in place now is not working. Congressman Wright Patman of Texas was brilliant when he warned us about central banks. Here are excerpts from what he said on September 29, 1941, as reported in the Congressional Record of the House of Representatives (pages 7582-7583):

"When our Federal Government, that has the exclusive power to create money, creates that money and then goes into the open market and borrows it and pays interest for the use of its own money, it occurs to me that that is going too far. I have never yet had anyone who could, using logic and reason, justify the Federal Government borrowing the use of its own money. . . I am saying to you in all sincerity, and with all the earnestness that I possess, it is absolutely wrong for the Government to issue interest-bearing obligations. It is not only wrong: it is extravagant. It is not only extravagant, it is wasteful. It is absolutely unnecessary."

"Wright Patman gave an example on bonds that explains this," Tom Said.

"Now, take the Panama Canal bonds. They amounted to a little less than $50,000,000 — $49,800,000. By the time they are paid, the Government will have paid $75,000,000 in interest on bonds of less than $50,000,000. So the Government is paying out $125,000,000 to obtain the use of $49,800,000. That is the way it has worked all along. That is our policy. That is our system. The question is: Should that policy be continued? Is it sane? Is it reasonable? Is it right, or is it wrong? If it is wrong, it should be changed."

"Wright Patman made this argument about changing the system," Tom said.

"Now, I believe the system should be changed. The Constitution of the United States does not give the banks the power to create money. The Constitution says that Congress shall have the power to create money, but now, under our system, we will sell bonds to commercial banks and obtain credit from those banks.

"I believe the time will come when people will demand that this be changed. I believe the time will come in this country when they will actually blame you and me and everyone else connected with this Congress for sitting idly by and permitting such an idiotic system to continue. I make that statement after years of study."

"If the Government can issue bonds," Genie inquired. "Why doesn't it issue money and save the interest?"

"Abraham Lincoln insisted that the Government should," Tom stated. "Quite a few clear-headed Americans have said the same. Thomas A. Edison explained it this way: If our Nation can issue a dollar bond, it can issue a dollar bill. The element that makes the bond good makes the bill good also. It is absurd to say that our country can issue $30 million in bonds, and not $30 million in currency. Both are promises to pay: but one promise fattens the usurer (banks), and the other helps the people."

As they approached the hotel, they were excited about the lively conversation. They knew their points concerning the 'Fed' and the Income Tax were solid. The team was now ready to move on to a new, but related, topic: Budgeting and Taxes.

CHAPTER FOUR | *The Economy Summary*

1. A growing, vibrant economy is a cornerstone of the American way of life.

2. A balanced budget depends on expenses not exceeding annual revenues.

3. Congress has the power to coin money and regulate the value thereof.

4. Printing devalued fiat, or free, money is stealing the value of the people's money. Fiat money harms the economy and creates inflation.

5. Bailouts do more harm than good as they prop up failure.

6. Corporate taxes provide little revenue while they encumber business.

7. Eliminating corporate taxes will cause the GDP to skyrocket.

8. Corporations do not pay taxes. In reality, the citizens pay those taxes.

9. A Congressional Budget Office study shows workers bear 70 percent of the corporate tax burden.

10. The USA has the highest corporate tax rates on the planet at about 40%.

11. Corporate taxes harm American workers and the economy at large.

12. Capital Gains Taxes penalize citizens when they invest in the economy of their country.

13. The Federal Reserve System is not a part of the United States government.

14. Private Banks own the 'Fed.' It is not a federal agency.

15. The Federal Reserve has been the root cause of inflation for 100 years.

16. The CPI Annual Average has mushroomed from 9.9 percent in 1913 when the Federal Reserve Act was enacted to 233 percent in 2013.

17. The Fed is a central bank that must be padlocked. Whatever replaces the 'Fed' must be more transparent in its actions and policies.

18. Younger citizens support the free market, competition and profit.

19. Millennials explained success by listing hard work, ambition, and self-discipline as the top three explanations for wealth.

20. The 20/20 Plan gives the American people an upgrade to prosperity.

CHAPTER FIVE

Budgeting and Taxes

"We contend that for a nation to try to tax itself into prosperity is like a man standing in a bucket and trying to lift himself up by the handle." — Winston Churchill

TUESDAY MORNING. WEEK 2.

The four met in the parking lot and opened car doors as Ron began speaking. "The budget must be based on revenues; not expenditures. Congress needs to appropriate expenditures based upon an agreed on formula whereas expenditures do not exceed revenues. A balanced budget must be implemented and it must be based on the percentage of the budgeted items, not on dollar amounts that can be easily manipulated and exceeded."
"Go on," Genie said. "I think you're on to something that makes perfect sense. Please explain yourself a little more, with some examples."

"Okay," Ron said. "Here's a good example that everyone can relate to. The two political parties argue incessantly over the amount to spend on defense. They should instead vote on the percentage of total revenue needed for defense to keep us safe and secure. Lets' presume the agreed upon budget for defense is 20 percent. With that figure in place, everyone in the country now knows twenty percent of their tax dollars are devoted to the defense budget. Voters then have the power to approve, or disapprove, the percentage of their tax dollars they want to budget and where, by electing representatives who comply with their intentions.

"The Budget and Accounting Act of 1921 established the framework for the modern federal budget. It was approved by President Warren G. Harding to provide a national budget system and an independent audit of government accounts. The official title of this act is 'The General Accounting Act of 1921,' but it is commonly referred to as "the budget act," or "the Budget and Accounting Act." This act meant that for the first time, the President would be required to submit an annual budget for the entire federal government to Congress. The object of the budget bill was to consolidate the spending agencies in both the executive and legislative branches of the government.

"It's mindboggling to think in terms of how many billions are going to defense and the other departments, or bills. The 20/20 Plan compels Congress to balance the budget and only allocate 100 percent of revenues to expenditures. People can understand a budget that calls for 110 percent of funds, for example. They know immediately that the government is spending 10 percent too much."

"Wow," Dave said. "That's going to take a really big paradigm shift."

"I have a suggested model for a balanced budget," Ron answered. "Just a broad brush look at it for talking purposes. The current budget is divided into mandatory spending and discretionary spending. The current proposed budget using round numbers to illustrate my point is approximately $4 trillion. Using that as the base and applying percentages, the budget can be built by adjusting spending as a percentage of the whole.

Projected budget (2015) for Mandatory and Discretionary Spending:

Mandatory Spending	65% or $2.70 Trillion
Discretionary Spending	29% or $1.16 Trillion
Interest on Federal Debt	6% or $0.24 Trillion

"As we can see, this is not a viable plan over a long period of time. No one can guarantee Mandatory Spending and Interest on the Federal Debt will not increase. This implies Discretionary Spending must eventually decrease. It is obvious that Discretionary Spending will eventually reach 1 percent by applying the current model employed by Congress. The result, little, or no, money remains for the military, education, transportation, agriculture, science, energy, international relations or operating the federal government to name some of the major budget categories. This process is deeply flawed. Now we know the reason the budget is never balanced. It cannot be. Thomas Jefferson stated this concerning spending the income of future generations:

"The principle of spending money to be paid by posterity, under the name of funding, is but swindling futurity on a large scale." - Thomas Jefferson

A simpler, more direct way to budget the nation's funding is:

Interest on Federal Debt and Debt Reduction 10%	$400 Billion
Education 15%	$600 Billion
Military and Veterans Benefits 20%	$800 Billion
Social Security and Medicare 30%	$1.2 Trillion
Employment and Training 10%	$400 Billion
Science 2%	$80 Billion
Infrastructure and Transportation 3%	$120 Billion
Federal Government Operation 10%	$400 Billion
Proposed Budget-Spending Model (20/20 Plan Balanced Budget)	$4 Trillion

"Obviously some minor adjustments need to be made to this example, but as a general rule the budget will look something like this. With strong economic growth, reserves will be possible to not only balance the budget but also to further reduce the national debt. An objective of the budget process should be to reduce the debt, and therefore reduce the amount of interest the taxpayers are misusing each, and every year, ad infinitum.

"The categories listed above focus on the priorities of the nation. The full faith and credit of the USA depend on payment of interest on the debt, paying down the national debt, and having a balanced budget. Education is critical if we are to educate our children to be creative and productive instead of being potential weak links. The military needs to be strong, and state of the art, to keep us safe and to do the things required to be the leader of the free world. Social Security and Medicare are important. It is our obligation to take care of our senior citizens. They carried the torch for us over their lifetimes. Employment and Training will grow and sustain an economy that provides funds to operate the government. The federal government must be efficient and effective, not in competition, or redundant to the state governments.

"This is great stuff." Tom said. "Lets' talk about other issues we need to work on. I'll take notes. Budget and Taxes set the stage. Next issue should be service and employment. Then Defense and Veterans Relations; Social Security; Health Care and Medicare; Energy, Oil, Gas, Mining and Minerals; International Relations; Education; Immigration; Alcohol, Firearms, Drugs and Substance Abuse; Prisons and Parole; The Judicial Process; The Congress and Term Limits; Political Correctness; The Operation of the Government; and finally Implementing the 20/20 Process. We can add anything else we discover. We may have several sub-topics under each major topic."

"The IRS employs 114,000 people. More than double the CIA and more than triple the FBI. Taxpayers receive no value from the IRS. Taxes hurt us all," Ron said.

"That simplifies it Ron. Dozens of hidden taxes are paid by citizens every day," Genie said.

"No one pays all of them, but we are all taxed into oblivion. When citizens are paying upward of 50 percent, and more, in taxes, the economy is stifled because money is better spent when it fuels the economy, not the government. Every tax dollar diverted from the economy suppresses the economy.

"Politicians have become extremely creative in finding ways to confiscate our money. Most Americans don't realize the extent of purchasing power that is taken from them.

"Using Pareto's Law of Mathematics, 20% of Americans pay 80% of all taxes, while 80% only pay 20% of the tax burden. While some people might think this is fair and equitable, how can anyone trust the 80% who only pay 20% receive any significant benefit from this tax scheme?" Ron queried. "Just because a person pays less, doesn't purport that citizen receives the full benefit of the taxes paid by those who pay more taxes.

"When taxpayers pay more than 50 percent of earnings to the government, they lose motivation to earn more money just to turn it over to the government. A small percentage of the population now pays more than half of what they earn to various government agencies. Fifty percent is fundamentally wrong. Twenty percent is equitable."

Tom led the discussion, "let's see if we can make some sense out of the tax debacle. Ron, this is your pet subject and you have shared some great ideas with me. This country really needs to do something different, not only to help the taxpayers, but to reduce the pointless price tag of revenue collection."

"Thanks Tom." Ron got right to the point. "We must eliminate each and every federal, state and local tax of every type in the entire USA. No more taxes, period."

Everyone in the car sat stunned as Dave almost ran off the road. Genie spoke up, "Ron, if you say that to anyone, you will scare them to death. How will the country generate revenue to pay for all of the goods and services the country needs? In addition, what will happen to the IRS? On second thought, do not answer that. Most people will answer that question using some very strong language."

"Here's some information we found on the internet," Tom inserted. "Examples of taxes levied on citizens. There are more taxes than listed here, and not all apply to everyone, nevertheless this list is an indicator of the overall problem. The following is a partial list of more than 100 taxes Americans pay every year, most of which did not exist 100 years ago:

Examples of taxes levied on citizens:

1 Air Transportation Taxes
2 Biodiesel Fuel Taxes
3 Building Permit Taxes
4 Business Registration Fees
5 Capital Gains Taxes
6 Cigarette Taxes
7 Court Fines (indirect taxes)
8 Disposal Fees
9 Dog License Taxes
10 Drivers License Fees (another form of taxation)
11 Employer Health Insurance Mandate Tax
12 Employer Medicare Taxes
13 Employer Social Security Taxes
14 Environmental Fees
15 Estate Taxes
16 Excise Taxes on Comprehensive Health Insurance Plans
17 Federal Corporate Taxes
18 Federal Income Taxes
19 Federal Unemployment Taxes
20 Fishing License Taxes
21 Flush Taxes (yes, this actually exists in some areas)
22 Food And Beverage License Fees
23 Franchise Business Taxes
24 Garbage Taxes
25 Gasoline Taxes
26 Gift Taxes
27 Gun Ownership Permits
28 Hazardous Material Disposal Fees
29 Highway Access Fees
30 Hotel Taxes (these are becoming quite large in some areas)
31 Hunting License Taxes
32 Import Taxes
33 Individual Health Insurance Mandate Taxes
34 Inheritance Taxes
35 Insect Control Hazardous Materials Licenses
36 Inspection Fees
37 Insurance Premium Taxes
38 Interstate User Diesel Fuel Taxes
39 Inventory Taxes
40 IRA Early Withdrawal Taxes
41 IRS Interest Charges (tax on top of tax)
42 IRS Penalties (tax on top of tax)
43 Library Taxes
44 License Plate Fees
45 Liquor Taxes
46 Local Corporate Taxes
47 Local Income Taxes
48 Local School Taxes
49 Local Unemployment Taxes
50 Luxury Taxes
51 Marriage License Taxes
52 Medicare Taxes
53 Medicare Tax Surcharge on High Earning Americans under Obamacare
54 Obamacare Individual Mandate Excise Tax (if you don't buy "qualifying" health insurance under Obamacare you will have to pay an additional tax)
55 Obamacare Surtax on Investment Income (a new 3.8% surtax on investment income)56 Parking Meters
57 Passport Fees
58 Professional Licenses and Fees (another form of taxation)
59 Property Taxes
60 Real Estate Taxes
61 Recreational Vehicle Taxes
62 Registration Fees for New Businesses
63 Toll Booth Taxes
64 Retail Taxes
65 Self-Employment Taxes
66 Sewer & Water Taxes
67 School Taxes
68 Septic Permit Taxes
69 Service Charge Taxes
70 Social Security Taxes (FICA)
71 Special Assessments for Road Repairs or Construction
72 Sports Stadium Taxes
73 State Corporate Taxes
74 State Income Taxes
75 State Park Entrance Fees
76 State Unemployment Taxes (SUTA)
77 Tanning Taxes (a new Obamacare tax on tanning services)
78 Telephone 911 Service Taxes
79 Telephone Federal Excise Taxes
80 Telephone Federal Universal Service Fee Taxes
81 Telephone Federal, State and Local Surcharge Taxes
82 Telephone Recurring and Non-recurring Charges Tax
83 Telephone Minimum Usage Surcharge Taxes
84 Telephone State and Local Taxes
85 Telephone Universal Access Taxes
86 The Alternative Minimum Tax
87 Tire Recycling Fees
88 Tire Taxes
89 Tolls (another form of taxation)
90 Traffic Fines (indirect taxation)
91 Use Taxes (Out of state purchases, etc.)
92 Utility Taxes
93 Vehicle License Registration Taxes
94 Vehicle Retail Tax
95 Waste Management Taxes
96 Water Rights Fees
97 Watercraft Registration & Licensing Fees
98 Well Permit Fees
99 Workers Compensation Taxes
100 Zoning Permit Fees

"Despite this oppressive taxation," Ron continued, "local, state and federal governments are drowning in debt. Balancing the budget has no priority. When the U.S. government first imposed a personal income tax back in 1913, the vast majority of the population paid 1 percent, and the highest marginal tax rate was 7 percent. However, as we now know, numerous increases in tax rates have occurred over the past 100 years with many more on the drawing board. The tax rate has exploded. Purchasing power has imploded.

When people rob banks, they go to prison.

When they rob the taxpayer, they get re-elected.

When banks rob the people, they get bonuses and bailouts.

"The entire tax issue is out of control. I read these facts in various articles. Hope the writers don't get mad at me for using them. In any case, this is not a simple matter. I don't know how anyone can possibly keep up with the ever-expanding tax laws.

"According to the National Taxpayers Union, the IRS currently has more than 2,000 publications, forms, and instruction sheets to download from the IRS website. The instructions to file a Form 1040 is 189 pages. 100 years ago, the instructions were two pages long. There have been over 4,428 changes to the tax code during the past decade. It is incredibly costly to change tax software, tax manuals and tax instruction booklets for all of these changes. Yet the taxpayers foot the bill for this obscene expense every year so the federal government can collect more tax money from them. Ironic, is it not?

"The U.S. tax code is now 3.8 million words long. The entire collection of William Shakespeare's works are only about 900,000 words long. Our tax system has become so complicated it is almost impossible to file taxes correctly. For example, in 1998 *Money Magazine* had 46 different tax professionals complete a tax return for a hypothetical household. All 46 came up with a different result. In 2009, *PC World* had five of the most popular tax-preparation software websites prepare a tax return for a hypothetical household. All five arrived at a different result.

"The IRS spends $2.45 for every $100 it collects in taxes. That is a penalty of 2.45 percent on every dollar collected by the federal government. It's similar to paying a fine to an agency no one likes. It is an unnecessary expense item for our budget.

"According to The Tax Foundation, the average American works through the middle of April just to pay federal, state, and local taxes. 'Tax Freedom Day' came on January 22nd back in 1900. Now we work an additional 3 months to earn tax money," Ron concluded. "It is evident the abolishment of the current tax system is necessary for the United States to change course and step on sound footing again. Twenty (20) trillion dollars in national debt, and its recurrent interest payments to service the debt, will soon cost the country one (1) trillion dollars per year, which is a poor key indicator for a once strong nation. Clearly, neither major political party seriously considers tax reform. They suffer from Paradigm Paralysis. So unless someone, I guess that's us, devise a better plan, we will be stuck with a tax code that crushes the country," Tom stated.

"Of course, we need a method to generate revenue, but revenue generation must be voluntary, not mandatory," Ron continued boldly. "Bear with me on this. All the obscene taxes we pay are mandatory except for sales taxes. We can choose to buy, or not to buy, taxable items. This is a murky subject, as some states do not tax the purchase of food, while some states collect full, or partial, sales taxes on food. Taxation on food and groceries should be uniform in all states. Sales tax on groceries cost low-income families proportionally more than high-income families since groceries are a higher percentage of their overall expenditures. The 20/20 Plan is not oppressive for low-income families who spend a larger amount on food in proportion to higher income families.

"The bottom 20 percent of earners receive $8.13 in federal spending for every dollar they pay in federal taxes. The top 20 percent receive $0.25. That's an enormous gap. The result is politicians use the tax code to play citizens against each other. One can argue this from both sides, because that is their belief, or paradigm. The best method to absolutely unite America is to absolutely eliminate the income tax.

"The controversy over corporate taxes is also extensive. In reality, corporations do not pay taxes. They pass their tax burden onto the general public and their own workers. They build their tax burden into the price of the goods and services they provide. Consumers indirectly pay corporate taxes through higher prices. The corporate tax may technically be a tax on business, but consumers, investors and workers ultimately bear the tax burden. When a corporation pays higher taxes, it takes measures to compensate for those lost dollars, whether in raising its prices, which hurt consumers, or docking wages or cutting back jobs, which hurts workers. Moreover, this tax steers businesses to expand abroad and retain profits rather than paying higher dividends to shareholders.

"Corporate taxes must be eliminated in order to build a robust economy. Why force businesses to jump through hoops to find the loops they need to reduce their tax burden. Reduced cost of tax preparation and auditing will further reduce consumer prices. More corporations will rush to the United States as a result. This in turn will produce a vibrant economy and many more high paying jobs.

"Capital Gains Tax. Many investors complain about this tax. The Capital Gains Tax is immoral and counter-productive. It is criminal to tax the citizens of our republic for investing their earnings in the economy of their own country."

"That's exactly what it does and it does need to be eliminated," Tom interjected. "This alone will bring in huge investments from citizens and investors all over the globe. The result will be a gigantic boost to the economy and many more jobs. Many report citizens, and corporations, have more than $2 Trillion parked in overseas accounts to avoid taxation. That money will come back to America when the economic and tax environment is favorable to them.

"Another thought I have," Tom went on, "is politicians promote 'tax free zones.' States, counties and local governments give tax breaks to corporations to relocate their business. Well if a 'tax zone' is good for one area, why isn't it good for the entire country?"

"It is," Ron stated emphatically. "Taxes are a costly burden to administer and collect. The income tax is the perfect example. The current income tax penalizes people for holding a job. Who but a politician could devise a cruel scheme so sinister as to tax people for working in their own country to build their own economy? We did not have an income tax 100 years ago and we should not have one now. Dave, you will have to slow down to 5 mph if I am to describe how harmful this list of taxes imposed on us is and how burdensome and ridiculous they are before we get back to the hotel for dinner.

"Before I get into the details of tax collection, I need to tell you what will not be taxed. This is critical because it is an important feature of the entire foundation of how this process is designed." Ron took a deep breath and continued, "All federal, state and local income taxes will be eliminated. Withholding taxes cease to exist and are not confiscated from paychecks. Payroll taxes will be eliminated as well. So let me move on to the ideal replacement plan."

"Does that mean Social Security Taxes will be eliminated," Genie interrupted.

"Yes. We need to explain the 20/20 Plan when we address the Social Security issue," Ron answered. "The 20/20 Plan eliminates all hidden taxes. For example, we receive a price when we sign a cell phone service contract. Nevertheless, when we receive the bill, the total is always at least 20 percent higher. The extra amount is the result of hidden taxes and fees."

"I'm for that," Dave said, "I just want to pay for what I buy. Not all of the hidden add-ons. Just tell me what the extras will be. Actually, I do not think they know. That is another thing wrong with the tax payments we make. We just do not know what they are. I really love the way we are looking at this. Hope others love what they see."

Ron further illustrated, "When a person searches for an airline ticket, the website quotes a price. Upon purchase, the total ticket price is 30-40 percent higher. Gasoline at the pump includes taxes, from several government agencies, commonly known as the fuel tax. The federal government first imposed it in 1932 at a mere 1 cent per gallon. Some states imposed fuel taxes earlier than that. They have now escalated to $0.184 plus $0.304 for federal and state taxes respectively. That totals $0.488 per gallon and by now, the average price per gallon is clearly more than 50 cents. Oil companies wish they could receive that much money for doing nothing but taxing it."

Dave pulled into the client's parking lot and found a parking space. "Okay team," Dave said. "We're here. I'm looking forward to a big day training supervisors, but I can't wait to hear what we'll talk about on the afternoon drive back to the hotel."

TUESDAY AFTERNOON. WEEK 2.

After Tom rounded up the other three team members at 5 o'clock, they packed up, got in the white rental car, buckled up and started for the hotel. Tom opened the conversation stating, "We accomplished a lot at work today. I made some mental notes. I'll share them with you to point our new project in the right direction. These issues are all connected and I am confident we can apply the very same principles and techniques to the 20/20 Plan. That's why we utilize a coordinated team to work on these issues."

Everyone was exhausted but sat up with a jolt when Ron said, "Remember, we need to eliminate each and every federal, state and local tax of every type in the entire USA. No more taxes, period."

"Okay. Let's cover that again," Genie requested. "The only tax is a 'Retail Tax?'"

"Correct, one tax, period." Ron stated emphatically. "A Retail Tax of 20 percent applied to all goods and services purchased at the retail level by individual consumers, or by businesses for their own use. There is no value added tax, or any other tax. No taxes are applied to process materials. Taxes eat up 40% of the average family's income; that is more than they spend on food, clothing and shelter combined. That's double the 20/20 Plan Retail Tax.

"These Retail Taxes are to be collected the same way state and local sales taxes are currently collected. This process eliminates billions of dollars spent on tax collection by the IRS. It simplifies the entire system since citizens no longer need to keep records for the IRS. All businesses and contractors registered with the several state entities are required to complete a simple state form for retail sales and taxes collected. They then electronically remit taxes to the Department of Treasury. This is a very simple process compared to present tax complications business owners' face.

"Here's how the collection process works. The Department of the Treasury receives weekly electronic payments from each of the fifty states, and other areas, or territories that collect and pay taxes to the US Federal Government. The Department of the Treasury then credits the collected retail taxes to the state and the county they are collected from, in accordance with the formula of 50%/25%/25%. 50 percent is retained by the federal government; 25 percent is remitted to the state that collected the taxes; and 25 percent is remitted to the county that collected the taxes for their budget which then is responsible for appropriating those received funds to the various agencies and municipalities they serve in accordance with its' budget requirements.

"Certain items will be excluded from the 20 percent retail tax and are not to be taxed under any circumstances. This list is inclusive to food and non-alcoholic beverages purchased in grocery stores, health food stores and/or at convenience type stores that sell retail grocery items. Money spent on approved education and materials is tax exempt.

"Rent for primary housing, banking transactions, investments, prescription drugs and hospital and doctor's fees that are related to personal health issues are tax exempt as well. For example, purchases made at River City Nutrition in Kirkwood, Missouri for nutritional supplements and other health aids are not taxed.

"Items to be taxed at the 20 percent rate are the same as all items presently being taxed with the addition of services that are now tax exempt. Businesses that sell services will now collect retail tax at the same rate as those businesses that sell goods. The tax playing field is now level."

"For example, purchases made from the 'Cardinals Clubhouse Shop' in the Mid Rivers Mall in St. Charles County, Missouri will be tallied at the end of the calendar week and entered on a State of Missouri Retail Tax form. The amount of Retail Taxes collected that week, on those purchases, are immediately transferred electronically to the State of Missouri. This process is similar as what is currently in place. "Give us an example of what is to be taxed?" Genie requested.

"Okay," Ron explained. "You and Dave are going to have to pay a 20 percent retail tax when you get your hair cut. Tom is going to have to pay retail tax on his massages, unless he has a doctor prescribe them for his bad back. Our client is going to pay retail tax on our consulting service. The landscaping service that mows my lawn every week when I travel will charge me retail tax. Moreover, Dave that supervisor you are working with in the maintenance department will pay 20 percent retail tax on the engagement ring he is talking about buying. Gasoline will be taxed at 20 percent of the retail price. There will also be an Extraction Tax on natural resources taken from United States land. I think we all get the idea.

"Prices will come down as businesses compete for the extra dollars everyone now have in their take home pay. The sum of about $50,000 dollars per year was mentioned earlier as median household income. Before the 20/20 Plan, the annual take home pay for the wage earner was about $35,000 of that $50,000. Under the 20/20 Plan, that same wage earner will now bring home about $65,000 per year. That $30,000 increase will go a long way toward making needed purchases since taxes and other labor expenses are not deducted from paychecks. The maximum Retail Tax paid on that additional $30,000, if spent entirely on taxable purchases, would be $6,000 per year. The obvious benefit to the consumer is a huge annual increase of an additional $24,000.00 in purchasing power. This effectively resolves the decreasing purchasing power problem."

"Will you explain that in detail for us?" Genie inquired.

"Yes. Let me work through the process first," Ron said. "Prices will naturally fall as competing businesses pass on the savings that result from their relief from corporate and other taxes. Not to mention less overhead from accounting and bookkeeping costs. Reprieve from expensive pointless regulations is another benefit of the 20/20 Plan as well.

"The relief each of us receives from huge breaks in real estate taxes, capital gains taxes, taxes on dividends and interest will result in greater wealth for everyone at every economic level. Furthermore, we are bound to invest some of that additional money which will further fuel the economy. Everybody wins when senseless taxes and oppressive government regulations and restrictions cease to impede business operations.

"What about real estate taxes," Genie asked? "They're a burden on everyone in every age group, especially seniors on fixed incomes."

"Good question. Real Estate Taxes will be a one-time tax at the rate of 20 percent of the real market value of primary residential property. That includes land, buildings and improvements. The 20/20 Real Estate Tax Plan is 20 percent or one-twentieth of the total sale over a period of 20 years. For example, a home with a market value of $200,000 will be taxed $40,000. That homeowner has the option of paying their real taxes annually at a rate of $2,000 per year for 20 years or making a one-time payment of $40,000. At that time, the homeowner's tax obligation is fulfilled. This same concept is applied when purchasing an automobile, boat or other large purchase. In short, the home is forever tax-free for the resident.

"Homeowners are permitted to finance their real estate taxes with their current mortgage provider, or a different provider if desired. This method is similar to the present method of real estate tax escrow payment and collection. This creates a healthy competitive environment for real estate tax loans while allowing homeowners to retire the tax burden on their own property.

"Senior citizens are provided additional relief from real estate tax payment. Seniors will only pay real estate tax until they are 85 years of age. Seniors over 66 will pay a prorated tax depending on the difference in years before they reach 85 years of age. Citizens over 85 never have a real estate tax obligation on their primary residence.

"Wait a minute," Genie interjected. "What about my mortgage deduction and the real estate tax deduction I take when I fill out my tax return? I need that deduction."

"Great question," Ron answered. "This is the wonderful part of the 20/20 Plan. You never have income tax deducted from your paycheck and since you do not pay income tax, you do not need a tax deduction. All previous deductions are instantly added to your paycheck. Tax records and tax deductions are outdated. That dreadful, distressing chapter in our nations' history is finally erased. Moreover, that applies to businesses as well.

"Retail tax rates on vehicles, boats and firearms are taxed at the 20 percent rate. This also applies to luxury type purchases such as yachts and private jets. Some states have punitive luxury taxes on these products that have proven counterproductive. Most highly paid craftsmen were laid off because the luxury tax discouraged retail sales of these products and therefore production. The only thing luxury taxes produced was unemployment. The 20/20 Plan puts skilled workers back to work at higher paid jobs.

"Businesses will pay a 20 percent retail tax on all business services purchased, or contracted, by registered companies or contractors. That includes consulting services, and contract labor. For example, repairs to office equipment such as a copy machine, or computer, will have retail tax applied to it. Repairs, or maintenance, on business production equipment is taxed one time at the rate of 20 percent. This eliminates burdensome and confusing depreciation rules. Loopholes are now extinct.

"Services purchased, that are included in the retail cost of products and goods are exempt from the retail tax as they are taxed in the retail sale of those products and goods when they are sold. The 20/20 Plan prohibits double taxation. For example, when a painter completes the painting job, the painter will invoice the total cost of paint used plus the expended labor cost. This is the only tax that is collected. No other business tax is collected, or levied. Let me explain further with an example: the All American Painting Company is contracted to paint a portion of the facility at Boeing in St. Louis for $100,000. The invoice submitted to Boeing will include the 20 percent retail tax added to the invoice for a total cost of $120,000. This is the only tax either company will ever pay for this service. Moreover, no corporate taxes are levied, period. Simple.

"Additionally the cost of exploration and drilling of natural resources such as oil, gas, minerals, etc. are included in the retail cost of that product. Extraction of those resources will be taxed at the 20 percent rate. This is the Extraction Tax. There is a very specific reason for this. Companies benefitting from the resources they extract from the land cannot replenish those resources. They are removed from America forever and therefore compensation needs to be made for that one time benefit. Calculation of that tax is based on the retail price of that resource. For example, a barrel of oil, to be refined and sold at the gasoline pump will equate to a certain amount of gallons of gasoline. Typically, a 42-gallon barrel of oil will produce 19 gallons of motor gasoline. The Extraction Tax on that barrel of oil will be 20 percent of the average cost of a gallon of gas at the pump multiplied by

19 gallons. The remainder of the barrel will produce other fuels such a jet fuel, etc. The 20 percent Extraction Tax is applied to them as well and therefore is a compilation of the retail prices of all these various byproducts.

"Internet retail sales will be taxed at the rate of 20 percent. This tax is to be reported and collected in the state of the seller. This is a complex issue as the seller may have an internet site located in one state and offices in another state, or many states. This is further complicated by inventory or warehouse location and shipping point. Internet taxation is an extremely complex issue. The 20/20 Plan provides a uniform tax in all states. The home state of the purchaser receives the credit for the retail tax.

"Utilities, including electricity, gas, water and oil are taxed at the 20 percent rate. Fuel oil and other energy products used for heating, and/or commercial uses will also be taxed at the 20 percent rate. With regulations reduced and corporate taxes eliminated, energy costs will shrink and be passed on to the consumer. Gasoline and diesel fuel will be taxed at the 20 percent rate. The 20/20 Plan dramatically reduces gas prices at the pump as the USA reduces its dependence on foreign oil. Consumers will experience gasoline outlays at half, or lower, of current prices.

"I've discussed the next area of tax collection with all of you individually during breaks and lunch as this is the final answer to the trillion dollar question," Ron stated. "Alcohol, tobacco, firearms, drugs and prostitution are now taxed and at higher rates. The 20/20 Plan adjusts the tax rate for these items. Further definitions and adjustments may be required as there are many product variations within these groups.

"Each state currently has its own spirits retail tax plus some type of excise tax on adult beverages. These taxes are imposed whether sold individually by the drink, or by package retail. For example, Washington State has the highest liquor tax at 100 percent. Expensive place to buy a drink. The states issue liquor store licenses to sell alcoholic products. The tax rates will be uniform for all states.

"Beer, wine and similar products, under 20 percent alcoholic content are taxed at 50 percent. Spirits of any type, 20 percent of alcoholic content are taxed at 100 percent. Retail sales, and use, of these products is prohibited to anyone under 21 years of age. Violations will carry progressive fines. Like alcohol, each state has its own retail taxes plus other taxes on tobacco products. The average price of a pack of cigarettes is now $6.00. The total average taxes (excise, sales and state) is $3.35. The total retail tax in every state will be 100 percent on all tobacco products. Sale and use of these products is prohibited to anyone under 21 years of age. Violations carry progressive fines.

"Firearms, and ammunition, will be taxed at the 20% rate. This conforms to the 2nd Amendment right to bear arms and enables citizens to protect themselves without being penalized. However, there is a one-time registration fee (similar to an auto title) of $100 per item. Possession of unregistered firearms carry harsh progressive fines. The purpose of this process is to remove any, and all, illegal guns from unauthorized users.

"Drugs are also taxed. Since most drugs are illegal in most states, this will be a difficult retail tax to administer, collect and monitor. However, these products need to be re-legalized. The cost to the taxpayer to conduct the 'War on Drugs' is massive and ineffective. Law-abiding citizens, who pay taxes on purchased products that do not require policing, pay an unjust burden, as taxes are not collected on products that are destructive and require expensive policing. This levels the playing field.

"In other words, drugs may be purchased and used with restrictions. There are many product variations within each type that further definitions must be made. Sales, and use, of these products are prohibited to anyone under the age of 21 years. Proof of purchase of these drugs must be available on demand by authorities. Violations will carry large progressive fines.

"States will register retailers of these products and issue licenses to be displayed at point of purchase. The 20/20 Plan requires re-legalized drugs be packaged in a manner that displays functional bar codes, retail prices and taxes collected. Retailers must report and remit collected taxes using the same reporting method as the sale of other retail products and services. Retailers of these products will be regulated and be subject to quality and sanitary inspections, similar to the food industry.

"Marijuana will be taxed at the rate of 100 percent; manufactured drugs such as meth will be taxed at the rate of 200 percent; cocaine and cocaine byproducts will be taxed at the rate of 300 percent; and heroin and other similar addictive drugs will be taxed at the rate of 500 percent. Progressive fines starting at $10,000 will be levied for violation of the business registration, display, retail, use and consumption of the drugs.

"Prostitution, the oldest profession, is a destructive act that is criminalized in most states. This is another example of an activity that costs the taxpayers disproportionate expenses to police with no tax revenue in return to offset the costs of supervision and safety. The 20/20 Plan legalizes prostitution for only those over 21 years of age in order to regulate the activity and generate revenue. Licenses must be displayed at the business location. The same strict regulations mandated on the sale of drugs apply to acts of prostitution. Progressive fines will be levied for violations. A monthly health and sanitary inspection and license examination will be made at the business location to ensure participants do not spread diseases and potential, under-age participants are not employed in the trade.

"That's a lot to take in," Genie said. "Many people will struggle to accept some of these retail taxes and activities. Nevertheless, they have to weigh the costs and benefits. Why should taxpayers pay to police products and activities that generate no revenue? More links in the chain will be stronger because this will now be a tax issue. Wasn't that Al Capone's downfall?"

Now it was Tom's turn to complete the circle as he said, "this brings us back to business registration. Each business entity must register in each state in which they have facilities, and/or employ personnel. There will be some exceptions and adjustments to be made later.

"All businesses must register with the state or states in which they operate. Small businesses operating out of one location or out of a home residence office fall into the basic business category. Independent contractors fall into this basic category as well.

Another business category is one that has more than one location within the state, and/or operates multiple locations in multiple states. Businesses that sell alcohol, tobacco, firearms, drugs and prostitution must register as a separate classification.

"A $500.00 annual registration fee is required for all businesses. This $500 fee applies to businesses with one to ten employees. These businesses incur an additional weekly registration fee of $1.00 per additional employee on the payroll over ten. A weekly report consisting of a roster of employees, hours worked, compensation paid to the employees' checking and benefits accounts must be submitted to the state. This measure eliminates under the table payments and protects employee benefit plans now and in the future. Registration fees are remitted in the same manner as Retail Taxes.

As Dave turned into the hotel parking lot, he looked at the gas gauge and thought about how much it cost each week to fill up the rental car before returning it to the rental agency at the airport. He also thought about how much of his take home pay went to filling the gas tank at home. "Taxes are killing all of us," he said. "Okay team, we're here."

"It appears we have covered every taxation category one could think of," Genie opined. "Surely, there are more issues to resolve, but this is a useful representative sample. A good start to get people thinking and a perfect example of the 20/20 Vision. Cover 80 percent of the examples. The remaining 20 percent will be addressed later." As the team retrieved their briefcases, Tom said, "Let's discuss Service and Employment tomorrow morning."

CHAPTER FIVE | *Budgeting and Taxes Summary*

1. Budgeting is the foundation of the operation of the government.

2. Balancing the Budget must be the top priority of Congress.

3. The budget process needs to be based on percentages spent, not dollars spent.

4. Taxes are oppressive, complicated and they stifle the economy.

5. 20 percent of Americans pay 80 percent of the tax burden.

6. The remaining 80 percent of Americans pay only 20 percent of the tax liability

7. Those who pay 20 percent receive no significant benefit from this tax system.

8. Too many taxes are levied by too many agencies.

9. Citizens pay more than 100 different taxes every year.

10. Local, state and federal governments are drowning in debt despite this oppressive taxation.

11. 100 years ago, most Americans were taxed at a rate of 1 percent.

12. Income taxes penalize citizens for working and building the economy.

13. Citizens are at the point where they pay more in taxes than they keep.

14. The 20/20 Plan eliminates all taxes except the retail tax on goods and services.

15. The IRS has more than 2,000 publications, forms, and instruction sheets.

16. The U.S. tax code is now 3.8 million words long.

17. The 20/20 Plan Retail Tax is 20 percent on goods and services with exceptions.

18. Higher tax rates will be levied on tobacco, alcohol, drugs and prostitution.

19. The 20/20 Plan makes the United States of America a tax free zone.

20. The 20/20 Plan eliminates the cost of the government intermediary.

CHAPTER SIX

Service and Employment

"Individual commitment to a group effort - that is what makes a team work, a company work, a society work, a civilization work." — Vince Lombardi

WEDNESDAY MORNING. WEEK 2.

The team was looking forward to a new topic to brainstorm as they started for work the next morning. Tom led the conversation with, "Dave came by the room last night and ran some excellent ideas past me. We both agreed it is imperative that every citizen participate to forge a bright future for the country. The high unemployment rate among teens and young people encourages us to find a path they can take to build solid careers. Typical government programs seldom work. If they did, the unemployment rate would not be more than 20 percent. Dave, go ahead and get us started."

"The analogy of the country being a chain with more than 300 million links led me to some practical ideas." Dave expanded, "everyone has to have skin in the game. Everybody needs to feel a part of something. Be involved. Have a common bond. Presently, students graduate from high school and they cannot get a job. They don't have experience or skills. They don't have a work ethic or discipline. They don't have direction or a clear path. They have no sense of purpose or future. They need guidance.

"They all need to participate in a similar experience that bonds them together through meaningful achievement and exposure to a positive reality that defines a clear path to their future. It must be a developmental experience that gives them specific job, and/or career skills. It must be a practical common sense path with a future.

"Each American has a personal obligation to develop the skills necessary to obtain and maintain employment. Some have those skills, however many young people have not had the opportunity to develop work skills. The United States must give them the training to learn those skills if the country is going to have a robust economy for all to enjoy and participate in.

"Entering a service program is the best tried and true method to accomplish this goal. The 20/20 Plan has a program that includes everyone. Fundamental training all will feel a part of; all belong to; and all are able to relate to afterwards. A fresh positive experience to give hope and help to become strong, solid links in the 300 million-link chain.

"Sounds like a big undertaking. Are you proposing that we start training the entire nation?" Genie questioned. "Who will begin the program?"

"Yes, I am. At least initially, all who need training to obtain and sustain a purposeful and successful career. This, of course, pertains immediately to those younger Americans who are left out of the job market; to those who cannot get a job because they have no suitable experience; to those the job market left behind or bypassed. The 20/20 Plan forges a perfect partnership between businesses who now are unshackled from taxation and the youth of the country who will now have valuable skills to be treasured employees. Remember, everyone has a role to play in the success of the nation. Everyone is a link in the chain.

"No undertaking is too big that puts the nation on a path of freedom and prosperity. Nothing is too big if it gives our young people hope and a sense of purpose. The future of our nation depends on having well-trained, qualified workers."

"How will this work?" Genie asked. "We've implemented processes with some large companies, but this seems huge. Who will administer this program?"

"A new department with a cabinet level secretary will administer this new program named the 'AmericaWorks Career Program.' This is a two-year, four-phase job training program for high school graduates. Enrollees in the program have the opportunity to choose their desired career field. They are presented the opportunity to take an aptitude test to help them determine their most suitable career field. Selecting a military service will be a viable alternative option in lieu of the AmericaWorks Career Program.

"It is huge, and we will manage it the same way we always do. After all, you're the one who taught me how to do this. Take it 'one step' at a time. Eating the elephant one bite at a time by training individuals and groups in a 'hands-on' program. Each young male and female citizen, at age of 18 is eligible to enter the two-year training program known as 'AmericaWorks.' This mandatory program will initially include everyone who is between the ages of 18 and 27. There will be an initial period where emphasis is placed on 'training the trainers.'"

"What if someone wants to attend college, or they already have a job?" Genie queried. "Will there be exceptions or deferments?"

"Of course," Dave replied. "Everyone, including males and females, 18 and older, who graduate from high school during the first year of the 'AmericaWorks' program will be called to enter the program. This will apply to the first year of the program and then later to all those who graduate from high school in subsequent years. This will be the starting point. Those who choose to enter college may request a deferment until they receive their bachelor's degree, or until they reach the age of 27.

"Those who have left high school previous to the start of the program will be systematically called to enroll into the 'AmericaWorks' program. Those without jobs receive first priority. This provides everyone with an opportunity to receive training and preparation for his or her future careers. Those young citizens who have collegiate degrees and have jobs will have the option to request a deferment. However, they may also elect to volunteer for the 'AmericaWorks' intern program.

"Okay. I think I got it,' Genie stated. "But I can think of some more exceptions. What about people who are ill, or are disabled? How will that work?"

"Genie, I can't imagine a day that you don't ask me a ton of questions," Dave answered. "In any process, there are going to be exceptions. Citizens with disabilities will be evaluated and it will be determined which special needs program is best for them. This is similar to programs in which they may have been enrolled in elementary school or high school. Everyone needs an opportunity. Most people would rather work, be productive and experience a positive sense of accomplishment than be relegated to unemployment with little hope for a sunny future. There are meaningful important jobs for everyone in society. Each person has a role to play. Everyone wants the good feeling of accomplishment and self-worth. Every link in the chain wants to be a strong link."

"What if an enrollee has problems?" Genie asked. "Not all trainees will be highly motivated. Some are likely to cause problems and disrupt the program. Some may want to drop out of the program or may want to drag their feet."

"This is an age old problem military units, schools and employers face," Dave answered. "The goal of the 20/20 Plan is a 100 percent success rate. There will be criteria established to deal with the inevitable exceptions. There will be consequences for troublemakers. Those with limitations will be treated with respect and applicable programs will be established to make them strong links in America's chain.

"Military service remains another viable option. Young citizens will be afforded continued opportunities to enlist in the United States Armed Forces as an alternative to the 'AmericaWorks' program. Emphasis is placed on both essential training and maintaining the military at optimum staffing and strength.

"Everyone will initially go through an introductory training period of twelve weeks of 'AmericaWorks' as a job intern. The interns will live on a base during this phase, which is conducted at a boot camp like training facility. Each intern will receive, at no cost to the intern, work uniforms and receive pay, quarters and subsistence as a part of the training program benefits. This initial phase includes physical fitness, nutrition, hygiene, first aid, outdoor survival techniques, communications skills, workplace safety and firearms safety along with intangibles such as teamwork, leadership, work ethics, confidence training, work discipline and personal budgeting and economics. The training program is a blend of physical and classroom activity. The goal is to give the interns a fresh start in life in the best physical and mental condition of their young lives. Trainees who complete the introductory training course receive a certificate validating their accomplishment that becomes an important part of their resume.

"The second or intermediate phase, of AmericaWorks, is a twelve-week program as well. Elements of the introductory phase, such as fitness, nutrition, workplace safety and communications skills continue, however, emphasis is now placed on job instruction, shop work and training in the discipline, or career field, of their choice.

"Examples of the many career fields trainees may elect, and receive training in, during the intermediate phase are: medical, foreign service, communications, technical trades, electronics, law enforcement, equipment operator, mechanical trades, electrical trades, vehicle repair, culinary arts, transportation, legal, arts, sales, business management, economics and many more. The 20/20 Plan provides training for a Peace Corps type organization. This is an important element of the AmericaWorks Program. Trainees who complete the intermediate training course receive a certificate validating their accomplishment that becomes an important part of their resume.

"The third phase, a twenty-four week advanced phase of 'AmericaWorks' will be either 'on the job' training, or advanced technical career instruction. Some career choices naturally lend themselves to 'on the job' training. These trainees are then placed with either public or private employers and they actually enter the workforce as interns. Some examples of this training are construction, vehicle repair, and culinary arts. Employers who provide advanced intern training programs are responsible for developing and implementing customized training programs for each intern.

"These training programs are very specific and detailed. Each documented curriculum contains comprehensive, precise tasks and activities that are performed under the supervision of the employer, or the employer's supervisors. The employer is also responsible for conducting a periodic assessment of each employee with the objective of continued improvement toward mastery of the career field. Trainees who complete the advanced training course receive a certificate validating their accomplishment that becomes an important part of their resume.

"Some career fields in the advanced phase may require training of a more specific, progressive nature. Examples of this training are in the medical field, such as nursing, or technicians, Foreign Service, electronics, law enforcement, firefighting, etc. Trainees who complete the advanced training course will receive a certificate validating their accomplishment that will be an additional important part of their resume.

"The fourth phase, or work phase, is a one-year actual work period as an advanced intern. Trainees are placed in intern employment programs where they may work for either public or private employers. Many of the third phase intermediate 'on the job' interns may continue to work for the same employer in the same or similar capacities. The objective of this phase is to prepare trainees for future full employment. The Assessments and Certificate processes remain in place for this phase.

"The fourth phase for those who received specific advanced training is similar to the 'on the job' program in the above paragraph. Again, this is a one-year, 'on the job, actual work phase, as an advanced intern. Examples of these jobs would be medical, foreign service, communications, technical trades, electronics, information technology, law enforcement, firefighting, security, forestry, etc.

"An example of performing 'on the job' training as an intern for an actual employer is working as a carpenter who works for a contractor learning how to build residences, commercial buildings, or forming for concrete work. Another example is a vehicle mechanic working as an intern at an automobile dealership, or perhaps for a truck repair shop. Another example is someone who prefers a career as a chef with employment as an intern in a restaurant, or by a catering company.

"Those are really good examples," Tom said. "Give us some specifics on the other advanced training programs for interns such as medical or foreign service."

"When I used medical as an example, I implied many career choices," Dave stated. "One intern may choose nursing, while another may elect to be a Magnetic Resonance Imaging (MRI) technician, whereas others may prefer to be a pharmacist, a lab technician or an Emergency Medical Technician (EMT). Many avenues are available to develop these skills.

"Foreign service has many opportunities as well. There is a service opportunity to travel to and work in foreign countries. These work assignments include medical assistance, teaching, residential, commercial and industrial construction, information technology and other jobs helping growing countries achieve their goals. This is more beneficial and productive than dumping money into despots' foreign bank accounts.

"Law enforcement, firefighting and related activities such as working as interns for state, county and local governments are excellent work options for those desiring to enter civil service type careers. Here again training programs will be documented and implemented to provide the intern with useful work experiences.

"Infrastructure construction is an important need in America. Some interns may opt to work in road and bridge building and repair while may choose upgrading the electrical grid.

"A training program to install a fiber-optic network includes learning many job activities and skills. Building a fiber-optic communications network to transmit data and information is vital to the future of the nation. Fiber-optic communication systems have revolutionized the telecommunications industry and have played a major role in the advent of the Information Age. Because of its advantages over electrical transmission, optical fibers have largely replaced copper wire communication in core networks in the developed world. Telecommunications companies use optical fiber to transmit telephone signals, internet communication, and cable television signals.

"Some of these paths may not be the eventual career field for the intern. Many people change jobs and careers," Dave mused. "I changed my college major after my sophomore year. That choice was best for me and I presume it may be for some others. However, one of the great aspects of this program is that it will prepare the trainees to work. That is most important. Many people change jobs, but many of them take work skills and work ethics with them. This program gives them that opportunity."

Genie leaned forward toward Dave in the front seat and said, "you have done a great job explaining this. Another question. What is the process for employing these interns? Who will be responsible for their compensation? What is their pay scale?"

"We need to delay the answer to this question. The entire 20/20 process is so interrelated and interconnected that we need to discuss the payroll foundation of the 20/20 Plan first," Tom replied. "The strength of the 20/20 Plan is its total connectivity and cohesiveness. Because the 20/20 Plan is completely integrated, it will be successful, where other programs have failed or not lived up to their expectations. This is the first time our nation will implement a wholly integrated training process. We all know that 'now is the time' for it."

As Dave pulled into the parking lot at the office, he said, "Looks like we need to take this up on the ride back to the hotel this evening. Much detail is involved and it'll take some math and understanding of how payroll systems work to explain and demonstrate the wage structure of the 20/20 Plan."

WEDNESDAY AFTERNOON. WEEK 2.

After some sharing of progress about their client's project at the end of the day, the team was eager to hear what Dave had to say. So much so, that Ron took the keys to drive back to the hotel this evening. Dave started out the discussion from the back seat, "guys, I'm probably going to get into more detail than we need to at this point, but I want to get your input. I want to make sure this makes sense. I'm using the same principles and techniques employed in models we utilize with our business clients."

"We're good with that," Genie said. "Whenever we watch politicians on TV, they can never answer how their policies work. We need practical solutions that work. I'm looking forward to learning the full scope and depth of this aspect of the process. Will this process apply to everyone employed in the United States?"

"Yes it will. It applies to full time and part time employees and their new 20/20 Plan compensation. It applies to both hourly and salaried employees at every level, and, of course, it applies to interns. In other words, if someone receives a paycheck, the 20/20 Plan process applies. I have examples of how the plan applies to independent-contract workers, self-employed contractors, wait staff, etc. Employees receiving a weekly, biweekly or monthly paycheck will receive their full paycheck. That paycheck will include the employee's wages and the employees full cost of employment. Employers are responsible for calculating the full cost of employment and they are mandated to make full disclosure of those calculations.

"Remember the example in Chapter Five (5) that explained how a wage earner who earned the median annual income of $50,000 per year takes home about $35,000 per year. $15,000 of that $50,000 is deducted for taxes and benefits. Under the 20/20 plan, that same wage earner now brings home about $65,000 per year. The $30,000 increase is the difference the government and others take from the employees hard-earned wages. The employee cost to be on the employer's payroll is $65,000, but the employee only takes home $35,000. Equivalent to a $30,000 raise.

Some more examples:

"A forty hour week employee making the 20/20 Plan minimum wage of $10.00 per hour is now paid a full $400.00 per week, plus, and this is a huge benefit, they will also receive their full, true compensation package. The details for this entire process are simple but a lot to understand. Start with minimum wage earners and it becomes apparent how this process will work for everyone else, no matter their pay level.

"The Federal Minimum Wage Rate established under the Fair Labor Standards Act was $0.25 per hour on October 24, 1938. It was increased to $1.00 per hour in 1950; $2.00 per hour in 1974; $5.15 per hour in 1997, and finally up to $7.25 per hour in 2009. I bring this up, not because I have judgments on the validity, or the purpose of the minimum wage, but because this is a very critical keystone in this entire process.

"An employee who earns the minimum wage of $7.25 per hour actually costs the employer much more than $7.25 per hour. The total employment package is always much more than what the employee receives. The employer pays these costs to various agencies. Employees never see these costs. To eliminate the complex tax situation our nation has become a slave to, and corrupted by, we have to start here.

"Each employer pays 50 percent of the Payroll Tax (FICA) while the other half is deducted from the employee's gross payroll amount. Furthermore, to dispute many politicians, these deductions do not go into the employee's lockbox. They go into the general revenue fund. This fund costs American workers more and more every year.

"Income Taxes (Withholding) are also deducted. The employer pays Workmen's Compensation, Unemployment Compensation and other benefits as well. These true costs of labor are deducted taxes, benefits and other payroll costs. However employees never receive their full fruits of the labor. They go into the rabbit hole, not into the paycheck.

"These costs vary by location, industry, etc. and can vary between 20 percent and 50 percent. They typically add an additional 25 percent to the employers cost to employ a worker. In some industries, they can be as high as 90 percent. This example will use 25 percent for illustration purposes. When the employer provides full or partial paid health insurance, this of course adds to the total labor cost of the employer and employee. Exceptions are left out of these calculations, as it is difficult to know which benefits each employer pays. Another aspect of this is vacation and holiday pay. These benefits vary from employer to employer, especially between public sector and private sector employees. The 20/20 Plan proposes benefits be applied voluntarily by each employer. Employees may elect to receive their vacation pay when their vacation is due, or they may elect to have it paid proportionally to them in their regular hourly or salaried pay.

"To determine the true cost of employment, using the minimum wage of $7.25 per hour, 25 percent, or $1.81 per hour, must be added to the base pay of $7.25 per hour. The true cost of employment is $9.06 per hour. This does not include health insurance, holiday pay or vacation pay. This cost is higher if they are included. Overtime pay remains at current levels.

"This illustrates a basic misunderstanding most employees have. The actual cost per hour to the employer is $9.06, plus those other benefits if they apply. However, the employee only receives net pay of $5.75/hour, or $3.31/hour less than their true cost to the employer. $5.75 per hour multiplied by 40 hours/week equals a net paycheck of $230.00 per week. $3.31/hour taken from the employee every hour multiplied by 40 hours/week equals $132.40 per week hidden and not paid in the weekly paycheck.

"The 20/20 Plan solves that mystery. The minimum wage employee now brings home $362.40 per week or $18,844.80 per (52-week) year. This places that worker above the poverty level. That same employee only earned $11,500 per year under the existing tax code. The lost purchasing power is $7,344.80 per year. That is huge.

"The 20/20 Plan, a clear vision transparent pay plan, mandates a Federal Minimum Wage Rate of $10.00 per hour be paid to all employees. Employees keep the entire $10.00/hour. They own their own money. The government does not take it away.

"The 20/20 Plan minimum wage decrees wage earners who earn less than $10.00 per hour have their pay rate adjusted upward to $10.00 per hour or higher to include their total labor cost. Those who earn $10.00 per hour or more or salaried employees who are paid $400.00 per week or more will have their pay adjusted up to reflect their new pay rate, which includes the 20-50 percent actual labor cost and employee benefit package.

"The 20/20 Plan minimum wage employees now take home annual pay of $20,800 per year. This almost doubles the take home pay of the current minimum wage earner who takes home less than $12,000 per year. This lifts bright, talented and gifted people with potential out of the poverty level. People that were told they would never succeed in this country but who needed nothing more than training, direction and hope."

"Does the 20/20 Plan benefit both the employer and the employee?" Ron asked.

"Yes. It benefits both as it simplifies the payroll system for both," Dave replied. "Employees keep their earnings and the employers save wasted expenses. The employer does not pay more wages to the employee under the 20/20 Plan. All compensation is only paid to the employee. The governmental bureaucracy is cut out as is government involvement in the business community," Dave affirmed. "The 20/20 Plan actually saves the employer money by not being burdened with tax preparation, compilation, and collection for each employee on the payroll. Employer accounting and payroll tasks and activities are reduced under the 20/20 Plan.

"The employee obviously benefits with the 20/20 Plan, as each employee now has full control over their entire earnings. The quality of life, and the increased standard of living, is twofold. This changes an employee's life in immeasurable ways. The 20/20 Plan mandates that employees be paid by "direct deposit" to the bank or credit union of their choice. There are two practical reasons for this. The first prevents employers from paying unreported cash to employees under the guise that it is a simpler and faster method to give them spending money. The second ensures employee wages are entered into their proper benefit accounts. Using the new minimum wage of $10.00 per hour, as an example, 80 percent, or $8.00 per hour, is direct deposited into the employee's general account. 20 percent, or $2.00 per hour, is paid in the form of a direct deposit to the employee's benefit accounts."

"What happens to that 20 percent, or in this case $2.00 per hour?" Genie asked.

"Great question," Dave replied. "This money is owned by the employee. The employee earns the full paycheck. Therefore, the full amount is deposited into the employee's account. Each employee is required to have a bank or credit union type account. Accounts for payroll purposes are set up for each employee and these accounts are under the sole ownership of the employee. The employer distributes earnings into the checking and benefits accounts by direct deposit immediately on the day of each pay period. Distribution of earnings is made automatically into the employee account. Employees have immediate access to $320.00 per week, or $90.00 per week more than under the income tax system.

"Individual Employee Accounts are established. They consist of five (5) separate, but linked, sub accounts.

These tax-free and fee free accounts are as follows:

Individual Checking Accounts (ICA). Eighty (80) percent is direct deposited into this employee owned account. (Optional Checking or Debit Account)

Individual Retirement Accounts (IRA). Ten (10) percent, or half, of the 20 percent is direct deposited into this employee owned retirement account. (Benefits Account)

Individual Health Accounts (IHA). Five (5) percent, or one-fourth, of the 20 percent is direct deposited into this employee owned health account. (Benefits Account)

Individual Employment Accounts (IEA). Five (5) percent, or one-fourth, of the 20 percent is direct deposited into this employee owned employment account. (Benefits Account)

Individual Savings Accounts (ISA). This is a savings account for employees to make voluntary deposits on an optional basis. Employees, and/or the employer, may direct deposit earnings into this account. Earnings deposited into this account may only be taken from the 80 percent portion of the total earnings. (General Account)

"Salaried employees earning $400 per week have 80 percent, or $320.00 direct deposited into their employee ICA. Twenty percent or $80.00 per week will be deposited into the employee's benefits accounts distributed in the form of a direct deposit to the employee's appropriate benefit accounts.

"For employees earning more than minimum wage, or more than $400 per week, the exact same percentages apply. Employees paid bi-weekly or monthly will have their earnings directly deposited in the same manner.

"Can you give us an example of how that would work for employees who earn the Median Annual Household Income of about $50,000.00?" Genie requested.

"I'll give you both a salaried example and an hourly example," Dave answered. "Using $50,000 as a Median Annual Household Income which is a federal government statistic rounded off to make the math easy to understand, but still a representative figure.

$50,000 plus 30 percent true labor cost (example explained in Chapter 5) or $15,000, elevates the 20/20 Plan total take home pay to $65,000.00. This is an increase in take home pay of $30,000.00 per year and disbursed as follows:

TYPE	PERCENT	WEEKLY	ANNUALIZED	OLD TAX
ICA.	80%	$1,000.00	$52,000.00	$0.00
IRA.	10%	$125.00	$6,500.00	$0.00
IHA.	5%	$62.50	$3,250.00	$0.00
IEA.	5%	$62.50	$3,250.00	$0.00
ISA.	Voluntary Contribution from Employer or Employee - Net Pay			
Total:	100%	$1,2500.00	$65,000.00	$35,000.00

"Example: An employee who previously earned $20.00/hour now receives $26.00/hour with the 20/20 Plan. Yearly pay is now $54,080.00. (New weekly pay is $1,040.00.) The 20/20 Plan increases take home pay by $24,960.00/year ($480.00/week) Table follows:

TYPE	PERCENT	WEEKLY	ANNUALIZED	OLD PLAN
ICA.	80%	$832.00	$43,264.00	$0.00
IRA.	10%	$104.00	$5,408.00	$0.00
IHA.	5%	$52.50	$2,704.00	$0.00
IEA.	5%	$52.50	$2,704.00	$0.00
ISA.	Voluntary Contribution from Employer or Employee - Net Pay			
Total:	100%	$1,040.00	$54,080.00	$29,120.00

If employer paid health insurance is part of the total wage package, it must be added to the total labor package cost which in turn adds to the total gross paycheck. An employee option to this distribution plan is for the employer and employee to mutually agree to direct deposit an amount equal to the health insurance previously paid in benefits to the employee.

"If an employee changes employment, their Individual Bank Account (IBA) plus benefit accounts remains with them for life. The employee is now the sole owner of that account and all money held in that account. Married employees may elect to have all accounts placed in joint names similar to present bank practices. This IBA does not preclude an individual having other bank accounts in other banks."

"What regulations, or restrictions, govern these accounts?" Ron asked.

"Now is a good time to clarify how these accounts benefit the employee," Dave responded. "Employees set up their own account while they are either employed, or beginning employment. Once this IBA is established, it remains the sole property of the employee for life. The employee can use the account with subsequent and/or multiple employers. In addition, if an employee, who is now a bank customer, decides to change banks, the accounts are immediately transferred to the new bank at no charge. Another benefit of the IBAs is the bank may not charge a bank service fee on these accounts. These accounts are established as interest bearing checking and savings accounts to further benefit the employee. Rules, regulations and restrictions on the IBA and each sub account are:

ICA. Earnings deposited into this account are as stated in the above examples. Several options are available. For example, partial wages may be elected to be deposited into the various benefit accounts including the ISA in lieu of the ICA. These deposits are optional based on the employee's desire to save additional funds. Vacation and/or holiday pay benefits may be direct deposited into the ISA.

IRA. Earnings deposited into this account will be as stated in the above examples. Several options are available, for example, additional voluntary earnings of the ICA deposits can be deposited into this account if the employee elects to invest additional amounts into this retirement account.

"Earnings deposited into this account may be entirely, or partially, invested in approved Retirement Investment Accounts that are solely owned by the employee. These approved accounts offer options that range from low yield to high yield accounts based on the employee's risk tolerance. Investments in the IRA would typically be money market or mutual fund type investments.

"All retirement account investments may be linked to, and governed by, this account. This is a safe guard to prevent funds from being diverted from this account for any reason, including fraud or early withdrawal. Existing traditional and Roth IRA Accounts, and/or 401K investment type accounts may be rolled over into this account.

"Those individuals under the age of 50 years, who have contributed into the Social Security System, are refunded the full amount of their total Social Security Account contributions. The Department of the Treasury on their date of birth deposits these contributions annually into the IRA. The total contributions credited to the account are prorated over the number of years the contributor has remaining to age 66. Example: a 46 year old with $100,000 total contributions is refunded $5,000 per year for 20 years to invest, or save, in their own IRA. No taxes are paid on IRA or SEP redemptions ever.

"Employees between the ages of 50 to 66 have the option to remain in the Social Security System or to opt out of the system. Those who opt to remain in the system will continue to contribute into Social Security at the rate of 15.3 percent per year until the age of 66. They will then receive their Social Security payments and benefits the same as those already receiving Social Security payments.

"A person, 50 to 66, who elects to opt out of the Social Security System, is refunded the full amount of their Social Security account contributions. Those contributions are deposited into the IRA by the Department of the Treasury annually on their date of birth and are prorated over the amount of years the contributor has remaining to age 66. Example: a 56 year old with $100,000 total contributions will receive $10,000 per year for 10 years to invest, or save, in any manner they elect.

"Withdrawal of funds from this IRA are not permitted until the employee is 66 years of age. A maximum withdrawal of 10 percent of the total funds invested will be permitted in any one calendar year starting at age 66. This provides retirement benefits to at least the age of 76 years. Minimum distributions are not required.

Beneficiaries are to be designated for this IRA account in the event retirement funds remain after the death of the owner. Estate taxes are eliminated; therefore, the beneficiaries receive the full amount of the investor's funds in the event of the death of the owner of the account.

IHA. Employee earnings deposited into this account are as stated in the above examples. Several options are available, for example:

"A portion of these funds may be utilized to purchase health insurance. Funds are not required to be withdrawn annually. Funds may accumulate over the lifetime of the contributor. The employee may wish to utilize the funds for self-insurance if so desired. Employees are permitted to change this option at any time because they own their money. Any combination of the above is permitted.

"Employees choosing alternative health resources such as walk-in clinics or apps such as 'Doctor on Demand' may pay their medical expenses from this account. Withdrawal of funds from this account may be used only for health and medical expenses such as physicians' fees, hospital bills and prescription drugs. No other withdrawals are permitted. Beneficiaries are to be designated in the event funds remain in the account after the death of the contributor.

IEA. Earnings deposited into this account are as stated in the above examples. Several options are available, for example:

Employees may only withdraw these funds for purposes of unemployment compensation. Withdrawals for other purposes are not permitted. Employees who become unemployed for any reason may utilize the funds in this account as a safety net until new employment is found. Withdrawals from this account may not start until after two full weeks of unemployment. Withdrawals from this account may not exceed 5 percent of the total funds in the account per week. At the rate of 5 percent, these funds ensure unemployment compensation for 20 weeks.

"Upon reaching the age of 66 years, the employee may withdraw all, or part, of the total funds in this account. Beneficiaries are to be designated in the event funds remain in the account after the death of the contributor.

ISA. Earnings deposited into this account may be utilized at the discretion of the employee. This fund serves as a voluntary safety net fund which is established by each individual based on that individual's personal requirement to maintain an emergency fund. All Americans are encouraged to become debt-free."

"There's a lot of well thought out detail in this process," Tom jumped in. "Anyone have thoughts on how citizens will accept this part of the 20/20 Plan."

"You bet," Ron said. "Some of the aspects of the 20/20 Plan are easier to understand than others. Unemployment is the easiest to accept. Many people know health insurance needs a complete overhaul. I believe people will naturally want to reject the IRA Plan much the same as they do all new ideas and concepts. This is because they are locked into their paradigms. Paying taxes and living under a socialist type program like the Social Security System has conditioned them to think there is no alternative. No better way. They tend to think just like the Swiss watch makers."

"I agree with you Ron," Genie interjected. "However, more and more citizens are starting to realize the politicians are bankrupting Social Security. It is sure to slowly collapse when the national debt exceeds $20 trillion. This is a report I want to share with you:

"The Medicare Trustees report states that Social Security including retirement and disability funds will go totally bankrupt by 2033. Many citizens are beginning to view the financial landscape in somber tones. Social Security collected over $750 billion in non-interest income in 2013, but it spent almost $825 billion. That is a $75 billion, or 10 percent loss. Social Security has run a cumulative deficit of almost $220 billion since 2010. The Social Security program will owe almost $9 trillion more than it is estimated to bring in over the next 75 years. By 2033, the program will only be able to fund 77 percent of promised benefits. That percentage will continue to plummet. Unless the system is overhauled, FICA will have to be increased to about 20 percent. Our 20/20 Plan is far superior because it permits citizens to own and control their own money.

The 20/20 Plan is synonymous with liberty and restores freedom to everyone, "Tom stated. "People are enabled to build, and own, their own wealth. The Founding Fathers had this in mind when they thought of property ownership. It is exactly the same concept. The federal government was never meant to be the 'middleman' in our lives. As special interests gain more influence over regulations and the tax code, we lose more and more of our freedom. The gate is closing raidly. The 20/20 Plan is the only remedy to bring freedom, liberty and ownership back into our daily lives."

As Ron parked the car, everyone was excited about the economic boom that will occur when unemployment is reduced and more people enter the work force, especially at an early age. Training is the key, but no one in government has ever been able to implement an effective process. They knew the 20/20 Plan was rock solid.

THURSDAY MORNING. WEEK 2.

Since Dave had more to share about 'AmericaWorks' Ron elected to drive again this morning. The team was still excited about the 20/20 Plan as Tom said, "Dave, you have the floor, actually the back seat, but we all want to learn more about this process. This vision will put America far ahead of all other industrialized nations."

"We need to get back to the question about "AmericaWorks" and how interns will be impacted by what we determined yesterday afternoon," Dave continued. "There are a variety of programs. All interns while enrolled in the Introductory Phase and continuing on to the Intermediate Phase will have the same pay scale. That covers their first 26 weeks of job training.

"Interns are paid a salary of $400.00 per week that equals the minimum wage of $10.00 per hour. Interns have $800.00 direct deposited into their account every two-week pay period. Each intern will have Individual Bank Accounts with the five sub accounts. This may be the first time new interns have a bank or credit union account. Managing money and investing are included in their instruction.

"Interns are paid by the Department of the Treasury and contribute the same percentages as all citizens into their ICA account and sub accounts of IRA, IHA, IEA and ISA. The interns are in a training program, living on a base, with all expenses including health care paid. This provides them the added advantage of maintaining a large percentage of their pay. This affords the interns the benefit of beginning their careers with a positive cash flow in their own accounts that is a key ingredient to forging future citizens into solid links in the 300 million plus link chain.

"The Advanced Phase occurs during the last six months of the interns first year of training. Interns follow two paths.

1. Those who are immediately accepted into a work program are eligible to work for either public or private employers. They continue to receive their same pay from the Department of the Treasury. However, if a public or private entity employs them as an intern, the employing entity is now responsible for payment of the 'Benefits' portion of $2.00 per hour (20 percent), into their accounts. The employers assume the responsibility of employing the interns for 40 hours per week, for the balance of the six-month (26-week) period. This payment method equals a 20 percent meritorious raise for completion of the first two phases of the program. Interns in this category also receive $500.00 per month subsistence allowance plus $500.00 per month housing allowance if they are not living on base. The benefit to the employer is they have the services of a program paid employee for the total tax-free payroll cost of $80.00 per week. Both employer, and intern, benefit immensely from this program.

2. Those receiving advanced specialized or technical instruction are enrolled in a program similar to the VA Technical Career Field (TCF) Program. They continue to be compensated $400.00 per week salary from the Department of the Treasury, the same as they were in the first six months of the intern-training program. If they are required to reside in off base quarters, they also receive $1,000.00 per month for subsistence and housing allowance.

"The Work Phase occurs during the second year of the interns' training program. All interns are employed by either public or private entities and are compensated by the training program as they continue to receive direct deposit pay from the Department of the Treasury. Employers are responsible for all specific work related costs such as travel expenses, uniforms, safety equipment, licenses, permits, etc. Those who maintain successful employment and achieve qualifying progress reports on their training assessments receive a 20 percent increase in their pay to the equivalent of $12.00 per hour. The employer will continue to be responsible to pay benefits into the intern's benefits account (20 percent) at the prescribed rate.

"Public and private employers may employ a number of interns equal to, but not to exceed, 20 percent of their current workforce. This ensures interns are able to receive specific training and employers are not taking advantage of the training program by employing, in effect, excessive numbers of free labor. The exception will be work in the medical field, law enforcement, firefighting and other public sector jobs, who are allowed a number of interns up to 50 percent of their current workforce under the strict conditions of adequate supervision and detailed training courses and schedules.

Example: the number of interns allowed at a facility is: (Totals may be rounded up.)

EMPLOYMENT TYPE	CURRENT WORKFORCE	INTERNS ALLOWED
Private Business	1	1
Private Business	2 - 10	2
Private Business	11+	20% of workforce
Public Entity	2+	50% of workforce
Medical/Specialized	2+	50% of workforce

"What will happen to those interns who are not employed, or who have not met qualification standards?" Genie asked. "Will they remain in the Advanced Phase?"

"No," Dave answered. "They will be assigned to, and under the supervision of, special Work Phase 'AmericaWorks Career Program Teams' based on their qualifications and aptitude until they find employment or their 2-year training program is completed. These multi-purpose teams might be used as emergency teams to support weather related disasters; to perform assistance at large public events; to perform infrastructure work; to perform demolition work in the case of condemned structures; to audit processes implemented under the 20/20 Plan; or any type of assistance the country, states, counties or municipalities require.

"These interns remain at the $400.00 per week pay rate plus their work related expenses which are paid by the 'AmericaWorks Career Program.' They also receive $500.00 per month subsistence allowance plus $500.00 per month housing allowance if those are not available during all or part of the second year of their intern-training program."

"The example you gave us relates to first time high school graduates who have reached 18 years of age," Tom remarked. "The National Center for Education Statistics projects about 3.3 million high school graduates per year. About 90 percent of those graduates are from public schools, and the remaining 10 percent from private schools."

"The unfortunate reality is that approximately 25 percent of the citizens in this age group are unemployed," Dave continued. "About 14 percent enroll in college programs (postsecondary degree-granting institutions). This adds up to approximately 3 out of 4 high school graduates do find jobs or attend college. The nation must do whatever it takes, and whatever it costs, to change this reality to one where every high school student utilizes their education to make a productive life for themselves and to continue to make America better. Many of these bright, talented graduates have never experienced an opportunity or the hope of a promising career. The 20/20 Plan is the best way for young Americans to sustain this country. Many just need an opportunity, and that opportunity means a good paying job in a meaningful career."

"The 'AmericaWorks' part of the 20/20 Plan focuses on new high school graduates," Genie stated. "What happens to the rest of the young citizens between ages 18 and 27? The unemployment rate for that age group is double that of the total population. They need jobs and opportunity also." Dave answered, "all high school graduates in the age group of 18 to 27 can be enrolled in 'AmericaWorks.' Enrollment priority is based on enrollment date, employment status, age and other criteria. Those citizens who volunteer early will receive their opportunity early on.

"About 4 million people in the United States are unemployed for 27 or more weeks. Young Americans make up a large percentage of the long-term unemployed. When employers can offer these employees jobs in exchange for paying their benefits at $2.00 per hour, they are more likely to hire interns than if they were required to pay an employee the full minimum wage.

"Citizens in the age group of 28 to 66 also need jobs. The unemployment rate published by the Bureau of Labor Statistics can be misleading depending on which rate is studied. The U3 Rate, currently 6.8 percent, is the most commonly used, or official rate, while the U6 Rate, currently at 12.9 percent, is a more accurate rate of how many people are not working. It is about double the U3 Rate. In any case, the tragedy is that many citizens remain unemployed, or underemployed. Many are forced to work part time or temporary jobs. When part of work force is not working full time, productivity is estimated to be between 20-30 percent of its potential.

"The nation does not utilize all of its available resources, especially its labor resources in an economy with high unemployment. Businesses enjoy higher output when the workforce is effectively employed. During long periods of unemployment, workers lose skills, or their previous skills no longer apply nor can they be utilized in the present economy. Being unemployed may reduce the life expectancy of workers by about seven years. High unemployment causes workers to fear that foreigners are stealing their jobs. High unemployment also causes social problems such as crime. When people have less disposable income than before, it is very likely that crime levels will increase.

"'America Works' also includes training and job placement programs for those citizens in the 28 to 66 age group. These programs are similar, but shorter in duration. They are six-month training programs divided into a basic course and a specific career course. There is no practical method to customize training programs for each individual. 'AmericaWorks' for this more seasoned and experienced citizen group takes into consideration age, skill sets, previous experience and physical capabilities along with aptitude assessments and career preferences."

Ron parked the car in the parking lot as they all sat silent while Dave finished his presentation. As they got out of the car and retrieved their briefcases, they all made comments about how they were on the right track.

The 20/20 Plan was developing in a similar fashion as the successful processes they historically implement. They were all convinced the future of the republic depended on the skills and work ethic of the youth of America. If the youth cannot develop into productive citizens, they will be unable to lead their children and that will ultimately spell doom for America. On the hand, the 2020 Vision provides them with the tools to make America great again.

CHAPTER SIX | *Service Summary*

1. All citizens must participate to have a successful future for the country.

2. High unemployment rates weaken the nation as fewer people are producing.

3. Low unemployment rates increase production and GDP.

4. People want to work, be productive and experience the positive sense of accomplishment.

5. Young citizens need the opportunity to learn and start careers.

6. Many bright, talented young people have no hope or opportunity to advance.

7. Each citizen at age 18 is eligible to enter the two-year intern-training program.

8. The intern-training program consists of four phases.

9. Private and public employers both benefit from having an internship program.

10. The 20/20 intern training programs will be very specific and career oriented.

11. Military Service careers will remain a viable volunteer option.

12. The 20/20 Plan sets the minimum wage at a tax free $10.00 per hour.

13. Current minimum wage take home pay is about $5.75 per hour.

14. Take home pay for a median household is about $35,000 per year.

15. The 20/20 Plan tax-free take home pay is about $65,000 per year.

16. The 20/20 Plan gives citizens complete ownership of their own money.

17. The 20/20 Plan creates fee free individual ownership accounts.

18. The 20/20 Plan creates Retirement, Health and Employment Accounts.

19. The 20/20 Plan is synonymous with liberty and personal property ownership.

20. The 20/20 Plan will create an unprecedented economic boom.

CHAPTER SIX | *Employment Summary*

1. America fails to utilize all of its valuable resources, especially its labor resources.

2. Four million people in the United States are unemployed for 27 or more weeks.

3. Young Americans make up a large percentage of the long-term unemployed.

4. The 20/20 Plan puts America far ahead of all other industrialized nations.

5. The 20/20 Plan initiates the "America Works Career Program."

6. The "America Works Career Program" contains four critical phases over 2 years.

   Phase 1. Introduction Phase (12 Weeks plus 1 Week Transition)

   Phase 2. Intermediate Phase (12 Weeks plus 1 Week Transition)

   Phase 3. Advanced Phase (24 Weeks plus 2 Weeks Transition)

   Phase 4. Work Phase (52 Weeks)

7. "America Works" prepares Americans with many invaluable, practical lifelong skills.

8. Examples are medical, trades, technical, law enforcement and Foreign Service.

9. 20/20 Plan training focuses on new high school graduates.

10. Interns are eligible to work for both public and private employers.

11. Interns in the "AmericaWorks" program are paid by the training program.

12. Interns are paid $10.00 per hour while in the 'AmericaWorks' Program.

13. Employers only pay interns the $2.00 per hour benefits portion of the wage.

14. Employers may pay additional benefits and bonuses to industrious interns.

15. Employers may retain interns at the conclusion of the training program.

16. Those between ages 18 and 27 are able to enroll in the intern program.

17. The 20/20 Plan includes training and job placement for citizens 28-66.

18. The 20/20 Plan includes training for college graduates with student loans.

19. Employers may employ as many as 20 percent of their workforce as interns.

20. The 20/20 Vision is to build an exceptional country through exceptional education and training of young Americans.

CHAPTER SEVEN

Defense and The VA

"...It is a proud privilege to be a soldier – a good soldier ... [with] discipline, self-respect, pride in his unit and his country, a high sense of duty and obligation to comrades and his superiors, and a self-confidence born of demonstrated ability." — George S. Patton Jr.

THURSDAY AFTERNOON. WEEK 2.

Tom was first to speak as Dave, back behind the wheel, drove out of the parking lot onto the main road. He said, "we completed a very long and detailed process plan for service and employment. That is the foundation of a free market economy. A skilled workforce is obviously an essential requirement for economic success and for the nation itself. We're ready to begin the process to optimize the Department of Defense and the US Department of Veterans Affairs. Ron, lets' get started."

"Okay Tom," Ron replied. "I think that we, along with all Americans understand the strength of the nation largely depends on establishing and maintaining a viable, well trained, powerful military force. The current budget of the Department of Defense is about $500 billion. The budget spiked, of course, in the past decade in order to fight the wars in the Middle East. The budget has been gradually decreasing this decade.

"In order to sustain the finest, most powerful military deterrent in the world, intelligent decision making is needed to define missions, establish research goals and allocate funds. The Department of Defense must be adequately funded to keep our great nation safe and secure. The US needs a stable military force. Not one that expands or contracts whenever a crisis occurs in the world. Our military forces are superior and we need to keep them that way.

"Our present military organizational structure is a result of the National Security Act of 1947 which created the United States Air Force, and restructured the "War Department" into the "Department of Defense." Currently, the Department of Defense contains four major branches of service: the US Army, the US Navy, the US Air Force and the US Marine Corps. Other United States Armed Forces include the US Coast Guard and the four services reserve forces, the National Guard and the CG Auxiliary.

"The U.S. Coast Guard is the only military organization within the Department of Homeland Security. Since 1790, the Coast Guard has safeguarded our Nation's maritime interests and environment around the world.

"The National Guard serves a dual role. It is under the control of individual states, with each respective state governor acting as commander in chief. However, the President of the United States can activate the National Guard and place it under federal control. When this occurs, guard units are typically utilized to supplement the regular Army. During call up times, the federal government funds the National Guard.

"The reserve components of the United States Armed Forces are military organizations whose members generally perform a minimum of 39 days military duty per year and augment the active duty (or full-time) military when necessary. The reserve components are also collectively referred to as the Guard and Reserves. The purpose of each reserve component is to provide trained units and qualified personnel available for active duty in the armed forces during time of war, in national emergencies, and at such other times as the national security may require.

"A thorough review of all stateside military bases and facilities must be conducted. All military facilities must be brought to state of the art conditions. Quarters and housing standards must be evaluated to determine optimum living conditions for all military personnel and their families. Overseas military bases and facilities must also be analyzed to determine their feasibility and disposition. Priorities will be given to maintaining bases and facilities in countries aligned with the United States of America in all areas of security and defense.

"According to latest statistics (rounded for ease of reading) the armed forces are staffed at these (approximate levels vary from year to year) levels:

	ARMY	NAVY	USAF	USCG	USMC	TOTAL
Active	540,000	320,000	335,000	42,000	195,000	1,432,000
Reserve	205,000	63,000	71,000	9,000	40,000	388,000
Total	745,000	383,000	406,000	51,000	235,000	1,820,000

"A comprehensive review must be made jointly between the Department of Defense and the Congress. Leaders of all branches of the military conduct this review. The review will include defined mission statements and objectives based on current and projected world conditions; reshaping and resizing all military forces to meet future challenges; continued research and development of state of the art weapons systems; terminating outdated systems; bolstering military intelligence capabilities; supporting all counterterrorism efforts; further development of unmanned aircraft for all missions; and superior support for all active and retired military personnel and their families including health care and other ancillary services.

"This is of course a brief overview, but it provides direction the government must take in protecting the republic and serving our service personnel and their families."

"Do you anticipate a draft, or conscription, to maintain the armed forces," Genie asked. "Also, what is the current role of the Selective Service System in the USA?"

"Good questions Genie," Ron replied. "The Selective Service System Website states the following instructions:

> If you are, a man ages 18 through 25 and living in the U.S., then you must register with Selective Service. It's the law. According to law, a man must register with Selective Service within 30 days of his 18th birthday. Selective Service will accept late registrations but not after a man has reached age 26. You may be denied benefits or a job if you have not registered. You can register at any U.S. Post Office and do not need a social security number. When you do obtain a social security number, let Selective Service know. Provide a copy of your new social security number card; being sure to include your complete name, date of birth, Selective Service registration number, and current mailing address; and mail to the Selective Service System, P.O. Box 94636, Palatine, IL 60094-4636.

"Earlier, we outlined the service program and described it as a voluntary program. The military is a voluntary force, but registration in the Selective Service System is required and the law will be amended to include females. The Selective Service System is utilized for enrollment in the 'AmericaWorks' service program.

"Those who do not volunteer, and do not receive a deferment, are called into the 'America Works' program. In other words, they are drafted into the training program. Enlistment in the Armed Forces will benefit those volunteers as they have a head start with their training program. Those who decide to delay their entry benefit less.

"All military personnel currently on active duty will benefit from the elimination of taxes. Armed Forces personnel will receive a twenty percent increase in pay across the board. This is different from civilians who will have their pay adjusted according to their labor costs. Military personnel will receive increased benefits for Basic Allowances, which include Quarters and Subsistence and all other benefits.

"Military personnel currently on active duty receive pay based on rank and years of service. A good example is a Sergeant with the rating of E-5 with four years of service who now receives base pay of $2,555.10 per month, or $30,661.20 per year. The 20/20 Plan gives a 20 percent pay increase to this same Sergeant (E-5 with four years of service) to $3,066.12 per month, or $36,793.44 per year. Military personnel of every rank and time in service can calculate their individual pay.

"New recruits, who volunteer for military service, start at the same rate as those who enter the 'AmericaWorks' training program. Their starting pay is $400.00 per week, or $20,800.00 per year. New recruits have the benefit of on base housing and subsistence by nature of their training status. They also receive military medical care at base hospitals and clinics. The current base pay for new recruits (E-1 with less than two years active duty service) is $1,416.30 per month, or $16,995.60 per year.

"These pay rates and allowances elevate military personnel close to their civilian counterparts in regards to pay. They will also contribute to their own Individual Retirement Accounts, Individual Health Accounts, Individual Employment Accounts and Individual Savings Accounts. The need to draw funds from these accounts will be minimal while military personnel are on active duty. They will be able to swiftly build their retirement accounts. An added benefit will be that all military personnel will now have a retirement account no matter how long, or short, their tour of active duty.

"Military training and education will be surveyed and evaluated to ensure military personnel receive the finest available training. This training enables military personnel success and a higher degree of safety on their missions; to be grounded in all core military skills and responsibilities; and be further prepared for life when their active duty career is concluded.

"Special emphasis will be given to basic training. Each military service branch will continue to maintain their own unique basic training principles and techniques. All new recruits must adhere to the highest standards. Everyone expects, and demands, the United States military to continue to be the standard-bearer for the free world.

"The military services will be given the additional responsibility of design and development of a uniform basic training program for the 'AmericaWorks Career Program.' This is required to ensure job training begins with a sound foundation of unconditional work ethic, integrity, responsibility, discipline, social skills, life skills, teamwork and a sense of meaningful accomplishment. This basic (boot camp) training will challenge all interns/trainees to be physically fit and to understand the benefits of good nutrition, proper hygiene, and good health standards to nurture them for a healthy lifetime.

"What will happen if a military recruit, or an 'AmericaWorks' enrollee, decides they want to leave the program, or they desert from the program?" Genie inquired.

"Every action has consequences," Ron replied." Provisions already exist to process these actions. Those provisions, or laws, depending on the circumstances, will be applied in that event. Remember, these programs are designed and developed to be positive influences, and promote positive endeavors for all enrollees."

"Okay. What about those who cannot pass, or advance, in their training? What happens if an enrollee, or recruit, has a negative attitude toward the program, or exhibits disruptive behavior, or is a troublemaker?" Genie further inquired.

"Those enrollees, or recruits, will be disciplined according to the circumstances and degree of disruption. The program is intended to benefit the enrollees, not to punish them. The 20/20 Plan recognizes enrollees will come from different cultures, backgrounds, conditions and experiences.

The principal purpose of the 20/20 Plan is to put America on the right course; to lift Americans up to bring them together; to make every link in the chain sturdy. Good leadership will find methods to inspire and motivate all enrollees. The military academies are synonymous with leadership.

MILITARY ACADEMIES

"The first military academies were established in the early 19th century to provide future officers for technically specialized corps, such as engineers and artillery, with scientific training," Ron added. "Today there are three major military academies: The United States Military Academy, The United States Naval Academy and the United States Air Force Academy. Each academy has an enrollment of a little over 4,000 students and is currently admitting a few more than 1,000 new students annually.

"Academy qualifications for admittance vary but generally, a candidate must be a U.S. citizen at least 17 but not yet 23 years old on July 1 of the year admitted. They cannot be married or pregnant or have any legal obligation to support a child or children. They are congressionally nominated or they have a service-connected nomination and must have strong scores on either college entrance exam (ACT or SAT). Current candidates receive 35% of base officer pay plus quarters and subsistence allowances among other benefits while enrolled in an academy.

"The 20/20 Vision fully supports these existing academies and also foresees two additional academies to support the efforts of the United States and its armed forces much the same as in the early 18th century."

UNITED STATES MEDICAL MILITARY ACADEMY (USMMA) and the UNITED STATES REGISTERED NURSES ACADEMY (USRNA)

The added military academies are the United States Medical Military Academy (USM-MA) for physicians, and the United States Registered Nurses Academy (USRNA). The purpose of these academies is to provide future professional medical personnel for the Armed Forces and to set high standards for medical training in the United States. The 20/20 Plan establishes, organizes and operates these academies in a manner identical to the existing academies. Similar entrance qualifications plus compensation, benefits and allowances will exist for the new academies.

The 20/20 Plan envisions initial enrollment in these two academies to be 1,000 candidates per year culminating in a total enrollment of 4,000 candidates. Graduates will be commissioned officers assigned to military units or hospitals, to serve, or to continue their education in the case of elected specialties. The newly commissioned officers will have a four-year active duty obligation upon completion of their medical studies.

THE VETRERANS ADMINISTRATION

"The US Department of Veterans Affairs has a total budget of about $164 billion. This includes $68.3 billion in discretionary resources and $95.6 billion in mandatory funding," Ron continued. "The VA employs nearly 332,025 people at hundreds of Veterans Affairs medical facilities, clinics, and benefits offices. The Office of the Secretary is a cabinet position who reports directly to the President. The United States Secretary of Veterans Affairs is responsible for administering benefit programs for veterans, their families, and survivors.

"The US Department of Veterans Affairs is responsible for the administration of Disability Compensation; Education and Training; Employment Services; Health Care; Home Loans and Housing-Related Assistance; Life Insurance; Memorial Benefits; Pension; Spouses, Dependents, and Survivors. This agency has become a bureaucratic nightmare much too large and much too unwieldy to properly serve and support the veterans who have honorably served this republic.

"The 20/20 Plan folds The US Department of Veterans Affairs, and its annual budget, as a separate department in the Department of the Defense. The entire VA must be streamlined. Funding invested on veterans, not squandered on bloated bureaucracy. As an agency of the military, the military is responsible for taking care of its own personnel from enlistment to death. The military would staff, and take over, all the VA Hospitals and Clinics and operate them in the same manner they operate military hospitals.

"Hospitals and clinics will be assigned to the Army, Navy and Air Force. Each service will individually operate hospitals, and clinics, and care for all veterans in their respective areas regardless of branch. Veterans who do not reside near a VA facility will be able to use their Tricare card at a doctor's office or hospital of their choosing."

"This is an interesting concept, Tom interjected. "Should the military really take care of its veterans? Should all veterans who received honorable discharges be given retirement status?"

"Absolutely." Ron declared. "They all served and the nation owes them a debt no one can ever repay. We would not have the freedom and liberty we now enjoy without them. Each veteran played an equally important role in the security and safety of this republic whether on active duty during peacetime or wartime. The military is in a continuous state of readiness. Every veteran served to make that happen."

"I never heard it explained that way before," Tom answered. "The 20/20 Plan concept is that a veteran who served in peacetime, for just a few years, is just as important as one who served during time of conflict. I now understand it was not their choice that it was peacetime, or wartime, they still carried the flag for the next veteran, so they are all equally important and equally deserving of benefits. That makes a lot of sense."

"Where will all of the doctors and nurses come from?" Genie inquired. "Are there enough personnel to staff the VA Hospitals? And what will happen to those that work for the VA now?"

"Good questions." Ron answered. "The DoD would not terminate the service of the care-givers and ancillary personnel at the hospitals and clinics. The responsible military service will administer, manage, supervise and direct the activities at each facility. This eliminates the bloated bureaucracy. The military will gradually fill their ranks with qualified doctors, nurses and technicians to staff the military hospitals. Doctors and nurses who desire to serve will be given the option to join the military for tours of duty or work as contractors." "Job trainees who are enrolled in the 'AmericaWorks' training program for health care careers will be eligible, and encouraged, to seek employment as interns at the VA hospitals and clinics. They may serve as interns in all positions from admittance through discharge. This is an excellent training program for their future careers."

Before they knew it, they arrived at the hotel. Tom again forgot to turn on the radio to catch the six o'clock news. As they departed their rental car, he said, "we addressed the VA. The US Department of Veterans Affairs is an area of great concern for our nation because it cares for those who served our nation well." Dave remarked as he was walking through the hotel parking lot, "The 20/20 Plan is such a thorough, comprehensive process that the interrelationships are endless. This is what our country truly needs. All working together to achieve a common goal."

CHAPTER SEVEN | *Defense and The VA Summary*

1. America fails to utilize all of its available resources, especially its labor resources.

1. America depends on strong, and sustained, armed forces.

2. The armed forces are well organized and constituted.

3. A thorough review needs to be made of all services and their missions.

4. The military budget has decreased this decade.

5. Our military forces are superior and we need to maintain them in that manner.

6. The military will assist in the training of the 'AmericaWorks' program.

7. The pay and allowances of military personnel will be increased 20 percent.

8. The 20/20 Plan military pay rates and allowances elevate armed forces personnel closer to their civilian counterparts.

9. The 20/20 Plan supports all existing US Military Academies.

10. The Veterans Administration is a bloated, ineffective bureaucracy.

11. The VA must be streamlined with the funding spent on the veterans, not on bureaucracy.

12. The Veterans Administration will be administered by the Department of Defense.

13. All Veterans Administration Hospitals and Clinics will become Military Hospitals.

14. Military Academies will be established for doctors and nurses.

15. The Department of Defense will provide benefits for all veterans.

16. All veterans are equally important whether they served in peacetime or times of conflict, and whether they served for a career or a short tour.

CHAPTER EIGHT

Social Security and Medicare

"I care about our young people, and I wish them great success, because they are our Hope for the Future, and some day, when my generation retires, they will have to pay us trillions of dollars in social security" — Dave Barry

FRIDAY MORNING. WEEK 2.

It was getaway day for the team. Everyone had packed their roller bags and checked out of the hotel. After they loaded briefcases and luggage into the trunk, it was time to discuss a most important topic as Dave drove out of the parking lot and headed toward the plant. The team was ready to address a new topic and this one contained much controversy and emotion. However, most of all it contained a deluge of misunderstanding by the American people. Citizens must confront this delusion in order to make informed decisions about their future. Social Security is a perfect example of a pipe dream government program rife with inordinate corruption.

"Since I'm the senior citizen on this team, I'll take the lead on the Social Security Program," Tom announced. "I've found from personal experience it is a very complex program. Few in the Social Security offices know and comprehend the entire program. It is a typical government created bureaucracy that costs billions to administer and yet is readily defrauded.

"165 Million citizens pay into Social Security every year and still it is on the verge of bankruptcy. A key issue here is ownership. Individual citizens should have the right to own their own money to spend on retirement and health care as they see fit. The Social Security Act took that right away from citizens when it created a nanny state for the elite to distribute, and redistribute, individual earnings to other citizens as they deemed fit. A collective of 165 million citizens pay into the government for services that the government then provides to others based a formula of need that bureaucrats created. This is a program of socialism and not a program of free market capitalism.

"I have researched many websites and have found a few that describe the Social Security Act of 1935." The following excerpt is from the Social Security Website:

"The Social Security Act -- In early January 1935, the President's Committee on Economic Security (CES) made its report to the President, and on January 17th the President introduced the report to both Houses of Congress for simultaneous consideration. The House Ways & Means Committee and the Senate Finance Committee Hearings were held during January and February. Some provisions made it through the Committees in close votes. The bill passed both houses overwhelmingly in the floor votes. After a conference which lasted throughout July, the bill was finally passed and sent to President Roosevelt for his signature."

"The Social Security Act was signed into law by President Roosevelt on August 14, 1935. In addition to several provisions for general welfare, the new Act created a social insurance program designed to pay retired workers age 65 or older a continuing income after retirement."

"We can never insure one hundred percent of the population against one hundred percent of the hazards and vicissitudes of life, but we have tried to frame a law which will give some measure of protection to the average citizen and to his family against the loss of a job and against poverty-ridden old age." — President Roosevelt upon signing the Social Security Act.

"The government's own website describes a swollen government agency that has over 1,230 offices (another page states over 1400 offices) with 60,000 employees," Tom stated. "The organization chart shows 12 columns with up to 10 levels of bureaucrats called commissioners of various flavors, deputies, assistants, directors, officers, ad infinitum, etc. The abuses are legend. The waste is extravagant. It is the epitome of foolhardy government grown into an irresponsible insatiable, out of control beast."

"What happened to the funds that were supposedly put in the 'lock box?'" Ron asked. "Was that real or just a cruel hoax imposed on the people?"

"Social Security and Medicare funds are actually a tax that is deposited into the general operating funds of the Treasury," Tom answered. "A report from the NCPA states the Social Security program is in trouble. Since 2010, benefit payments have exceeded revenues, and the deficit is rapidly growing. Workers retiring today have paid into the system more than they will get out of it, and future retirees will find themselves in an even worse position.

Financial consequences of each program to an average-earning man born in 1985 are: The baseline option -- raising taxes and keeping the benefits structure in place -- would mean that such workers would pay 13.5 percent of their lifetime income in Social Security Taxes. In exchange, they will receive benefits equal to 9.6 percent of their income, resulting in a 3.8 percent net tax.

However, in a reform program, those men would pay a 10.2 percent tax rate and receive benefits equal to 8.2 percent of their income, resulting in a 2 percent hike.

Very low earners might gain under reform. A low-income earner born in 1985 would pay 13.5 percent of his income in taxes and receive benefits of 15.8 percent under the baseline program. Under a reform program, he would pay just 10.2 percent of his income in taxes and receive benefits worth 14.5 percent of his income -- resulting in net lifetime benefits of 4.3 percent of his earnings.

"The above is confusing to say the least. No one has a clue if these options will actually work. Every projection made has been faulty and grossly inaccurate. It is all guesswork. The brightest of the bright have no solutions for this abomination. None of these alternatives are viable for our citizens," Tom stated emphatically. "These are feeble methods to place bailing wire, duct tape and band aids on a crippled system. These proposed tweaks and adjustments to the Social Security System only prolong the misery this debacle will inflict on all citizens and the total misery it will surely bring when the system suddenly and certainly collapses.

"The United States was founded on the principle of ownership. It is a tenet differentiating our republic from other governments. Ownership, by all, sets us above every other nation on the planet. The Social Security Act takes ownership of its citizen's labor and currency and gives it to the government to redistribute and do what it deems best for the citizens who earned that ownership: their own money. The Founding Fathers would have found the Social Security abomination foolhardy and careless.

"The Trustees Report *(A SUMMARY OF THE 2014 ANNUAL REPORTS - Social Security and Medicare Boards of Trustees)* makes clear that the Social Security Program (including its retirement and disability funds) will go entirely bankrupt in 2033. The financial picture is bleak. Social Security collected $752.2 billion in non-interest income in 2013, yet it spent $822.9 billion. Since 2010, the Program has run a cumulative deficit of $219.7 billion, and the program will owe almost $9 trillion more than is estimated to bring in over the next 75 years. The reports do not give a clear picture of what is actually happening as far as fiscal responsibility is concerned. The data and information reported appears prepared with smoke and mirrors. It is as if the government is so lost in its own jumbled mess that it has lost track of reality. Do the American people deserve the monstrosity that will ultimately destroy all they have worked for? Absolutely not.

"The Medicare program is also in debt and continues to run up annual deficits. After analyzing government reports, it is clear that nothing they report is clear. The program states it received $232.5 Billion from General Revenues in 2014. The illustrated report contains graphs that demonstrate funds do not cover the program cost. In summary, the entire Social Security System is a complex government program that is top heavy and is sinking fast from its own over regulated policies. American citizens deserve much more from their government and certainly much more from the tax dollars they pay into this failed ill-advised program.

"When funds are depleted in 2033, the American Action Forum report explains that the program will be able to fund just 77 percent of promised benefits -- a number that will continue to fall. Without some sort of reform overhaul, the Payroll Tax (which funds Social Security) would have to rise by 24 percent or cut benefits by one-quarter.

"The Social Security Disability Insurance (SSDI) program is also in poor financial straits: "The program spent $143.4 billion in 2013, despite taking in just $106.5 billion in non-interest income. Since 2005, SSDI has added more than $179.8 billion to the debt. "The SSDI trust fund will be exhausted by 2015 with a 75-year liability of $1.2 trillion. Tom further shared From SHRM (Society for Human Resource Management) Website.

The following information and data is reprinted:

A. FICA Adjusts: Income Subject to Payroll Tax Increases in 2014

B. Earnings up to $117,000 will be hit by Social Security FICA tax; more will face additional Medicare Tax. -- Source: Stephen Miller, CEBS 10/30/2013 (last updated 1/30/2014)

C. On Oct. 30, 2013, the Social Security Administration (SSA) announced that the maximum amount of earnings subject to the Social Security payroll tax would increase to $117,000 from $113,700, beginning Jan. 1, 2014. Of the estimated 165 million U.S. workers who will pay Social Security payroll taxes in 2014, about 10 million will pay a higher amount as a result of the inflation-based increase in wages subject to Social Security withholding.

Social Security and Medicare payroll withholding are collected together as the Federal Insurance Contributions Act tax. By Jan. 1, U.S. employers should have:

A. Adjusted their payroll systems to account for the higher taxable maximum under the Social Security portion of FICA.

B. Notified affected employees that more of their paychecks will be subject to FICA.

C. Withholding Rates Unchanged

D. The portion of the Social Security FICA tax that employees pay remains unchanged at the 6.2 percent withholding rate. Correspondingly, the portion of the tax that employers cover also remains at 6.2 percent of employee wages. This amounts to a total Social Security FICA tax of 12.4 percent.

E. These rates are set by statute and are not adjusted annually based on inflation. Except for a temporary 2 percent cut in the employee portion of the Social Security payroll-tax rate, which took effect in 2011 and ended in January 2013, they have been in place since 1990.

At the close of 2013, the IRS issued payroll-withholding tables for 2014:

1. Notice 1036: Early Release Copies of the 2014 Percentage Method Tables for Income Tax Withholding.

2. (Circular E), Employer's Tax Guide for 2014.

3. Additional withholding information is available at www.IRS.gov.

Maximum Withholding: In 2014, with the higher income ceiling, the maximum yearly Social Security tax withholding amount rises to $7,254 (6.2 percent withholding on earnings of up to $117,000), up from $7,049.40 (6.2 percent withholding on earnings of up to $113,700).

Medicare's Bite: For most Americans, the Medicare portion of the FICA tax remains at 2.9 percent, of which half (1.45 percent) is paid by employees and half by employers. Unlike Society Security, there is no limit on the amount of wages subject to the Medicare portion of the tax. This results in a total FICA tax for most wage earners of 15.3 percent (Social Security plus Medicare), half of which is paid by employees and half by employers.

Self-employed individuals are responsible for the entire FICA tax rate of 15.3 percent (12.4 percent Social Security plus 2.9 percent Medicare).

Additional Medicare Tax: For high earners, Medicare takes a somewhat larger bite, under a provision of the Patient Protection and Affordable Care Act. Beginning in 2013, the employee-paid portion of the Medicare FICA tax became subject to the 0.9 percent Additional Medicare Tax. The threshold amounts are $250,000 for married taxpayers who file jointly, $125,000 for married taxpayers, who file separately, and $200,000 for single and all other taxpayers. These wage thresholds are not inflation adjusted, and thus apply to more employees each year.

An employer must withhold the Additional Medicare Tax from the wages or compensation it pays to an employee in excess of $200,000 in a calendar year. The Additional Medicare Tax raised the individual wage earner's portion on compensation above the threshold amounts to 2.35 percent from 1.45 percent; the employer-paid portion of the Medicare tax on these amounts remained at 1.45 percent.

Tom went on to say, "the best alternative is to gradually phase out the Social Security Act. We must protect senior citizens already receiving social security benefits and they must be given livable funds and benefits. Next, those about to retire, who are ages 50 to 66, must have a plan to care for themselves and their families. Finally, those under age 50, the citizens who will reach 66 when the system goes belly-up, must not be stripped of their future benefits after they paid into the system. That has a profound impact on everyone under 50 years of age."

"Tom, you make it sound so easy, but won't the politicians try to frighten the seniors as they always do. You know, throwing grandma over the cliff in a wheelchair," Genie interrupted. "So far the 20/20 Plan is perfect for finally giving the young the opportunity they so desperately need. However, seniors are in a different position in life. They are not looking for jobs and they do not have the same tax situations young Americans who are just starting their careers have."

"Good point Genie. Let's take it one step at a time. It is evident, Social Security will be bankrupt before the year 2033, and therefore action must be taken immediately."

The 20/20 Plan phases out the Social Security System in the following three stages:

1. Senior citizens who are eligible for Social Security benefits, and have reached age 66 keep their Social Security benefits for the rest of their lives, and they receive the following tax-free increases to their monthly pay amounts.

a. They all receive a 20 percent increase in their base monthly pay amount. (Example: A senior who receives $1,000.00 per month will automatically receive a 20 percent increase to $1,200.00 per month.)

b. One who receives less than $834.00 per month will have their monthly base pay amount automatically increased to the minimum Social Security pay amount of $1,000.00 per month.

c. The Medicare medical insurance (Part B) will remain in effect however the monthly deduction of approximately $100.00 per month will be eliminated, and will not be deducted from the monthly pay amount.

d. An additional payment amount, to compensate for Supplemental insurance for Medicare Part B, of $100.00 per month will be added to each eligible senior citizens monthly pay amount.

e. An additional payment amount, to compensate for Supplemental insurance for Medicare Part D, of $50.00 per month will be added to each eligible senior citizens monthly pay amount.

f. The bottom line for each senior citizen receiving Social Security monthly payments is an increase of 20 percent plus $150.00 per month. (Example: a senior citizen who previously received $1,000.00 per month minus $100.00 Medicare insurance deduction received $900.00 per month. That senior citizen will now receive a new pay amount of $1,350.00 per month. This is a $450.00 ($5,400 annual) per month tax-free increase in funds to live on and pay bills.

2. Those citizens who are between the ages of 50 and 66 have the option to remain in the Social Security System, or opt out of the Social Security System.

a. Those who exercise the option to stay in the Social Security System will receive their full pay package from their employer (which includes the 15.3 percent FICA and Medicare deductions) in accordance with the 20/20 Plan as described in Chapter 5. They will now have that same 15.3 percent of their total net pay deposited into their present Social Security Account. (This is the exact same amount as is currently deducted plus the amount currently contributed by their employer who has compensated the employee in their pay increase. The result is net neutral. See above information from SHRM.)

b. The citizens in this age group may also exercise their option to invest in their own Individual Retirement Account (IRA) and contribute to their own Individual Health Account (IHA). They may volunteer to invest as much, or as little as they determine best for their own individual situation. These tax-free funds will be 100 percent owned by the individual.

c. Those citizens who exercise the right to opt out of the Social Security System will contribute into their own Individual Retirement Account (IRA). They will contribute a minimum 10 percent as described in Chapter 5.

d. However, those who opt out of the Social Security System will not receive Social Security or Medicare benefits when they reach the age of 66.

e. Nonetheless, those who opt out of the Social Security System are refunded the full tax-free amount of the total Social Security (FICA) and/or Medicare funds they contributed, plus their employers' contributions, and direct deposited in their Individual Retirement Accounts (IRA) and Individual Health Accounts (IHA) prorated over the remaining years they have until they reach age 66. This refund is in addition to their own future individual contributions. Example: A citizen, age 50, whose total contributions to FICA and Medicare, self and employer, from about 30 years might be $150,000.00. That citizen will be refunded the total $150,000.00 over 15 years from age 51 to 66, or $10,000.00 per year direct deposited into the individual's IRA and IHA.

3. Citizens, ages 1-49, who have contributed to Social Security will be removed from the active Social Security System.

a. They receive their full pay package from their employer, in accordance with the 20/20 Plan, as described in Chapter 5.

b. These citizens receive refunds of their total Social Security (FICA), and/or Medicare funds contributions. The refund is direct deposited into their Individual Retirement Accounts (IRA) and Individual Health Accounts (IHA) prorated over the years until they reach age 66.

c. This refund will be in addition to their own individual contributions. (Example: A citizen, age 41, whose total self and employer contributions to FICA and Medicare for about 20 working years might be $100,000. That citizen is refunded the full tax-free total $100,000 over approximately 25 working years from age 41 to 66, or $4,000.00 per year. This tax-free refund is direct deposited into that individual's IRA and IHA.

d. This new individual investment plus the government refund produces a more superior retirement benefit package than the soon to be bankrupt, soon to be non-existent Social Security benefits.

"When Medicare was instituted in 1965, it was estimated that the cost of Medicare Part A would be $9 billion by 1990. In actuality, it was seven times higher—$67 billion. Similarly, in 1987, Medicaid's special hospital subsidy was projected to cost $100 million annually by 1992 (just 5 years later); however, it actually cost $11 billion—more than 100 times more. And in 1988, when Medicare's home care benefit was established, the projected cost for 1993 was $4 billion, but the actual cost was $10 billion."

— Michael D. Tanner, Senior Fellow, CATO Institute

"The Medicare program is so intricately linked to the Social Security System that it must be phased out along with the Social Security System. It must continue, however, to provide benefits to senior citizens as described above. The federal government taxed the citizens for this program, therefore the government owes it to those citizens to either provide the benefits that were fraudulently promised to them, or refund their money in full."

"Reforms are needed for many reasons, but the compelling fact is that Medicare is unaffordable in its current form. Already expensive to seniors and burdensome to taxpayers, its costs will soon outstrip its own resources by a wide margin, putting enormous pressures on the federal budget and the economy. Left unchecked, Medicare's claim on national resources will rise from 2.7 percent of GDP in 2007 to 5.9 percent in 2030, and eventually to 15.6 percent in the following years. ...

In 2007, Medicare tapped the general fund of the Treasury for $179 billion, or about 1.3 percent of GDP. To put this in perspective, this was equivalent to about half of all federal corporate income receipts. On the spending side, this was more than enough to cover the total outlays of the Departments of Homeland Security, Housing and Urban Development, Interior, Justice, and State." — J. D. Foster, Ph.D., Senior Fellow, Heritage Institute

---

"The 20/20 Plan establishes Individual Health Accounts for its citizens. Citizens keep their health care, keep their doctors and keep their health plan with them wherever they go, and/or wherever they work. No one can take it away from them, because they own it."

CHAPTER EIGHT | *Social Security and Medicare Summary*

1. Social Security Act of 1935 signed into law.

2. The SSA has become a bloated bureaucracy of more than 1,200 offices.

3. Social Security and Medicare taxes continue to rise every year.

4. 165 million citizens pay 15.3 percent of their wages into Social Security every year.

5. Despite this huge annual tax, SSA is on the verge of bankruptcy as deficits continue to grow.

6. Alternate solutions are only temporary tweaks to sustain a program on life support that must be terminated before it bankrupts the republic.

7. SSA deprives enrollees the right to own their own retirement funds and their own health care.

8. SSA is not self-sustaining and requires funding from General Revenues.

9. Social Security is predicted to go bankrupt in 2033 when funds are depleted.

10. Bankruptcy will occur prior to 2033 with continual losses of $70 billion per year.

11. Medicare spends billions more every year than it collects.

12. Seniors can expect a cutback to 77 percent of their Social Security check.

13. The 20/20 Plan gives all eligible senior citizens a 20 percent increase in their Social Security check plus additional tax-free benefits of $1,800.00 per year.

14. The 20/20 Plan increases many seniors monthly SSA check to $1,000.00.

15. The 20/20 Plan creates an Individual Health Account for its citizens.

16. The 20/20 Plan will give most Social Security recipients an additional $5,000.00-$6000.00 per year in extra income.

17. Individual citizens should have the right of ownership of their own money to spend on retirement and health care as they see fit.

18. The 20/20 Plan refunds the total payments made by all citizens who choose to opt out of the Social Security System.

19. When funds are depleted in 2033, the Social Security program will be able to fund just 77 percent of promised benefits.

20. Without some sort of reform overhaul, the Payroll Tax (which funds Social Security) would have to rise by 24 percent or cut benefits by one-quarter.

"What is responsible for this change? Jauhar describes the mid-twentieth century as the "golden age" of American medicine, when life expectancy jumped and the field saw new advancements such as the polio vaccine and heart-lung bypass surgery. Doctors set their own fees and hours, and the lack of a massive insurance market meant that they could work with patients on fee arrangements.

"The introduction of Medicare in 1965 saw more people seeking medical care, which continued to push doctors' salaries upward. Eventually, people began to perceive doctors as making too much money. Health care spending began to grow faster than the rest of the economy, and concerns about fraud and waste within government health care programs rose. This led to the growth of health maintenance organizations (HMOs) in the 1970s, which brought new controls to curb prices and reviews over the necessity of medical procedures.

"With the development of so many new screening options and preventive services, doctors began finding it harder to spend quality time with patients, not to mention the headache that came with a large third-party-payer insurance system. Today, doctors spend $83,000 per year dealing with insurance company paperwork.

"As Jauhar explains, physicians began to display less and less satisfaction in their careers. By 2001, almost 60 percent of doctors surveyed said that their enthusiasm for their jobs had fallen during the previous five years.

"Salaries have also fallen; while the average general practitioner salary was $185,000 in 1970, it fell to $161,000 in 2010 -- despite, Jauhar points out, that doctors see nearly twice as many patients today as they did in 1970.

"For most doctors, says Jauhar, taking care of patients is the best part of their job. He writes that the United States needs to develop a health care system that restores the relationship between doctor and patient -- something that has been lost over the last several decades.

"The 20/20 Plan addresses the concerns of both the doctors and the patients. Patients can look forward to being better served, and better cared for, if physicians are satisfied with their work as opposed to being dissatisfied. That holds true for any profession or career. It also addresses doctor and patient hospital care. Admissions and discharges are streamlined to eliminate redundant record keeping. Doctors, nurses and technicians have the freedom to spend quality time with patients instead of time consuming needless paperwork that is currently exhausting so much time and effort."

"Are there other means by which citizens can receive medical care that helps both patient and physician?" Tom inquired. "I've read about alternatives that could reduce the time and costs for routine visits or doctor's visits that address minor ailments such as colds and flu for example."

"There are many today," Genie replied. "There is an alternative marketplace for health care. How many times have any of you had a bad cold, a sinus infection or flu and tried to make an appointment with your family doctor, or primary care physician, and found you could not get an appointment because the doctor was 'too busy?'"

"And even worse, when we get an appointment, we have to wait for hours in a crowded doctor's office while we all spread our various germs among each other," Ron chimed in. "There has to be a better way."

"And what about preventive health care?" Dave inquired. "We design and develop predictive and preventive maintenance programs for our clients. Why not encourage people to take care of themselves? We know from experience our clients spend more time and effort caring for their equipment and machinery than people do on themselves. More time and money is spent to care for automobiles and lawnmowers than on personal health. We have facts that prove treating emergencies on the factory floor is costlier than preventing those emergencies. Abusing equipment and machinery by running it too hard, or too long, is destructive. Isn't it also true for people who abuse themselves with poor nutrition habits, poor sleep routines, alcohol and drugs?"

"Dave, you hit the nail on the head," Genie replied. "We could spend hours discussing these issues, but since we're so close to the airport, let me just list a few. Americans are intelligent enough to figure this out on their own. The people know there are massive abuses in the present health care system. One controversial point, however, is well worth making.

Genetically Modified Organisms (GMO) foods are harming Americans. I found some information on the IRT (Institute for Responsible Technology) website. It gives 10 Reasons to Avoid GMOs. They are:

1. GMOs are unhealthy.
2. GMOs contaminate forever.
3. GMOs increase herbicide use.
4. Genetic engineering creates dangerous side effects.
5. Government oversight is dangerously lax.
6. The biotech industry uses "tobacco science" to claim product safety.
7. Independent research and reporting is attacked and suppressed.
8. GMOs harm the environment.
9. GMOs do not increase yields, and work against feeding a hungry world.
10. By avoiding GMOs, you contribute to the coming tipping point of consumer rejection, forcing them out of our food supply.

"People should choose healthier non-GMO brands and tell others about GMOs so they can do the same. This is true about all processed foods. We are what we eat.

"Today, an insured person can just go to the doctor, or hospital, instead of employing preventive care, because the insurance company will pay for it. People do not understand we are all paying these insurance premiums and therefore we pay higher premiums each time someone abuses the system. The 20/20 Plan causes citizens to become more responsible for their own health care. This is a natural benefit since people will not abuse their own Individual Health Account as they are want to do when someone else, i.e., the insurance companies pays the price.

"Some ways Americans can improve their health and their health care is:

a. Practice good, effective preventive medicine.

b. Adopt an effective physical fitness regimen.

c. Develop healthy nutritional eating habits.

d. Go to urgent care facilities when necessary.

e. Go to medical facilities in super stores, etc.

f. Get an app for internet services like 'Doctors on Demand,' etc.

g. Utilize services such as Nurse-on-Call.

"There are two more issues we have talked about among ourselves that we need to include in the 20/20 Plan. That is billing practices and malpractice insurance. It is difficult to identify true medical costs in most cases. If the doctor does not know what the cost is and the patient does not know what the cost is, how can costs be controlled? How can anyone know if too much or too little is being billed?

"Many medical practices contract with billing companies, who deal with insurance companies. Doctors do not know what they are being paid for a given service, or why. The reimbursement process for a doctor's services is just as complicated, and ridiculous, as any other part of healthcare.

"Insurance companies have managed to develop an almost perfect system of profit through incompetence. If a mistake is made, they don't pay. If they make a mistake, they don't pay. Hours on the phone with insurance companies are spent tracking payments or following up on denials. This is a costly waste of time and effort.

"Some doctors are tempted to eliminate insurance and take cash. Most doctors are happy to see an uninsured patient with medical problems they can resolve in their own office. Doctors typically, charge less than most insurance providers pay because they get the money immediately instead of having to travel through the insurance nightmare. The 20/20 Plan resolves this issue as patients now have more options.

"When a doctor, or medical provider, bills the insurance company, they bill for an amount that is well in excess of the expected payment. The reason is that insurance companies reimburse at different rates for services. Therefore, the doctor bills an amount above what 'all' insurance companies pay in order to receive the maximum that 'each' insurance provider will pay.

"Most doctors perform a narrow range of activities. This simplifies their lives in two ways: they do what they know best and it is easier to bill for what they do. Knowing exactly what the insurance companies will, and will not, pay is advantageous. Doctors benefit when they bill an amount that exceeds what they expect from any insurance payer. This guarantees they receive the maximum amount each insurance payer is willing to pay. Since most insurance companies reimburse office visits in a narrow pay range, billing 25-30 percent above the expected amount usually covers all circumstances.

"Doctors malpractice insurance premiums vary by type of practice and by the amount of claims paid each year. The more claims paid, the more malpractice insurance policies cost. Doctors build this cost into their patients' fees. Malpractice insurance policies are difficult to quantify but they range from about $4,000 to $50,000 per year depending on type of practice and procedures. Most physicians do not know the cost of malpractice insurance as they have accountants who take care of their finances. In 2010 there were just under 10,000 malpractice claims paid in the United States. The total dollars of claims paid were over 3.3 billion dollars. The average claim was just over $336,000.

"Malpractice claims and lawsuits need to be scaled much the same as insurance payments are determined. Some malpractice claims and lawsuits are frivolous by nature and need to be denied and/or eliminated. This brings down medical costs and insurance. The result is less patient cost and more time for doctors to do what they do best.

"Malpractice claims and lawsuits need to cap out at 1 million dollars for the most serious of cases. Medical Review Boards should be established to resolve these claims."

The team arrived at the airport just as Genie was completing her discourse. They would further develop the 20/20 Plan next week as they address and resolve new issues.

MONDAY MORNING. WEEK 3.

SCIENCE AND RESEARCH. (NASA) (NIH) (NOAA) AND MORE

Everyone was early on Monday morning and eager to get started. The agenda for this week was exciting. They were looking forward to building the blueprint for America's future.

One that would 'rev' up the country. Tom asked everyone about his or her families, activities and flights from the weekend as everyone settled in for the drive to work. Ron was eager to begin and said, "I've talked with a lot people who told me how energized the country was back in the fifties and sixties. Everyone was electrified back then because the country was involved in scientific research projects and space exploration. We need to get everyone excited about America and the future of our children and grandchildren. They deserve to experience the enlivened feeling of purpose and accomplishment."

Tom expressed a feeling of agreement. "The 20/20 Plan is great, but people need to be inspired and motivated to successfully implement the entire process. Every link in the 300 million-link chain needs to feel excited and a part of the success in the country. Our citizens need to feel confident and certain America is on the right course."

NATIONAL AERONAUTICS AND SPACE ADMINISTRATION (NASA)

"Speaking of space exploration and scientific research," Ron went on. "We have brilliant scientists, engineers and technicians who embrace the challenge of rejuvenated projects. The federal government is currently conducting research projects in many various departments. Some have budgets controlled by different departments or agencies. Let's just use a few examples for the 20/20 Plan.

The latest budget figures (rounded) for these agencies are:

NASA	$18 Billion		$30 Billion
NIH	$31 Billion		$40 Billion
NOAA	$6 Billion		$10 Billion
Total	$55 Billion	20/20 Plan Proposed Budget	$80 Billion

"A resourceful budget will put thousands of people to work and stimulate the economy. This, of course, is only one segment of the economy. Support of these exciting enterprises will not only create countless new industries, but bolster and restore existing industries as well. The country must place emphasis on educating young students in the sciences. They require inspiration and purpose. The 20/20 Plan ensures our young students have the educational background to take our country to new scientific heights. The entire nation will be invigorated and inspired.

"NASA must review its current missions and determine its course for the short and long term. Indirect economic returns from spin-offs of human space exploration has repaid the initial public investment many times over. A good start is the International Space Station (ISS). The USA should end its agreement with Russia. A new generation Space Station in an optimum apogee is the logical next step. Developing and employing a new shuttle is another imperative. Evaluation of what the USA currently has in orbit and is supporting in space is crucial. Is the Hubble Telescope, or its successor, state of the art and should it be part of a new USA Space Station to facilitate periodic upgrades? Our exploration of space prompts many questions that need answers."

"This is important. What is the future of America in space?" Ron asked himself. "The USA should vigorously consider its own space station. We should not depend on Russia for this, or anything. We can have partners. The USA should revive its astronaut program. Space station crews should continue to learn how to function and live in space and learn how to build technology and hardware that will survive and function in the future. The space station should be the launching pad to the moon and other planets. This is essential if we are to explore deep space.

"Former NASA Administrator Michael D. Griffin says the International Space Station has a role to play as NASA moves forward with a new focus for the manned space program, which is to go out beyond Earth orbit for purposes of human exploration and scientific discovery. ISS is the ninth space station to be inhabited by crews, following the Soviet and later Russian Salyut, Almaz, and Mirstations, and Skylab from the US. The ISS is the most expensive single item ever constructed with a cost of more than $150 billion. It includes NASA's budget of over $60 billion for the station plus the cost of 36 shuttle flights to build the station, estimated at $1.4 billion each, or $50.4 billion total.

"The ISS requires extensive maintenance by expensive Extra Vehicular Activities. The magazine 'The American Enterprise' reports, for instance, that ISS astronauts 'now spend 85 percent of their time on construction and maintenance alone. The Astronomical Society of the Pacific states the orbit is rather highly inclined, which makes Russian launches cheaper, but US launches more expensive. This was an intended design point, to encourage Russian involvement with the ISS—and Russian involvement saved the project from abandonment in the wake of the Space Shuttle Columbia disaster, but the choice has increased the costs of completing the ISS.

"The International Space Station has been the target of much criticism over the years. Critics contend the time and billions spent on the ISS could be better spent. Some critics, like Robert L. Park, Physicist and Author, argue very little scientific research was convincingly planned for the ISS in the first place. The bottom line is that the ISS is too expensive; in the wrong orbit; and its end of mission is nearing. On May 13, 2014, in response to US sanctions against Russia over the conflict in Crimea, Russia's Deputy Prime Minister, Dmitry Rogozin, announced Russia would reject a U.S. request to prolong the orbiting station's use beyond 2020, and would only supply rocket engines to the U.S. for non-military satellite launches. The Russian ISS program head Alexey B. Krasnov, said in July 2014 "the Ukraine crisis is why Roscosmos has received no government approval to continue the station partnership beyond 2020."

"The Hubble Telescope launched by the Space Shuttle Discovery in 1990 is designed to be serviced by astronauts. Since then, it has been upgraded and repaired along with systems replacements four times. A fifth mission was canceled on safety grounds following the Columbia disaster. However, after spirited public discussion, NASA administrator Mike Griffin approved one final servicing mission, completed in 2009. The telescope is still operating as of 2014, and may last until 2020. Its scientific successor, the James Webb Space Telescope (JWST), is scheduled for launch in 2018."

Ron concluded, "The 20/20 Plan includes a revitalized space program that encompasses a new US mission, a new space station and a new shuttle program."

NATIONAL INSTITUTES OF HEALTH (NIH)

"Americans are living longer and healthier," Genie declared. "Life expectancy in the United States has jumped from 47 years in 1900 to 78 years as reported in 2009, and disability in people over age 65 has dropped in the past 3 decades.

"The National Institutes of Health (NIH), the nation's medical research agency, is a part of the U.S. Department of Health and Human Services. "NIH is the largest source of funding for medical research in the world, creating high-quality jobs by funding scientists in universities and research institutions all across America and around the globe. The NIH consists of 27 Institutes and Centers, each with a specific research agenda, often focusing on particular diseases or body systems.

The Office of the Director is responsible for setting policy for NIH and for planning, managing, and coordinating the programs and activities of all the NIH components. The NIH Director is responsible for providing leadership to the Institutes and relentlessly identify needs and opportunities, especially for efforts involving the multiple Institutes. The NIH has a budget of over $31 billion. More than 80 percent of the NIH budget goes to more than 300,000 research personnel at more than 2,500 universities and research institutions. Additionally, 6,000 scientists work in the NIH Intramural Research laboratories, mostly in Bethesda, Maryland. It is the home to the NIH Clinical Center, the largest hospital in the world totally dedicated to clinical research.

"The NIH supports many training programs and funding mechanisms with the goal of strengthening our nation's research capacity; broadening our research base; and inspiring a passion for science in current and future generations of researchers. Funding for the NIH must be reviewed, and a determination made to determine which programs should be preserved and what new programs should be introduced to sustain our nation's health and well-being. This and increased funding is a twofold benefit to the country by increasing our scientific efforts along with stimulating the economy."

NATIONAL OCEANIC AND ATMOSPHERIC ADMINISTRATION (NOAA)

"The National Oceanic and Atmospheric Administration "NOAA" is another primary federal government organization that provides an important service to the citizens of the nation," Dave said. "NOAA is a scientific agency within the United States Department of Commerce that focuses on ocean and atmosphere conditions. NOAA has 12,000 civilian employees and 300 uniformed service members who make up the NOAA Commissioned Officer Corps. NOAA was formed in 1970 when Richard Nixon proposed creating a new department to serve a national need "… for better protection of life and property from natural hazards … for a better understanding of the total environment … for exploration and development leading to the intelligent use of our marine resources …" NOAA formed a conglomeration of several existing agencies that were among the oldest in the federal government. They were the United States Coast and Geodetic Survey, formed in 1807; the Weather Bureau, formed in 1870—Geodetic Survey and Weather Service had been combined by a 1965 consolidation into the Environmental Science Services Administration (ESSA); and the Bureau of Commercial Fisheries, formed in 1871. NOAA is under the Department of Commerce.

"NOAA supplies people and agencies pertaining to the state and condition of the oceans and the atmosphere. NOAA issues weather warnings and forecasts through the National Weather Service and coordinates with federal, state, local and international authorities. NOAA manages the use of these environments by regulating fisheries and marine sanctuaries as well as protecting threatened and endangered marine species.

"The missions and goals of scientific research must be reviewed and analyzed. Programs should be funded to ensure the nation is advancing on the right course of making the US the leader in all aspects of science and technology. Although only three primary organizations are mentioned in the 20/20 Plan, the same concepts apply to all other scientific research and development the federal government undertakes."

As the team concluded their drive to work on Monday morning, they were all inspired thinking about how the entire nation was excited about the accomplishments of the fifties and sixties. A common purpose pulls people together. The country, divided by ideology with no clear path to travel, is dying a slow death. The four realized the 20/20 Plan is necessary to bring the people back together again and to renew the excitement of previous decades.

CHAPTER NINE | *Health Care Summary*

1. The 20/20 Plan allows citizens to own the healthcare they desire.

2. The 20/20 Plan permits employees to keep their health care if they change jobs.

3. The 20/20 Plan ensures health insurance policies will be custom-made.

4. Doctors are becoming more dissatisfied with their careers.

5. Most costs and prices in health care are hidden from both doctors and patients.

6. Any hidden cost is confusing and easy to inflate.

7. Health insurance does not equate to getting a good deal on your health care.

8. Price transparency in health care will lower health care costs.

9. Malpractice lawsuits and claims need to cap out at 1 million dollars.

10. Medical Review Boards must be established to resolve claims.

CHAPTER NINE | *Science and Research Summary*

1. The 20/20 Plan is designed to inspire the nation through exploration.

2. The 20/20 Plan puts the nation on the right course through research.

3. Space exploration and scientific research will stimulate the economy.

4. Young students need renewed interest in all scientific disciplines.

5. Increased funding will put people to work with a purpose.

6. The US needs to sever its costly ties with the ISS.

7. Construction of an American space station by NASA is essential.

8. Increased research in all areas is crucial for NIH.

9. Oceanic exploration must be a top priority for NOAA.

10. It is imperative that all other agencies in the USA continue research.

CHAPTER TEN

Energy, Oil, Mining, and Minerals

"We usually find gas in new places with old ideas. Sometimes, also, we find gas in an old place with a new idea, but we seldom find much gas in an old place with an old idea. Several times in the past we have thought that we were running out of gas, whereas actually we were only running out of ideas."

- Adapted from Parke A. Dickey, by American Potential Gas Committee.

MONDAY AFTERNOON. WEEK 3.

Tom began the conversation from the shotgun seat by saying, "we all have experience in the energy and mining industries. I was thinking about all of the places we worked. For example: power generation stations, chemical plants, refineries, steel mills, cement plants, zinc plants, lead smelters, aluminum plants, uranium mills, silver and gold refineries, quarries, above ground and underground mines that extract coal, copper, zinc, iron, uranium and aluminum.

We've worked on properties all across the nation and they all have many common traits. They are very nice people who work hard, know their business and take their work very seriously in order to earn a respectable wage for their families plus doing something meaningful to benefit humanity. They do everything they can to do things right and the clean water we drink and the clean air we see and breathe is evidence of that."

"We all agree the people at every level in these plants and mines do everything they can to provide and maintain a safe work place and do everything in their power to eliminate environmental incidents and emissions," Ron stated.

"I remember riding to the airport in a shuttle one clear Sunday afternoon. We passed a power plant and the driver said 'look at that pollution. That smoke is killing people.' The other passengers looked and they all chimed in to relate how dirty the plant must be and how it should be shut down immediately. They were surprised when I asked them how much pollution the power plant was emitting.

"None knew the answer and didn't say a word until the driver said, 'Anyone can see it. Just look at all of that smoke.' I then explained what they were witnessing was a cooling tower and the pollution they thought they saw was only water condensation. I went on further to explain the cooling tower was a self-enclosed system and it was physically impossible for toxic emissions to be generated from a cooling tower that contained only water. I don't know if I made any friends on that trip, but the rest of the ride sure was quiet."

"I guess that would be known as a teachable moment. Wouldn't it be great if more people knew, and understood, how things work instead of just buying into a false ideology? Especially controversial issues such as the environment. We're back to busting paradigms aren't we?" Dave asked.

"That's true. These companies take a beating from the EPA, OSHA, MSHA and all types of environmental activists," Genie added. "I've witnessed where companies bend over backwards to please everyone and are still fined. I've even been on site when the state and federal EPA were both in a cement plant at the same time and giving conflicting messages because they had opposing agendas. So what can be done about this?"

"The big picture is the United States must produce its own energy and mineral elements," Tom said. "If we do not because we are stymied by environmental activists, we will become a third world nation ripe for implosion. It is a matter of survival. Without energy and metals, we will not be able to produce goods and services nor have the ability to travel anywhere. Production and transportation will cease to exist, as will our republic.

"The 20/20 Plan calls for a swift, but thorough permitting process. This will stimulate our energy producers to explore and produce our own materials. The 20/20 Plan to eliminate corporate taxes will accelerate the economy, reduce costs, and therefore reduce consumer prices. We need to be an exporting nation not an importing nation. It is simple, keep our resources here and export the excess to bring home cash.

"The next step is to conduct an objective and practical analysis of all current regulations and roll back all regulations that provide no real value to the nation and the environment twenty years. Companies must be unshackled so they can hire people and make profits to invest back into the economy.

"There is much concern about the U.S. Environmental Protection Agency's (EPA) proposed carbon emission standards for existing power plants. This government agency is implementing regulations without Congressional approval. The 20/20 Plan expresses a strong objection to current carbon proposals. The federal government is overreaching and these costly regulations leave Americans paying senseless billions of dollars per year.

Reliable, low-cost power generated by coal drives local economies, sustains jobs, protects families from out-of-control energy costs, and truly keeps the lights and AC on in homes and businesses. The EPA's carbon regulations jeopardize the country's access to affordable power, putting America's energy and economic future in peril.

"Each state has its own agencies. The people know what is best for their state. They should have the power to regulate what is in their best interest. I remember when many US cities had smog and foul air. That condition just doesn't exist anymore. Our country has clean air and clean water. The federal government overreaches in areas in which they are ill informed just for ideological purposes," Tom concluded.

"I can see that you have some strong feelings in this area," Genie said. "What should the 20/20 Plan address in the area of mining?"

Tom replied. "This gets us back to a swift and thorough permitting process. Rolling back non-value added federal government regulations is the first step. The country needs to analyze and assess future requirements. A good example of this is rare earth elements. Very few people have knowledge of the importance of these elements.

Tom cited from the Tasman Metals Ltd. Website "rare-earth elements (REE) are described as naturally occurring non-toxic materials, whose unique properties make them essential to emerging technologies that contribute to environmental, energy efficiency and health solutions. REE's consist of 16 elements, being the 15 lanthanide-series elements plus the metal yttrium. The REE's are grouped together as they display similar chemical properties, in particular the ability to readily discharge and accept electrons, making them indispensable and non-replaceable in many electronic, optical, magnetic and catalytic applications."

Tom continued. "REE's and scandium, zirconium, hafnium, niobium and tantalum are considered strategic metals due to the essential role they play in high technology and defense applications. It is critical to ensure the development and growth of strategic metals and to secure their supply to further capital-intensive technology and green industries.

"Despite their name, REEs are in fact not especially rare. Each is more common in the earth's crust than silver, gold or platinum. Cerium, yttrium, neodymium and lanthanum are more common than lead. Thulium and lutetium are the least abundant REE's with crustal abundance of approximately 0.5 parts per million. However, they are never found as free metals in the earth's crust and all their naturally occurring minerals consist of mixtures of various REE's with other metals and non-metals. REE are classified into two subgroups, as light rare earth elements (LREE) comprising the first five elements with atomic numbers 57-62 and the heavy rare earth elements (HREE), comprising the elements with atomic numbers 63-71 as well as yttrium.

"The Pea Ridge Mine, a dormant mine near Sullivan, Missouri holds a deposit of our increasingly high-tech world rare-earth elements, used in everything from cellphones to missile systems to hybrid cars, according to Ryan Schuessler writing in Al Jazeera America. The Missouri mine is one of the few places in the world where such an abundant deposit of rare earth metals are found. Nevertheless, nothing about rare earth metals is simple. Rare-earth metals are essential for production of $5 trillion worth of products.

"China, and the United States, due to their scarcity and huge value, are in a complex geopolitical competition. It is a contest pitting China and the United States, and just about every other powerful nation on earth, into a new great game of diplomacy, business brinksmanship and a fight to dominate the market for these scarce elements. China is winning. Over the past few decades, China has bought up nearly the entire supply chain of rare-earth metals and the products they're used for, leaving other powers struggling to catch up.

"Russia discovered rare earth elements in Afghanistan in the '80s but somehow lost the information when they pulled out of their war in the country. The United States discovered this information but did not bid on it and the Chinese now hold the contract in Afghanistan, a country where our people shed blood and treasure.

"Getting American mines like Pea Ridge up and running won't suddenly rescue the U.S. rare-earth metals industry. China's monopoly in the market is beyond simply mining the metals. In fact, nearly all the manufacturing based on the high-value "heavy" rare earths has moved to China over the past few decades. China's export restrictions and supply-chain acquisition have taken U.S.-based operations to that country to receive a reliable source of rare earth metals needed for modern manufacturing. This process has played out over the last 25 years or so. In 1992, the then-leader of the Communist Party of China, Deng Xiaoping, said: 'The Middle East has oil and China has rare earth.' China has since lived up to that promise.

"Thirty years ago, U.S. production of rare earth metals was nearly three times that of China, just under 30,000 tons. However, U.S. production shut down in the early 21st century after being outdone by Chinese production, which had grown to approximately 70,000 tons and has continued to increase ever since. The most notable single example of China taking on the U.S. was in 1995, when Chinese companies acquired Magnequench, a GM subsidiary built in conjunction with the Department of Defense that developed high-tech magnets using the rare earth neodymium. By 2002, their facilities were duplicated in China, and all U.S. operations were shut down.

"China's upper hand, including the acquisition of Magnequench, was the result of a well-thought out carefully crafted dynamic long term strategy. Today China's rare-earth metal production is almost equal to global rare earth consumption, around 135,000 tons. That gives China power, especially as the world economy becomes ever-more high tech. If advanced countries such as U.S.A. and several European countries aspire to build an economy, which moves towards the Green Energy systems, then China, being a major supplier of rare earth metals will hold the world ransom.

"China's leverage also exists when it comes to military technology based on rare earths, used in radar systems, missiles and satellites, to name a few. This gives China powerful influence in global diplomacy. In September 2010, reports emerged alleging China had suspended exports of rare earths to Japan over an incident surrounding disputed islands in the South China Sea. Chinese officials continue to deny this claim, but rare-earth consumers nonetheless have been scrambling to find an alternative supply ever since.

"The alternative to Chinese production dominance lies in mines in the United States such as Missouri's Pea Ridge Mine and other places like it scattered across the United States. However, it is not just mining the rare earths that matters. It is what you can, or cannot, do with them once they are aboveground that matters too. A domestic supply of raw materials means nothing without the manufacturing capacity to turn them into high-value products. Some in the industry say China still has the upper hand.

"The neodymium magnet, also known as the 'neo magnet' is used in dozens of weapons systems, including the Patriot missile, the F-22 Raptor and the joint air-to-ground missile. These magnets, and their component parts, are manufactured in China. We are totally dependent on these products and their parts in the supply chain, in which China has the monopoly.

"The 20/20 Plan makes it possible for the United States to build the infrastructure to manufacture rare earth metals into the modern technological products that have made them so important. The world is completely dependent on China and the export of U.S. rare-earth assets into China will only intensify this dependence."

The discussion for the trip home was closing as they were nearing the hotel. Tom turned on the radio to catch the six o'clock news only to learn foreign policy and international affairs dominated the news again. "Sounds like decisions are being made for political purposes as usual," Ron spoke over the commercial break. Tom interjected, "that is our topic for tomorrow. Should be interesting." About that time, Dave pulled into the parking lot to conclude a long day.

CHAPTER TEN | *Energy, Oil, Gas. Mining and Minerals Summary*

1. American industry is committed to a cleaner and safer environment.

2. Few citizens are aware of the efforts made by their own industries.

3. Americans enjoy clean air and water.

4. The federal government, especially the EPA, is overreaching.

5. The US must become energy self-sufficient to survive as a world leader.

6. The 20/20 Plan ensures assessment of the nation's energy requirements.

7. The 20/20 Plan facilitates permitting to produce needed energy.

8. The 20/20 Plan makes mining in America a top priority.

9. Rare Earth Elements are essential to the future of American technology.

10. China dominates the RRE mining infrastructure and market.

CHAPTER ELEVEN

International Relations

"International politics, like all politics, is a struggle for power"

- Hans J. Morgenthau, Author, Politics Among Nations

TUESDAY MORNING. WEEK 3.

After watching the TV news last night all four team members were thinking about the future of the country and how the United States of America is the only hope for the rest of the world. Still, people within and outside the country have different agendas and different ideals they pursue. People at all levels in the government, and the media pundits, are at odds with each other as to whether the USA should lead the world or if it should be just another country. Tom opened up the conversation by saying, "discussions about our foreign policy should include the United Nations and foreign assistance. Terrorism has rocked the world and must be resolved. Immigration will be discussed as a separate subject and developed into a specific policy.

"Discussion on the United Nations should begin with a brief history of United States involvement. First was the League of Nations, an international organization, created after World War I to provide a forum for resolving international disputes. Headquartered in Geneva, Switzerland the League of Nations was initially proposed by President Woodrow Wilson in 1919 as part of his Fourteen Points plan for an equitable peace in Europe. The United States never joined the League. Most historians consider the League operated much less effectively without U.S. participation than it would have otherwise. The United States did however agree with many of its goals. Most of the propositions of the League were unenforceable. The league had 58 members at its highest point and finally disbanded on April 20, 1946.

"The United States public and the Roosevelt Administration supported and became founding members of the new United Nations. The United Nations has accomplished some good things according to its most ardent supporters but it has also been a gathering place for forces of corruption, greed and deceit as it fosters the self-serving interest of dictators and despots. When UN members negotiated the Arms Trade Treaty (ATT) it was a bewildering experience. It was not a negotiation as Americans perceive negotiations. It was a series of puzzling unconnected national interventions on particular points of interest. The actual drafting happened out of sight. Iran and North Korea were treated with as much formal respect as the United States and South Korea.

"The American public is now ready to move in a different direction. Membership in the United Nations does not serve the best interest of the nation and the cost of membership is misused on worthless programs that do little or no good for the people they purport to help. It is definitely time for the United States to get out of the United Nations and the United Nations to get out of the United States."

"Bravo. Do you think our citizens can accept a big departure from something they have grown used to for more than sixty years?" Genie asked. "Do you think the United States would be better off as a country if it didn't belong to the United Nations?" "Of course they will when they learn the facts," Tom said.

"Examples to remind us of the rampant hypocrisy of the United Nations and of its members and leaders are:

  a. The UN sessions are filled with eloquent blather but nothing ever is done.
  b. The UN inability to handle international conflicts and protect member nations.
  c. The veto power by any one permanent member on the Security Council.
  d. Does not follow its mandate to maintain international peace and security.
  e. The UN Peacekeepers are utterly ineffective. A good example is Somalia.
  f. The refusal to condemn attacks on Israel while annually condemning Israel.
  g. The abysmal record on human rights especially by members put in authority.
  h. Aggressors like China and Russia never being censured.
  i. Support for population control programs, but no support during the Ebola crisis.
  j. The 15 member Security Council stymies all proposals they individually agree to.

"The late Daniel Patrick Moynihan, speaking in 1976, after stepping down as U.S. ambassador to the UN said the UN was a "squalid circus," and wondered how long the US would take to resign. Since then the UN's moral failings have not diminished. The UN system is secretive while mechanisms of accountability are lacking. The officers are not loyal to any public constituency. They do however, hold diplomatic immunity and are subject to few laws. Advancement in the UN is centered on bribery, not merit.

"Some in our government want the US to sign on to the UN's International Criminal Court (ICC), which would allow the UN's ICC to arrest and try US troops for War Crimes, without the legal protections guaranteed under US Law, and from which there is no appeal. The US cannot allow our service personnel to be subject to this folly.

"Only twice since 1946 has the UN acted to turn back a breach of the peace: Korea in 1950 and Kuwait in 1990-91. Then, the Security Council gave the United States a writ of authority to do the job instead of acting through the peace-enforcing machinery spelled out in the Charter. The United States receives little or no benefit from membership. Below are the actual voting records of various Arabic/Islamic States which are recorded in both the US State Department and United Nations records:

The aggregate voting record is 88 per cent in opposition to the United States:

COUNTRIES OVERALL VOTING RECORD	RECENT VOTING RECORD
Kuwait votes against the United States 67% of the time.	86%
Qatar votes against the United States 67% of the time.	88%
Morocco votes against the United States 70% of the time.	89%
United Arab Emirates votes against the U. S. 70% of the time.	88%
Jordan votes against the United States 71% of the time.	88%
Tunisia votes against the United States 71% of the time.	89%
Saudi Arabia votes against the United States 73% of the time.	90%
Yemen votes against the United States 74% of the time.	88%
Algeria votes against the United States 74% of the time.	88%
Oman votes against the United States 74% of the time.	88%
Sudan votes against the United States 75% of the time.	86%
Pakistan votes against the United States 75% of the time.	87%
Libya votes against the United States 76% of the time.	89%
Egypt votes against the United States 79% of the time.	86%
Lebanon votes against the United States 80% of the time.	90%
India votes against the United States 81% of the time.	79%
Syria votes against the United States 84% of the time.	89%
Mauritania votes against the United States 87% of the time.	90%

"Other UN voting records surveyed and considered our closest allies were:

Australia votes against the United States 44% of the time.
Canada votes against the United States 51% of the time.
Israel votes against the United States 11% of the time.
Japan votes against the United States 58% of the time.
UK votes against the United States 40% of the time.
France votes against the United States 46% of the time.

"The United States seems to be at odds with the rest of the world, or the rest of the world is at odds with us. Example: United States Foreign Aid to those countries that hate us: (Verified as true at: http://www.snopes.com/inboxer/outrage/unvote.asp)

Egypt, for example, after voting 79% of the time against the United States, still receives $2 billion annually in US Foreign Aid plus military equipment.

Jordan votes 71% against the United States and annually receives $1,416,900,000 in US Foreign Aid.

Pakistan votes 75% against the United States receives $2,019,000,000 annually in US Foreign Aid.

India votes 81% against the United States receives $1,667,600,000 annually.

North Korea receives 98,100,000 annually and they never agree with the US.

"We know other countries never come to our aid. It is always the other way around. This is genuine evidence it is time to get out of the UN and give the tax savings back to American families who have to skimp and sacrifice to pay the taxes to fund these blathering corrupt fat cats. Everyone needs to know this. This organization is a disgrace. Still we wonder why the world has no respect for us. Perhaps it's their propaganda.

"The 20/20 Plan puts forth an invitation to a select few nations to join the United States in a new global organization. The present United Nations is not what the United Nations started out to be. This new organization must be established on honesty and integrity with the mission of helping make the world a better place; not a richer and more powerful place for dishonest despots and corrupt dictators. This new Association of Nations might include some NATO members and some former SEATO members (Australia, France, New Zealand, the Philippines, Thailand, and the United Kingdom) could be prospective members.

Tom looked out the window for a moment and took a deep breath before continuing. "The biggest issue with the UN is that is has no unifying purpose that can be enforced. This new 'Association of Nations' organization needs clearly defined missions that bring all nations together. Three areas where all nations can benefit mutually are Exploration, Technology and Protection. When the United States creates this new organization, it will stop filling its recent role of 'world police' and return to the role of being the shining example for humanity. When all nations in the organization are focused on exploring our oceans and solar system and developing new medical, energy and transportation technologies, other nations outside the organization will begin to recognize that working together is mutually beneficial. This leads to protection. If all nations work together towards common goals such as exploration, thoughts of these nations warring with each other will disappear.

"This is the perfect solution to form a more perfect union with countries who have the best interest of the planet in mind rather the fraudulently evolved United Nations whose only interest is themselves and their spoils. The nations in this new alliance would agree to support each other in times of strife, especially including the security and protection from terrorists and their organizations."

"Do you have a name of this new organization?" Genie inquired. "Who will organize it and who will write the charter?"

"The name can be decided by the diplomats from the countries that establish the new association. For talking purposes, we can call it the "Association of Nations." There are people with vast diplomatic and foreign experience to write the charter. The United States should take a lead role in the process, but the other member nations must also have input and involvement."

"Tom, you make a passionate and informed case in withdrawing from the flawed United Nations; and for forming a new union to build a safer, more secure and more constructive force to help other countries in need," Genie spoke up. "But what about foreign aid? Most people think we cannot exist in the world without buying the friendship of foreign countries and their leaders with our aid. Many think giving countries military resources is the best method to keep the United States safe."

"That's a good point," Tom replied. "Let me give some recent background to make my point. Congress passed the Foreign Assistance Act in 1961. This act reorganized the U.S. foreign assistance programs and separated foreign aid into military and non-military aid. This Act mandated the creation of the U.S. Agency for International Development (US-AID), which was established by President Kennedy two months later. USAID became the first U.S. foreign assistance organization whose primary focus was long-term economic and social development.

"Foreign aid is about 1 percent of the total U.S. federal budget at about $40 billion per year. This includes foreign military assistance and spending on diplomacy. These are tax dollars that could be better spent on job training and education that would be of a much greater benefit to our own citizens.

"This is not to say that the United States should not lend a helping hand to developing countries. It is imperative that the republic do just that. It just has to be accomplished in a more intelligent, beneficial and effective manner. It should be assistance given with the intent of helping both countries. Developing countries and their citizens will feel much better about themselves and the United States if we provide the methods for them to accomplish meaningful goals.

"The 20/20 Plan provides training for a peace corps type organization. This is an important element of the AmericaWorks Career Program. This approach is infinitely more effective in helping countries that not only need our help, but actively agree to cooperate and participate with the United States in building their countries and bringing them into prosperity. This cadre of citizens take on an assignment, or tour of duty, to assist in building needed infrastructure such as roads, bridges, schools, power generation stations, electrical grids, fresh water resources, water treatment plants, industrial and manufacturing facilities and more. The mission is to educate and to train builders to carry on this work in order to build strong, healthy societies."

"Our people make better emissaries than our dollars which always seem to go to a dictator's Swiss bank account. This is similar to the philosophy of 'give a man a fish and you feed him for a day. Teach a man to fish and you feed him for a lifetime.' The United States is the most generous nation in the world. We feed people and give people aid, but we never give them what they need to sustain themselves," Dave interjected. "This fulfills that objective and provides people with the critical means to advance and be prosperous instead of perpetually waiting for handouts. This is a perfect undertaking to provide meaningful employment for our own citizens. It contributes to each individuals work experience, and to the country itself."

"Good points Dave," Tom said moving on. "Our nation has serious problems with acts of terrorism committed here in the United States and abroad. These acts jeopardize our safety and security and in turn cost many lives and billions of dollars. In 1785, Thomas Jefferson claimed that war would be the only way to stop the pirates. Barbary Coast Pirates preying on our ships and hindering our trade was similar to the terrorism that we face today. When Jefferson came to office, the amount of tribute had exceeded $2,000,000. He refused to pay tribute, saying it was "money thrown away," he asked that the Europeans join with the United States in rising against the Barbary Pirates. Europe refused, however, deciding it best to continue paying tribute, or bribes.

"The 20/20 Plan advances a strategy similar to that of Thomas Jefferson because the situation is very similar today as it was in the early 1800s. A strong republic will not bow to terror and piracy and will preclude those acts from happening in the first place. The line in the Marine Corps Hymn, 'To the shores of Tripoli' refers to the First Barbary War and specifically the Battle of Derne in 1805. After Lieutenant Presley O'Bannon and his Marines hoisted the American flag over the Old World for the first time. The phrase was added to the battle colors of the Corps.

"Today we have operations in Afghanistan and the Middle East. The United States pays foreign assistance to nations to act in accordance with the wishes of the USA. This foreign assistance is similar to paying bribes to obtain favorable foreign policy outcomes under ever-growing military constraints. Other nations are getting into the act as well. The future may see the greatest growth in foreign assistance to be between China and smaller nations in Africa and Latin America. The United States must be ahead of this curve in order to strengthen these countries to develop essential trade with us and to secure vital supplies of raw materials."

"A good place to start would be Central American countries," Genie stated. "The US should bring them to prosperity instead of letting China infiltrate our hemisphere."

The four associates arrived at work on Tuesday morning excited about the prospects of working with developing countries by helping them to truly develop their own infrastructure and to train their people to build their own country. Foreign Service is the best way to help countries build themselves.

"Peace, commerce, and honest friendship with all nations...entangling alliances with none"
— Thomas Jefferson

CHAPTER ELEVEN | *International Relations Summary*

1. The United States needs to get out of the United Nations.

2. "The late Daniel Patrick Moynihan, U.S. ambassador to the UN, said the UN was a "squalid circus," and wondered how long the US would take to resign.

3. The UN is a "squalid circus" and is largely ineffective blather.

4. Supposed friendly members vote against the U.S. 88% of the time.

5. The United Nations does not serve the interest of the American people.

6. The 20/20 Plan initiates an Association of Nations with common purposes.

7. Too much foreign aid is frittered away with too little return.

8. A strong nation will not bow to terror and piracy.

9. The 20/20 Plan helps countries by training their people.

10. The 20/20 Plan implements a new strategy to combat terrorism.

11. The United Nations needs to get out of the United States.

"Whatever it is that the government does, sensible Americans would prefer that the government do it to somebody else. This is the idea behind foreign policy."
— P.J. O'Rourke

Education and Poverty

"An investment in knowledge pays the best interest. - Benjamin Franklin

TUESDAY AFTERNOON. WEEK 3.

As the team piled into the car to drive back to the hotel, it was Genie's turn to present the newest topics: education and poverty. Genie began by saying, "everyone in the United States believes in, and understands the importance of education. Poverty is a result in part of a faulty educational system. When people have positive educational experiences, they shun the ways of poverty and strive for a more productive life. There are many opinions about the best method of education for our citizens, both young and old, who should administer education, who should pay for education, and the relationship between education and poverty. I'll lay out some history and data and then describe the 20/20 Plan for education.

"The United States Department of Education (ED or DoED) is a Cabinet-level department of the United States government created by The Department of Education Organization Act, and signed into law by President Jimmy Carter on October 17, 1979. It began operation on May 4, 1980. The Act divided the Department of Health, Education, and Welfare into the Department of Education and the Department of Health and Human Services. The Department of Education is administered by the US Secretary of Education and is the smallest Cabinet-level department; with about 5,000 employees, conversely it has a budget of more than $67 billion.

"Carter wanted to transfer the education-related functions of the Departments of Defense, Justice, Housing and Urban Development, and Agriculture, as well as other federal agencies. Many saw the department as unconstitutional, arguing that the Constitution does not mention education and deemed it an unnecessary and illegal federal bureaucratic intrusion into local affairs. Some however see it as constitutional under the Commerce Clause and the funding role of the Department as constitutional under the Taxing and Spending Clause.

"In 1979 the Office of Education had 3,000 employees and an annual budget of $12 billion. Today the Department of Education budget is ever increasing and it is involved in a great many aspects of the federal government and the lives of its citizens. Unfortunately, as the budget increased, the level of education in America declined. We spend more money every year to degrade the educational level of the students.

"From the Department of Education website, ED currently administers a budget of $67.3 billion in discretionary appropriations (including discretionary Pell Grant funding) and operates programs that touch on every area and level of education. The Department's elementary and secondary programs annually serve nearly 16,900 school districts and approximately 50 million students attending more than 98,000 public schools and 28,000 private schools. Departmental programs also provide grant, loan, and work-study assistance to more than 13 million postsecondary students. It is important to point out that education in America is primarily a state and local responsibility, and ED's budget is only a small part of both total national education spending and the overall Federal budget. Lets' address elementary and secondary education first.

"The ongoing result of this massive budget and overreaching bureaucracy is abject failure. According to website statistics from the Program for International Student Assessment (PISA), American 15 year olds turned in flat test results measuring proficiency in reading, math and science. The United States doesn't rank in the top 20 worldwide. In mathematics, 29 nations outperformed the US by a significant margin. The US was ranked 23rd 3 years ago. The US ranked 22nd in science. That ranking fell from 18th 3 years ago. The US ranked 19th in reading, down from 9th place.

UNITED STATES	YEAR	MATH	SCIENCE	READING
RANKING	2009	23	18	9
RANKING	2012	29	22	19

"The top overall scores came from Shanghai, Singapore, Hong Kong, Taiwan, South Korea, Macao and Japan, followed by Lichtenstein, Switzerland, the Netherlands and Estonia. Student math scores in Shanghai showed they are 'the equivalent of more than two years of formal schooling ahead of those observed in Massachusetts, itself a strong-performing U.S. state.'

"The U.S. spends more per student than most countries. This should equate to exceptional performance. The United States spends more than $115,000 total per student. The Department of Education spends double what other countries spend per student (varies by state). According to the DoED website, foreign student's results are much, much superior. Parents and private foundations fund more and more of the cost of education. New and experienced teachers out earn their counterparts around the world.

"Where does this money come from? In the 2009-2010 school year, total revenues were $593.7 Billion. The best (latest) data available shows these three sources:

Local Revenues:	$261.4 billion	(44 percent of total revenues)
State Revenues:	$258.3 billion	(43.5 percent of total revenues)
Federal Revenues:	$74 billion	(12.5 percent of total revenues)

"Of the $602.6 billion budget spending by U.S. schools in the 2009-2010 school year only $19.3 Billion, was spent on debt interest and payments to other governments. $56.1 billion was spent on construction, land, existing structures and equipment. The largest amount (88.5 percent) was spent on a broad category called "current spending."

The $527.2 billion that falls into this category is as follows:

$317.8 billion: Instruction
$48.7 billion: Operation and Maintenance
$28.6 billion: Pupil support services
$27.8 billion: School administration
$27.1 billion: Other current spending
$24.8 billion: Instructional staff support services
$22.1 billion: Pupil transportation
$17.5 billion: Other and non-specified support services
$9.6 billion: General administration

"This reveals 53% of budgeting is used for instruction. The other budget items may be important to some extent, but 47% of the budget spent on items other than instruction does not make sense. Spending per student varies by state, from a high of almost $20,000 per student per year in New York, to $6,000 per student per year in Utah. The results are are inversely related. The more money spent, the lower the results. The less money spent, the higher the results. Reliable statistics are extremely difficult to find. There are disparities between sources and some stats lag up to 3 years. One point is certain. The United States is throwing away money at a dysfunctional system in the hopes that, some day, more money will make the educational system better. That will never, never, ever happen!

"America must lead the world in education if America is going to help the world. Poorly educated citizens cannot successfully guide the future of the country. If the country fails to educate its citizens, the nation will unquestionably fail. American exceptionalism only works if Americans act, and study, exceptionally. The first step to success is to admit the country has an education problem. The educational results are self-evident.

"The traditional public school system utilizes a one-size fits-all approach to teaching. This results in disengaged, unmotivated students who have a wide variety of learning styles and interests. School choice allows students to attend schools that best fit their learning aspirations. When students choose their schools, schools have an incentive to compete by offering effective and engaging lessons. More schools need to feature the academic disciplines of science, technology, engineering and mathematics. The 20/20 Plan encourages students to become engaged in these essential subjects.

"Charter schools work. The Freire Charter School found itself on the nation's "Best High Schools" list by U.S. News and World Report in 2013. 94 percent of its 2013 graduates went straight to college. The graduation numbers are especially impressive in Philadelphia, a city with a high dropout rate. Freire works hard to get scholarships for its students as they head to college. In 2014, average student scholarships were $59,665.

"The school has focused on keeping parents involved. Its "Power School" software program informs parents of students' grades, attendance and behavior. Students struggling in classes are matched with peer tutors, who are paid to help struggling students, under the supervision of adults."

"Most people recognize our educational system is flawed," Ron said. "They do not believe it can be repaired. They say 'it is what it is' and give up instead of doing a root cause analysis, or looking at history. The United States once ranked first in education. Then the government became heavily involved and the entire system became a political football that's been kicked around at every level of government from school boards to the federal bureaucracy. We need change that functions at every level. The four of us are doing pretty well for ourselves, but what about the youngsters that didn't have our advantages. The many young people who live in inner cities need something better than they're receiving.

"We read about the people who live below the poverty level and we find it has not changed since the 1960s. Since 1964, U.S. taxpayers have spent over $22 trillion on anti-poverty programs. This spending (which does not include Social Security or Medicare) is three times the cost of all U.S. military wars since the American Revolution. Progress against poverty, according to the U.S. Census Bureau, has been miniscule. President Johnson's main goal of reducing the "causes" rather than the mere "consequences" of poverty, has completely failed. A significant portion of the population is now less capable of self-sufficiency than it was when the War on Poverty began. Exceptional education is the best way out of poverty."

"Many argue that poverty is caused by inner city conditions, one parent families, cultural problems, employers moving to the suburbs, middle class flight, apathy, no self- reliance skills, dependency of the welfare system, etc. Clearly a controversial subject with little agreement from anyone," Dave stated. "We hear arguments from all sides on every level, but no one has ever implemented a solution. The 20/20 Plan for education is the only true process to educate and lift people out of poverty."

"The 20/20 Plan addresses all levels of education and works as a means toward citizens escaping poverty by being prepared to be employed in meaningful careers," Genie stated. "Educated citizens will aspire to and qualify for high paying jobs. That is the path out of poverty. This process must start at an early age. It will take up to fifteen years to completely implement the entire 20/20 Plan. Some students will have to enter the educational process, in progress, but that is far superior to their current prospects." Genie declared. "Let's start at the beginning."

DAY CARE AND PRESCHOOL

"The 20/20 Plan creates jobs for everyone. Many working families require day care for their children. The 20/20 Plan provides day care assistance for working families with children up to 5 years old. Qualifications are full time, 40 hour per week, employment by the parents. Parents may enroll their children in qualified Day Care Centers and Preschool Learning Centers. State, county and local governments will license and approve these centers. The federal government will directly fund the centers through the local/county/state governments on a per enrollee basis. Funding will be $100.00 per week per child. Families who wish to spend more for care, or schooling, will have the option of selecting facilities that meet their specific requirements."

ELEMENTARY, INTERMEDIATE AND SECONDARY LEVEL EDUCATION

"Schools will be privately owned by proprietors, or partners, who found, administer and manage these schools with a specific purpose in order to attract enrollment. Schools will be competitive in nature by emphasizing specific curriculum and attributes in order to appeal to students. Entrepreneurism, coupled with parental participation, guarantee quality education. Some schools will be similar to traditional schools and will attract enrollees who prefer a traditional type education. Some will be religious schools already the backbone of the educational system. Some may be private academies. Others may pattern themselves after charter schools or magnet schools. Parents now have a choice.

"Maximum class size will be 30 students per class per grade. One certified teacher is required for each grade. Interns from the AmericaWorks Program may be employed as teacher aides and administrative assistants. Schools will be limited to employing one aid per class plus two general assistance interns for each four classes. An additional benefit of the intern program is to instruct future teachers as they gain experience from on the job training.

"Each parent is required to devote two (2) hours per week, or forty (40) hours per semester, per student, to their school at all three levels. These participative activities are fourfold:

1. to assist the operation of the school to reduce and control costs; 2. to participate in school management activities in order to better understand the quality of education; 3. to ensure accountability, integrity, responsibility and discipline is adhered to; and 4. to be an integral part of the students education.

"Other suggested activities are Parent Teacher Association, mentoring student projects, tutoring, after school care, field trips, athletic team coaching, and mentoring school clubs such as music, chess, scouting, community service, debate and book clubs. Operational assistance might be office administrative work, cafeteria work, housekeeping, landscaping, building maintenance, security, etc.

"Each school selects a unique uniform for its students to wear. Uniforms have a positive effect on both students and teachers. They promote a single standard of dress. School environments become less competitive and more focused on learning. With uniforms, students find ways to express themselves creatively through the arts, music, sports, personality and academic achievement rather than through their clothes.

"There is a link between student appearance and teacher expectations. High expectations lead to high achievement. Uniforms build a sense of community within the school as they create an atmosphere of kinship and loyalty. Unity is a positive effect on a child's attitude toward school and leads to better learning and improved attendance. A child excited about school is a child prepared to learn. Uniforms promote a safe, healthy learning environment, as a safe school environment is essential for learning. The safer the environment, the more likely children will attend. Uniforms bring simplicity, organization, and neatness. Uniforms are the most cost-effective dress for school.

"Personal electronic devices such as laptops, cell phones, smart phones, iPhones, iPods, beepers and other types of electronic devices are strictly prohibited from being used, carried on, or brought on school premises at any time for any reason under the 20/20 Plan. This is a zero tolerance offense that applies to all teachers, students, school employees and any other person on school grounds. These devices, when used for personal purposes, become distractions from focusing on the task at hand, which in this case is education.

"In addition, students will not be allowed to use the internet for any reason except those that pertain to a specific subject being taught in that course. Texting, gaming, surfing the web, etc. are not permitted on school grounds at any time at any level."

"The 20/20 Plan for education is solid and sound," Dave interjected. "What is the 20/20 Plan for discipline and violence in schools?"

"The act of parents choosing a school and being actively involved in the school prepares students to focus on education rather than destructive activities," Genie answered. "Students are taught the benefits of the 300 million link chain and that each student is equally responsible and accountable to make each link in the chain strong. Uniforms will provide a sense of loyalty to the school and therefore encourage good behavior. Students held to high standards of behavior, in the classrooms, and outside, including off school grounds tend to behave. Of course, nothing is perfect. The 20/20 Plan anticipates there will always be problems.

"Schools will be mandated to follow a uniform policy of 'zero-tolerance' on physical and/ or verbal violence and bullying. Acts of violence may result in expulsion. Parents are then responsible for entering their child in a behavioral therapy course for treatment to change destructive and potentially self-destructing behaviors. Parents are responsible for the cost of this treatment. In cases of conflict, mediation is available.

"There are process steps to resolve conflict through mediation. Students are free to take their peers, or their teachers, to mediation with the 20/20 Plan. If the mediation is successful, the parties sign a contract to resolve the specific issue. Violations of the contract result in another round of mediation, or expulsion, if warranted.

"Since education is so critical to the future of America, students must focus on what they are in school for – their future. Distractions and disturbances cannot be tolerated and must be eliminated for the benefit of all students. Materials other than those required for school activities are not permitted. All weapons are banned.

"Students will be allowed to use school approved computers, calculators and the internet for learning purposes. These electronic devices must be utilized specifically for the course being taught. Schools may require students to furnish their own computers, or laptops. However, to be competitive, they may furnish computers, or laptops, for their students. Computers, or laptops, utilized in classrooms must be loaded with identical software, and programs. They may not have personal software or programs installed on computers utilized for classroom work. This applies to all schools, at every level, including homeschools.

"English is the official language of the schools. It is folly to think non-English speaking students can fully succeed in America. To not mandate English be taught and spoken in school, is in fact the cruel prison sentence of poverty. To instruct in languages other than English is to prevent young students from assimilating in the American culture and economy. This does not preclude students from speaking another language away from school, or that study of other languages is not permitted.

"International and local students typically choose to study English courses. Career prospects are strengthened by the proficient and skilled use of the English language. English opens up countless opportunities for those who learn English. There are many good reasons to study English, which is the most widely spoken language. English is spoken in many parts of the world and is often the common language of people whose first language is not English. In business and matters of trade, the English language is the common currency. With English, a person is able to conduct business transactions, write and respond to documents such as emails, memos, contracts, agreements and reports. Career prospects and employment opportunities increase for fluent English speakers as companies seek after them. The purpose of getting an education is to be able to work to build a prosperous life.

"As the world becomes closer and more connected, opportunities to travel and explore different parts of the world become more available. Travelers who speak English enjoy safe and pleasant interactions when they have a command of English.

"English is the language most commonly spoken by academics worldwide. Important research tends to be conducted, composed and published in English. Scholars who have knowledge of English find sharing their ideas and findings with their peers globally is better facilitated by their mastery of the English language.

"Technology is vital and crucial to the economy. English is often the language utilized by those who are technologically minded and ambitious. Those who master English make an investment in their education, and acquire great value for their effort.

"All schools must be licensed, certified and able to meet all qualifications in the state in which they are located. The federal government will fund the schools through the local/county/state governments with vouchers for each enrollee. Families who wish to spend additional amounts for education, above the voucher level, have the option of enrolling their children in schools that offer that alternative. Parents now have a choice of the type of school they choose their children to attend. It is imperative that parents participate and be an integral component of each child's education. This is not possible in a government school system staffed with union teachers with no incentive to provide a quality education for their students.

"All schools have a mandate to provide detailed lesson plans in order to be certified and licensed. Semester lesson plans must be presented to the students prior to enrollment. Each school must have a fully functional website to post lesson plans plus all required books, materials, supplies, uniforms and other school needs. Schools have the option of providing these materials for their students on a scholarship basis. Schools that do not wish to participate in this endeavor must post the cost of all extra school materials and supplies including lunches and snacks on-line before each semester. All additional educational costs including materials are tax exempt.

Funding for each student is as follows:

Elementary School Vouchers are $4,000.00 per semester ($8,000 per year).
Intermediate School Vouchers are $5,000.00 per semester ($10,000 per year).
Secondary School Vouchers are $6,000.00 per semester ($12,000 per year).
Home Schools are funded at the same rate per student as private schools.

"All schools operate on a two semester per year basis for all levels. School semesters including home schools start in late summer and are 20 weeks in duration with one 3-week break between semesters and a nine-week break between school years. School days are 8 hours in duration with homeroom, lunch and physical education/recess periods. A minimum of 90 class days of instruction per semester is required. 5 days are allocated for holidays and other non-school days. The remaining 5 days are reserved for end of each semester testing to ensure progress takes place. Students who do not meet standards must make up deficiencies.

ELEMENTARY SCHOOL

"The 20/20 Plan for Elementary School education consists of grades one through four. Private schools and home schooling are the sole source for elementary school education. Schools will have the option of providing as many classes as they choose to administer, therefore being as large, or small, as they determine for their location.

"English, Reading, Mathematics, Vocabulary, Handwriting, Science, Art, Health, History and an elective subject are basic requirements depending on grade. Three projects are required each semester. Projects are administered during the homeroom period and completed after school.

INTERMEDIATE SCHOOL

"The 20/20 Plan for Intermediate School education consists of grades five through eight. Private schools and home schooling are the sole source for intermediate school education. Schools have the option of providing as many classes as they choose to administer, therefore being as large, or small, as they determine for their location.

"English Grammar and Composition, Reading, Literature, Spelling, Language Arts, Mathematics, Science, Art, Social Studies, History and an elective subject are basic requirements depending on grade. Three projects are required each semester and will be administered during the homeroom period and completed after school hours. Schools that wish to include voluntary sports and athletics programs may do so.

SECONDARY SCHOOL

"The 20/20 Plan for Secondary School education consists of grades nine through twelve. Private schools and home schooling are the sole source for secondary school education.

Secondary schools have the option of providing as many classes as they choose to administer, therefore being as large, or small, as they determine for their location.

"Academic subjects and course requirements are identical for schools and homeschooling. Completion of one science project and one writing project are required each semester and are administered during the homeroom period and performed after school hours. Secondary Schools have the option to include extracurricular activities, athletics programs and clubs. Students who do not meet standards must make up deficiencies.

Minimum Secondary School requirements for grades 9-12 are as listed:

SUBJECTS/CREDITS (BY SEMESTER)	NUMBER OF COURSES
English (Grammar and/or Literature)	8
Science	4
Mathematics	4
Social Studies	4
American History	2
United States Constitution	1
Personal Finance	1
Foreign Language	2
Electives*	6
Physical Education	8
Total Semester Subjects/Credits	40

Suggested Subjects to earn credits are:

English: Grammar, Composition, Literature, American Literature, Referencing.
Science: Physics, Chemistry, Biology, Earth/Space, Astronomy, Botany, Computer.
Mathematics: Pre-Algebra, Algebra I, Geometry, Algebra II, Trigonometry.
Social Studies: World History, U.S. History, Civics, Economics, Geometry.
Foreign Language: Latin, Spanish, French, German, Italian.
Electives: Speech, Communication, Information Technology, Art, Music, Health

* Electives may include subjects from those listed above plus electives that are
 unique to the geographical area.

HOMESCHOOLING *(Elementary, Intermediate and Secondary Level)*

"Many parents choose to teach their children at home, in lieu of enrolling them in a formal setting. These parents accept full responsibility and accountability for their children's education. It is intense parenting, as parents spend more time with their children, doing the hard work and having the patience to educate their children. Advances in digital learning and availability of resources over the internet make homeschooling better and more effective than ever.

Parents cite these reasons on why they homeschool their children:

Learning environment at school is flawed.

Child could not get into desired school.

Provide child better education at home.

Religious reasons to teach faith in depth.

Family reasons. Enable family to travel.

Object to what school teaches. To develop character/morality.

School does not challenge child. Student behavior problems.

Child has special needs/disability. Child not old enough to enter school.

Transportation/convenience. Other problems with available schools.

"Homeschooling reaps rich rewards and can deliver many benefits in educating children. According to the Academic Statistics on Homeschooling, many studies have found that homeschooled students on average outperform their peers on standardized tests. Another study from the National Home Education Research in 2003 also found that homeschooled graduates are active and more involved in their communities, are more involved in civic affairs, and are "very happy" with life, compared to the general US population. An article in the Journal of College Admission notes higher scores on homeschoolers' ACT and SAT than those of public school students, and home-educated college students perform as well or better than traditional students.

"Homeschooling is typically one-to-one ratio teaching as most students are taught individually. Studies show smaller student teacher ratios enhance student performance. Parent teachers ensure all students master a basic skill or concept before advancing, ensuring genuine learning has taken place. Homeschooling customizes education to specific educational needs. Parents have the ability to assess strengths, weaknesses, learning styles and interests. This makes kids highly motivated to learn, and thus results in developing a love for learning. Homeschooled students tend to think independently and are unlikely to follow the ideas of a group without first making up their own minds. Homeschooling eradicates boredom since students do not waste time on what they already mastered while others catch up.

"Homeschooling provides a safe learning environment as it eliminates teasing, bullying, negative peer pressure, bad influences, and in some cases, bad or even ineffective teachers.

Homeschooling promotes a sense of security and it strengthens closeness of the family. Families are able to travel, practice their individual religious beliefs and observe holidays and holy days.

"Homeschooling accommodates special needs. Homeschooling prevents children who are hyperactive or who do not behave according to the norm, but otherwise have good intellect, from being unfairly labeled as needing special education."

"These are all excellent points on the benefits of homeschooling," Tom said. "How will homeschooling compare with the other schools in the 20/20 Plan?

"Homeschooling is an alternate source for education and is held to the same standards and expectations as schools that offer education to students in a classroom environment," Genie answered. "Home schools must be licensed, certified and able to meet all qualifications in their state. Travel during the semester is permitted, but class schedules must be adhered to, or made up in accordance with the requirements. Students who do not meet standards must make up deficiencies."

"Enrollment in homeschool is typically one or more students from the same immediate family. The teacher will typically be a parent, grandparent or other close relative. The 20/20 Plan allows several families the option to combine homeschools. This option requires adequate space, facilities and materials for multiple students. The homeschooling limit for one teacher is nine students. One additional certified teacher is required for ten or more students. Homeschool days will be 8 hours. Part time teachers to instruct specific subjects are also an option. An example is a science teacher. Ten students or more will qualify for a full time paid intern as a teacher's assistant.

The 20/20 Plan for homeschool elementary school education consists of grades one through four. Homeschooling cannot be a day care endeavor to park children.

The 20/20 Plan for homeschool intermediate school education consists of grades five through eight. Extracurricular activities such as athletics and clubs are optional.

The 20/20 Plan for Homeschool Secondary school education consists of grades nine through twelve. Extracurricular activities such as athletics and clubs are optional.

SUMMER CAMPS FOR CHILDREN

"Does the 20/20 Plan provide other programs for children and students," Dave asked. "I know people who enroll their children in summer camps and activities and they are ecstatic over the results. How do they fit into the 20/20 Plan?"

"Summer camps are an integral part of the 20/20 Plan,' Genie beamed. "They are a wonderful option for children to experience fun, creative activities while not in school. These camps are privately owned, and managed. They are held to the same high standards as schools. All camps must be registered and bonded as businesses. Camps must post all employee's resumes on the camp web site. Camp web sites must contain complete activity plans and costs for the campers for the duration of the camp. This information must be available to campers before they enroll in their camp session.

"Day camps are local non-travel, non-overnight camps that can operate for one day, one week, or multiple weeks. They can be single subject, single purpose, single focus camps, or multiple subject camps. Day camps offer enrichment activities, such as academic, technology, adventure, military, sports and fitness, arts and crafts, music, science, etc. These are examples of day camps, or daytime activities. Many families use them as a substitute for summer daycare. Enrolling their children in day camps during the summer ensures supervision during the day. However, the main purpose is to foster children's social, physical, emotional and creative growth through a wide range of interactive activities and relationships with role model counselors.

"Children attending these camps are typically between the ages of six and seventeen. Camp hours are 4 hours or 8 hours in duration to accommodate morning and/or afternoon campers. These camps operate up to eight weeks during the summer-school vacation period. Many of these camps are located in city parks, sport complexes, schools or community centers such as a YMCA/YWCA, ACA Accredited Camps, Boy Scouts, Girls Scouts or Boys and Girls Clubs for example.

"Older children can be employed during the summer to serve as camp aids or counselors. Interns from the AmericaWorks program may be employed as camp counselors. Day Camps, counselors and aids must all be certified by the state, county or local governments. Parents have many options to choose from when selecting Day Camps for their children. Funding for Day Camps is up to $100.00 per day per enrollee.

TRADITIONAL OVERNIGHT OR SLEEPOVER SUMMER CAMPS

"The 20/20 Plan has a program for children between the ages of 7 and 17 to attend these summer camps. The primary purpose of this program is to bestow the opportunity of the many positive benefits the camping experience brings young children. Many camps offer educational or cultural development. Summer camps are supervised programs for children, or teenagers, conducted during the summer months. The traditional view of a summer camp is an outdoor wooded setting with hiking, canoeing and campfires. This is evolving with greater acceptance of newer summer camps that offer a wide variety of specialized activities. For example, there are camps for the performing arts, music, magic, computers, teen camps, sports camps, wilderness expeditions, sailing trips, specialty camps, special needs, academic camps, language study, and weight loss. Many camps continually add new programs.

"There are also religiously affiliated summer camps. Children whose parents' desire a faith based overnight camp are offered this positive camping experience under the 20/20 Plan. These camps are funded at the same rate as other overnight camps.

"Children with special needs are afforded the positive camping experience under the 20/20 Plan. These camps are funded at the same rate as other overnight camps. Some examples are for children with ADD-HD, Asperger's, asthma, burn, cancer, developmental disabilities, diabetes, epilepsy, fitness, learning disabilities, physical disabilities, speech and hearing, visually impaired, and weight loss as examples.

"Traditional sleepover, or overnight, camp sessions operate from 1-7 weeks during the summer vacation period. Parents can choose from co-ed overnight camps or non-co-ed overnight camps. Each camp has the option of its own philosophy, daily scheduling, and activities. Most incorporate activities that include land sports, water activities, creative and performing arts, and basic wilderness skills. Many sources, including the internet, help parents select which summer sleepover camp is best for their child. Many are operated by the YMCA/YWCA, ACA Accredited Camps, and Boy Scouts, Girls Scouts or private camps such as the Red Arrow Camp in Wisconsin or KidsCamps.com as examples. Parents have countless options when selecting these Camps for their children. Funding for Day Camps is up to $700.00 per week per enrollee.

"Older children may be employed during the summer to serve as camp aids or counselors. 'AmericaWorks' interns may be employed as camp counselors as well. Overnight Camps, counselors and aids must be certified by the state, county or local governments.

Dave was pulling into the hotel parking lot as the team was wrapping up one of the most comprehensive and detailed parts of the 20/20 Plan. They all knew educating and training our future citizens is a large task. They also knew that education and training is the only permanent solution to the elimination of poverty. The 20/20 Plan cost of $120,000 per student compares favorably to the total cost of public education at $115,000 per student. The well-being of citizens and the future of the USA are closely related and the fate of the USA depends on a skilled work force with everyone having a role to play in the success of the country and everyone becoming a stronger link in the chain. Tom suggested, "let's get together after dinner and work on this some more." All agreed.

TUESDAY EVENING. Week 2.

The team met after dinner in a small conference room off the hotel lobby. Tom began the conversation with a question. "What is the 20/20 Plan for college students and adults who need education and training in order to be employed in the work force?"

COLLEGES AND UNIVERSITIES

"The 20/20 Plan encourages students to attend college and earn a degree," Genie answered. "A college education is a tremendous step toward a bright and successful career. However, college is not for everyone. That does not mean some people should not be allowed to attend college or that some people do not deserve a college education. A college education is very expensive. Massive college tuition loans saddle many graduates with debt they cannot repay or they struggle for years to pay. Worse yet, many enter into bankruptcy, which is an abhorrent way to begin a new life. Young students who wish to pursue a college education immediately after graduation from secondary school are encouraged to do so. The 20/20 Plan cautions them that the federal government will no longer issue, or guarantee, college loans or assistance. Enrolling in college will not preclude young citizens from entering the 'AmericaWorks Career Program.'

"The 20/20 Plan eliminates the danger of a risky entrance to college with an onerous lifetime loan hanging over the student's head. The 20/20 Plan offers great careers to recent secondary school graduates to enter AmericaWorks or the Armed Forces. These beneficial training programs can offer credit while in training in service of their country. The 20/20 Plan also compensates them with an excellent starting wage for the young with little life experience. Since both programs provide many living expenses and health care expenses, they have the opportunity to save money for college if they decide to enroll after their initial obligation. This is a threefold benefit: course credits; savings to enter college; and a more solid grasp for their future careers.

"What assistance does the 20/20 Plan give to those who have backbreaking college loans?" Dave brought up. "Some have good jobs, but most are working at entry level minimum wage jobs if they indeed have a job. Many are driven to live in their parent's basements. They want a satisfying, successful career as well. They need the 20/20 program."

"The 20/20 Plan does not leave those with student loans to fend for themselves. The country cannot afford to leave these well-educated, young citizens on the outside looking in. However, it would not be prudent to forgive their loans. Most graduate applicants to the AmericaWorks program would find that option distasteful anyway. They want to earn their way and demonstrate what they can accomplish. They all want to be leaders who earn the joy of high self-esteem.

"The 20/20 Plan has work programs available to allow college graduates to use earnings to repay a portion of their student loans during the course of their work program. After they complete their work program, the federal government will pay off the remainder of the student loan debt. College graduates who opt to retire their student loan debt may enroll in a program in the field of their degree or another field if they choose to be tested, and they accept counseling in another field. Career testing is utilized to ensure the best career choice. The remainder of the loan balance is a deciding factor in the length of the work program contract. The 20/20 Plan will develop formulas for each individual applicant that are in accordance with the 20/20 Vision.

"Examples of some of the work programs for college graduates will be in the public sector working at the federal, state, county and municipal levels. There is a need for qualified trainers to coach the young people entering in the 'AmericaWorks' Program. There are opportunities with the State Department, with embassies, in information technology careers, or other federal agencies. Compensation for these students will be in accord with government pay rates.

"Private sector employers continually need qualified personnel to fill jobs in the field of their degrees. The employment process is the same as for AmericaWorks interns with the exception that they would have an individual contract with a higher pay scale depending on experience, qualifications and demand. The average pay for these work program contracts is $40,000.00 per year.

ADULT EDUCATION

"The 20/20 Plan has a program for citizens age 27 and older who need a career. Testing and experience is utilized to ensure the best job is assigned to each individual. Examples of these work programs are identical to the college graduate program for both public and private sector opportunities. Some are introduced to new careers and new training. The employment process is the same as for AmericaWorks interns with the exception they have an individual contract and work at a higher pay scale depending on experience, qualifications and demand. The average pay for these work program contracts is also $40,000.00 per year.

POVERTY

"The 20/20 Plan is the primary escape method for Americans in poverty. It is widely recognized there are many other contributors to poverty in America. Attaining a purposeful quality education cannot cure every cause of poverty but it does provide most with the poverty busting knowledge and skills to acquire and maintain rewarding careers," Genie stated.

Empty pockets never held anyone back.
Only empty heads and empty hearts can do that.

- Norman Vincent Peale

"Many in America say poverty has always been with us in America and also throughout the world since the beginning of mankind," Dave interjected. "Poverty in America is different than poverty in other parts of the world, but the government still maintains a poverty level based on income. Presently it is about $24,000.00 per year for a family of four. The 20/20 Plan establishes a minimum wage of $10.00 per hour, or about $20,000.00 per year. How will a family ever escape the poverty level in the USA?"

"Good point Dave," Genie replied. "The minimum wage was never meant to be a lifetime wage for American families. Even though the 20/20 Plan minimum wage is almost $3.00 higher than the present federal government wage, it is a starter wage for people who are beginning first jobs. The 20/20 Plan promotes a robust economy that creates higher paying jobs from increased investment home and abroad. The 20/20 Plan also delivers lower purchasing prices across the board from huge savings in gas, oil and energy.

"People want to advance. The 20/20 Plan believes the American spirit not only wants to advance, it craves growth, enrichment and prosperity. To put the poverty level in a different perspective, the poverty level for a single person in America is less than $12,000.00 per year and $16,000.00 per year for a family of two. The 20/20 Plan moves single individuals well above the poverty level. If they start a family, they still exceed the poverty level by 25 percent. A family with two adults working minimum wage jobs can earn $40,000.00 per year with the 20/20 Plan. A powerful, booming economy rewards employees who develop skills with much higher wages. The 20/20 Plan anticipates the number under the poverty level to be less than 2 percent within four years.

"The War on Poverty began 50 years ago. The people who supported President Johnson at the time have since admitted the War on Poverty has been a monumental failure. The taxpayers of the United States spent $22 trillion over the past 50 years and the poverty threshold has remained the same. The U.S. Census Bureau, according to latest available statistics in 2009, reported more than 16 percent of the population is living in poverty, including almost 20 percent of American children, which is up from 14.3 percent and is now approximately 44 million people. This is the highest level since 1993. In 2008, 13.2 percent, or approximately 40 million Americans lived in poverty. Since 1980, relative poverty rates have consistently exceeded those of other wealthy nations. California has a poverty rate of 23.5 percent, the highest of all states."

"Many people say the country should be giving more to poor people," Dave stated. "They say the country should reduce the military budget and cut other spending to bring people above the poverty threshold. Should the country and the rich pay more?"

"Dave that has been tried many times," Genie replied. "Every time the military budget or other spending is reduced, the politicians find new ways to squander taxpayer dollars. The country has spent more than $22 trillion on the War on Poverty and the country is in debt to the tune of $20 trillion. That is obviously not the solution to poverty. The argument the rich should pay more sounds good to ideologues with political agendas. If the rich were taxed 100 percent of their earnings, the total amount would only be about $600 billion. If that one-time event occurs, the rich have no means to earn more and the $600 billion would soon evaporate along with the jobs they could create by hiring people and making investments. That would be disastrous for the country and the poor would be further devastated.

"In 2009, the number of people below the poverty threshold was approaching the 1960s levels that led to the War on Poverty in the first place. The government is doing a lot, but it will never be able to do enough. The government is just not the answer many people want it to be. In 2013, the government spent $943 billion providing cash, food, housing, and medical care to poor and low-income Americans. That is 25 percent of the revenues American taxpayers pay yet it still has not solved the poverty problem. It just is not working for poor or rich Americans.

"Today, more than 100 million people, or one-third of the population, receive some type of welfare at an average cost of $9,000 per recipient. Still Americans are at the 1967 poverty level. The definition of poor, defined by the Census Bureau, is confusing at best. It classifies a family as living in poverty if their income is below a predetermined level. Conversely, it discounts the effect of welfare spending making the figures of the poor very misleading.

Some examples of people living under the poverty line are:

   80 percent of poor households have air conditioning

   67 percent of poor have two or more automobiles

   67 percent have cable or satellite television;

   50 percent have a personal computer; and

   40 percent have high-definition televisions.

"Less than 2 percent of the poor are homeless and 10 percent live in trailer homes. Being labeled poor by the government is indeed misleading. People don't strive to live below the poverty threshold. They want to have more and better things. A life that starts with a quality education is the answer to eliminating poverty.

"President Johnson's goal was to turn "tax-eaters" into "taxpayers." The War on Poverty was constructed to make poor Americans self-sufficient and productive. Sadly, the opposite occurred. Less people are proficient at self-reliance and self-supporting today than before the War on Poverty began. This is a perfect example of government policies that simply do not work. The reason for this failure is found in penalties on marriage, the incentive to not work and a flawed governmental educational system. When the War on Poverty began, seven percent of American children were born outside of wedlock. Presently 41 percent of American children are born out of wedlock. Education of children cannot excel in one-parent households.

"The current administration plans to spend $13 trillion on welfare programs over the next 10 years. That will raise the burden on the taxpayers to $35 trillion over a sixty-year period with no prospect of self-sufficiency in sight. Social institutions and self-sufficiency are doomed to suffer more degradation as politicians continue to repeat the errors of the past. The nation must turn to the 20/20 Plan to give every citizen the tools of success, not more handouts." The team knew they found the best solution: education.

The purpose of the 20/20 Plan for education is threefold:

1. To provide all citizens with the knowledge they need to live a prosperous life.

2. To get a good job to enable all to have and maintain a high standard of living.

3. To strengthen the 300 million-link chain so all citizens can be productive and contribute to the future success of the republic and to their own personal success.

The 8-point education process timeline for the comprehensive 20/20 Plan is as follows:

1. Day care for children which assists working parents (up to six years of age)

2. Elementary School for children in grades 1 through 4 (ages 6 through 9)

3. Intermediate School for children in grades 4 through 8 (ages 10 through 13)

4. Secondary School for children in grades 9 through 12 (ages 14 through 17)

5. Day camps and overnight camps for school children (ages 6 through 17)

6. AmericaWorks Program for employment training (ages 18 through 27)

7. College Education (Optional for secondary school graduates)

8. Adult education (Optional training and work programs for citizens 27 – 65)

CHAPTER TWELVE | *Education and Poverty Summary*

1. The Department of Education began operation in 1980.

2. Since 1980, education spending has escalated while results plummet.

3. The US does not rank in the top 20 in education worldwide.

4. The 20/20 Plan offers parents and students a choice of schools to attend.

5. English is the most suitable language of instruction for American education.

6. School uniforms provide unity and focus on learning and creativity.

7. Private schools and home schooling will be the sole source for education in America.

8. Many Americans now regard public schools as government indoctrination centers.

9. The 20/20 Plan provides for day care and summer camps for children.

10. The 20/20 Plan does not include funding to universities and colleges.

11. Universities and colleges are state and private institutions.

12. The 20/20 Plan appraises Student Loans and designs a program to pay off the loans.

13. The 20/20 Plan has an adult training and jobs program.

14. The poverty rate has not improved despite the massive amount of wasted dollars.

15. Poverty has many causes, but only one permanent solution: education.

16. Over 100 million people receive some sort of government assistance.

17. Twenty-five percent of the federal budget is now spent on low income Americans.

18. The War on Poverty began 50 years ago. No progress is evident.

19. Most supporters of the War on Poverty now admit it was a huge mistake.

20. $22 Trillion has been spent on the War on Poverty over the past 50 years.

21. $13 Trillion are planned for assistance over the next 10 years.

22. Reducing military spending would have no effect on reducing poverty.

23. Taxing the rich 100 percent cannot reduce poverty. It will only eliminate jobs.

24. The 20/20 Plan reduces poverty to less than 2% through education and job training.

CHAPTER THIRTEEN

Immigration

"In the first place, we should insist that if the immigrant who comes here in good faith becomes an American and assimilates himself to us, he shall be treated on an exact equality with everyone else, for it is an outrage to discriminate against any such man because of creed, or birthplace, or origin. However, this is predicated upon the person's becoming in every facet an American and nothing but an American... There can be no divided allegiance here. Any man who says he is an American, but something else also, isn't an American at all. We have room for but one flag, the American flag... We have room for but one language here, and that is the English language... and we have room for but one sole loyalty and that is a loyalty to the American people." -Theodore Roosevelt

WEDNESDAY MORNING. WEEK 3.

The four consultants climbed into the rental car ready to ride to work. The consulting project was going extremely well. The 20/20 Plan was progressing better than they expected. The 20/20 Plan for education and the reduction of poverty were certain to solve those problems. Now they were prepared to address immigration, another issue for which politicians cannot find the answer. They were confident the 20/20 Immigration Plan would be well designed and implemented for the very reason that they are not politicians. Ron began the conversation. "Immigration is a sore subject for most citizens in the United States, and also with people who are not citizens as well. In any case, the politicians are not representing the views of their constituents.

"There is a reason Americans are so conflicted about immigration. Almost all Americans favor immigration, but they know it is imperative the nation have control over the immigration process. Immigration laws are in effect but there is no consistency in enforcement. Presently there are a record 40 million foreign nationals in the US. About 12 million of them are unauthorized foreign nationals.

"There is a reason foreign nationals come to the United States. Most are seeking a better life, freedom from oppression and/or a good paying job. What is so disconcerting is some foreign nationals can enter the country without documentation and expect to be treated as citizens or even better than citizens. It is unfair to many foreign nationals who entered the country legally, and have applied for citizenship and are going through the entire legal process. It is wrong for those who enter illegally because they want to circumvent the immigration process without documentation.

"If a Root Cause Analysis were performed on unauthorized immigration, the results would undoubtedly be that people want a better life. Nevertheless, why don't they have a satisfying life in their home country? Immigrants, both authorized and unauthorized, were living in countries that afforded them little or no opportunity, were oppressive, were backward, were lawless, or rife with corruption and brutality. Some countries, like Mexico, are beautiful with bountiful resources, but are corrupt and have little affection for their own citizens. Their citizens find it preferable to leave their homeland where officials prefer to perpetrate the corruption and evil the immigrants loathe. They prefer their lawlessness and their bribes to the betterment of their citizens. So their citizens come to the USA."

"A nation without borders is like a house without walls - it collapses. That is what is going to happen to our wonderful America." — Governor Jan Brewer of Arizona.

"An intelligence report compiled by the U.S. Customs and Border Protection agency (CBP) reveals large numbers of immigrants originating beyond Latin America are illegally crossing the southern U.S. border. The report states the illegal immigrants originated from more than 75 different countries. Overseas countries listed in the report are Syria and Albania, from which smugglers send immigrants first to Central America and then northward across the U.S. border.

Other nations from which immigrants were caught entering the United States illegally in the first half of 2014 are:

COUNTRY	CAUGHT CROSSING	CAUGHT AT PORTS	TOTAL
China	1,443	1,803	3,246
Pakistan	28	211	239
Egypt	13	168	181
Yemen	4	34	38
Somalia	4	290	294

"This is just a sample to illustrate what is happening at our borders and ports. It is not possible to know the number of people who illegally cross our borders escape detection. The above figures suggest many people from across the globe have crossed our southern border, including some with terrorist connections. The CBP data reveals at least 71 individuals from the three nations affected by the Ebola outbreak have either turned themselves in or have been caught attempting to illegally enter the United States in the first half of 2014.

"Unaccompanied children from Central America who cross our border pose a special problem for immigration authorities because deporting them involves special logistical difficulties. There are also many children from Mexico crossing our border. A Pew Research Center analysis of Mexican government data obtained from the Mexican Ministry of Foreign Affairs released on August 4, 2014 found:

"The number of apprehensions of Mexican child migrants rivals those of Honduras, Guatemala, and El Salvador but many of them attempted to cross multiple times. More than 11,000 apprehensions of unaccompanied Mexican minors occurred over a recent eight-month period. An explanation for the large number of Mexican children who have illegally crossed into the United States multiple times is its close geographic location to the U.S. border. It is easier for Mexicans than Central Americans to attempt multiple crossings. It is nearly impossible to deport unaccompanied minors to Central America without first letting them appear before an immigration judge. Because of the backlog, the wait for court appearances can be two years and longer."

"Texas Governor Rick Perry, speaking on August 3, 2014 on CNN's State of the Union, said the wave of unaccompanied minors crossing the border is a "side issue" and that he is "substantially more concerned about" criminals crossing the border. Perry asserted terrorists are using a porous southern border to enter the United States."

"A porous southern border is now on the advertising list for those who want to do nefarious activities entering the United States, everything from criminal activity — gangs, we've seen that surely — human trafficking, and now you're seeing these groups who we believe are connected in some way with terrorist organizations at least having the understanding, and now you're seeing the apprehensions behind it. — "Rep. Mike Rogers, (R-Mich)

"It appears they figured out the southern border is a weakness in our national security.

"Mexico has a radical idea for a rational immigration policy that most Americans would love. However, Mexican officials do not share this same policy with the United States. Mexico annually deports more illegal aliens than the United States. It is a felony to be an illegal alien in Mexico.

The US should look at how Mexico deals with immigration and how we might learn to solve our illegal immigration problem. Mexico has a single, streamlined law that ensures that foreign visitors and immigrants:

Are in the country legally;
Have the means to sustain themselves economically;
Are not destined to be burdens on society;
Are of economic and social benefit to society;
Are of good character and have no criminal records; and
Contribute to the general well-being of the nation.
That immigration authorities have a record of each foreign visitor;
That foreign visitors do not violate their visa status;
That foreign visitors are banned from interfering in the country's internal politics;
That foreign visitors who enter under false pretenses are imprisoned or deported;
That foreign visitors violating the terms of entry are imprisoned, or deported;
That those who aid in illegal immigration will be sent to prison.

"The Mexican constitution strictly defines the rights of citizens, and the denial of many fundamental rights to non-citizens, legal and illegal. A felony is a crime punishable by more than one year in prison. Mexican law makes it a felony to be an illegal alien in Mexico. If the United States adopted such statutes, Mexico no doubt would denounce it as a manifestation of American racism and bigotry.

"Mexico accepts only foreigners who will be useful to Mexican society. Immigration 'officials must make sure' immigrants are useful elements for the country and that they have the necessary funds for their sustenance and for their dependents.

"Foreigners may be barred from the country if their presence upsets 'the equilibrium of the national demographics,' when foreigners are deemed detrimental to 'economic or national interests,' when they do not behave like good citizens in their 'own country, when they have broken Mexican laws, and when 'they are not found to be physically or mentally healthy.' The Secretary of Governance may 'suspend or prohibit the admission of foreigners when he determines it to be in the national interest.' Mexican authorities must keep track of every single person in the country:

"Federal, local and municipal police must cooperate with federal immigration authorities upon request, i.e., to assist in the arrests of illegal immigrants. A National Population Registry keeps track of 'every single individual who comprises the population of the country,' and verifies each individual's identity.

"A national Catalog of Foreigners tracks foreign tourists and immigrants, and assigns each individual with a unique tracking number. "Foreigners with fake papers, or who enter the country under false pretenses, may be imprisoned. Foreigners with fake immigration papers may be fined or imprisoned. Foreigners who sign government documents 'with a false signature or different from that which he normally uses' are subject to fine and imprisonment. Foreigners who fail to obey the rules are fined, deported, and/or imprisoned as felons. Foreigners who fail to obey a deportation order are to be punished. Foreigners who are deported from Mexico and attempt to re-enter the country without authorization can be imprisoned for up to 10 years. Foreigners who violate the terms of their visa may be sentenced to up to six years in prison. Foreigners who misrepresent the terms of their visa while in Mexico, such as working without a permit, can also be imprisoned.

"Under Mexican law, illegal immigration is a felony. The General Law on Population says 'A penalty of up to two years in prison and a fine of three hundred to five thousand pesos will be imposed on the foreigner who enters the country illegally.' Foreigners with legal immigration problems may be deported from Mexico instead of being imprisoned. Foreigners who 'attempt against national sovereignty or security' will be deported. Mexicans who help illegal aliens enter the country are themselves considered criminals under the law. A Mexican who marries a foreigner with the sole objective of helping the foreigner live in the country is subject to up to five years in prison. Shipping and airline companies that bring undocumented foreigners are fined.

"This is contrary to what Mexican leaders are demanding of the United States. The contrast between Mexico's immigration practices and American immigration laws is simple. It gives a clear picture of the Mexican government's agenda to have a one-way immigration relationship with the United States.

"Politicians cannot agree on a policy, or program, for immigration. Nevertheless, we do have laws on the books governing immigration. Each administration decides which laws they want to enforce, and which laws they do not wish to enforce based on the number of votes they think they can receive in the next election, or their popularity in the next poll numbers. They have no real interest in solving problems. If they did, the United States would not be existing in chaos over this issue.

"The main issue is whether U.S. citizens and legal immigrants should have to pay for schooling, housing, food and medical care for illegal immigrants who want free or reduced cost social services. States are also considering whether to allow children of illegal immigrants who are not U.S. citizens to take advantage of college financial aid.

"Refugees admitted to the United States undergo a thorough identity and background screening by the United States. The President's office sets the cap on how many refugees are permitted each year, usually about 75,000 to 80,000. The main issue is how to provide for this number of people."

"Where do we start Ron?" Tom questioned. "Is it policy, borders, or quotas?"

THE 20/20 VISION REQUIREMENTS FOR IMMIGRATION

"The 20/20 Plan is an initiative with many facets and all must begin at once to be effective and to maintain control over the process," Ron explained. "The 20/20 Plan lists the major conditions first. Without writing an entire regulation, they are:

"Secure the southern border. The border southern must be completely locked down. This requires the services of The United States Border Patrol and other agencies plus the United States Coast Guard and the National Guard. This is a zero tolerance mandate to provide the United States with control of our sovereign borders plus a starting point to determine who is in the United States and the nature of their status. The US must:

1. Institute a temporary freeze on registration of the *Citizenship through Naturalization Process* to become a US Citizen for one year, to enable the Bureau of Immigration and Customs Enforcement (ICE) to sort out all applicants.

2. A realistic immigration quota must be set to determine the number of naturalized citizens that can be granted citizenship each year.

3. Conduct a thorough review of current qualifications, requirements and testing to become a naturalized citizen. Make and implement those changes within one year.

4. Unauthorized nationals who exercise the option for legal naturalized citizenship must take all the steps to meet all requirements to apply for citizenship. These immigrants are positioned in a queue based on criteria set up by the 20/20 Plan. Length of residence, verified work record and clean criminal record are priorities.

5. Make it a felony offense to enter the country illegally and also to reside in the country illegally. This crime carries a fine and automatic permanent deportation. If the illegal trespasser does not have means to satisfy the fine, the country of their citizenship is fined, plus payment for expenses and transportation. This places all countries on the alert that it is now very costly for them to permit their citizens to illegally enter, or illegally remain in, the United States of America.

6. Require businesses/employers to document citizenship, or immigration status, or face stiff penalties and/or consequences.

7. Allow all foreign nationals who are unauthorized immigrants and are now living within US borders to register, free of penalty, fine or charge, with the United States Bureau of Immigration and Customs Enforcement (ICE) within 90 days or be in violation of the regulation. These foreign nationals will be required to show proof of identity including residence, phone number, email address, birth certificates, and/or passports. They will

be required to verify ownership of $2,000.00 in a US bank account to ensure they have sufficient funds to subsist for a minimum of one month. This Registration Form requires a declaration of intent by the foreign national.

The declaration will contain four mandatory options:

    a. Intent to apply for US citizenship.
    b. Intent to reside in the US as a temporary guest worker for a 3-year period.
    c. Intent to be a student in the US for one year with the option of renewals.
    d. Intent to vacate the United States within 90 days.

"Foreign nationals who register are issued an ICE Identification Card containing all their pertinent information including their Intent Status. These ICE ID Cards will have an issue date and an expiration date similar to DMV ID Cards.

"The exception to this rule is visitors on business trips, or vacations, of less than three months. All travelers are required to complete a 'Customs Declaration' when entering the United States. This form is turned in at airports and seaports. Visitors must declare the location of their stay and report any changes immediately. Canadian citizens and those citizens of the newly formed 'Association of Nations' are given preference to extended stay within the United States. Those visitors who own residences in the United States will be permitted to stay in the US for one year before renewing their visa.

"Laws currently in effect in the US remain in force with the exception of the above new regulations which supersede all existing laws. The various federal agencies are expected to enforce all federal laws and there is an initiative to cooperate and work jointly with state and local law enforcement entities.

'United States Bureau of Immigration and Customs Enforcement (ICE) will keep up to date records on all foreign nationals who reside within the borders of the United States. These records will include all known information and be updated daily.

"Employers are mandated to verify the status of all employees and contract workers. Forms are currently in place to accomplish that initiative. Failure to do so will result in progressive heavy fines for each occurrence.

"Employees who are registered with ICE as authorized immigrants are required to complete all necessary forms to verify their identity and their status. All 20/20 Plan wage regulations will apply to immigrants just the same as American citizens.

"Employees who are registered with ICE as a guest worker are required to complete all necessary forms to verify their identity and their status. They are included in the same 20/20 Plan wage plan with one exception. They must register with a payroll services company such as ADP, Intuit, etc. They will receive their pay through direct deposit from the payroll service contracted by the employer. This ensures all employee accounts are administered properly, equally and lawfully. The payroll service may charge a fee of up to 2 percent of the employees' wages.

"Foreign nationals must present a current health certificate at the time of registration. Entry into the United States is not granted to pregnant women.

"Children born to foreign nationals in the United States are not granted citizenship until their foreign national parents take the Oath of Allegiance administered by the USCIS at an administrative ceremony or by a judge in a judicial ceremony.

"Foreign nationals who commit misdemeanors receive an immediate court date. If convicted of a crime, they are fined double the established amount for the first offense. The second conviction carries a redoubled fine. A third conviction results in deportation. The USA can only prosper with law-abiding citizens.

"Foreign nationals who commit a felony receive an immediate court date. If convicted of a felony, they are fined double the established amount for the first offense. The second offense carries a redoubled fine in addition to deportation. Property may be seized for payment. This is a zero tolerance policy.

REGULATIONS FOR AUTHORIZED IMMIGRANTS

"Some regulations will apply to all foreign nationals who are in the United States, including those who are registered for Citizenship through Naturalization. All foreign nationals are issued an ICE ID Card stating their 'declaration of intent' along with all other pertinent information. They are required to display this ID Card at all times. (Naturalization being the process to grant U.S. citizenship to a foreign citizen or national after they fulfill the requirements established by Congress in the Immigration and Nationality Act [INA].)

All foreign nationals plus authorized visitors must adhere to the following nine regulations. (Failure to comply will result in fines and/or dismissal from the immigration process.) They are:

1. Must carry, and retain, an official ICE ID Card at all times.
2. Must report all changes of address, phone and email address within 30 days.
3. Must maintain an active email address and monitor it for messages weekly.
4. Must enroll in English Classes and pass periodic proficiency tests.
5. Must be proficient in English to conduct business with the government.
6. Must abide by all federal, state and local laws. Ignorance is no excuse.
7. Must maintain an ongoing bank balance of at least $1,000.00 in a US bank.

8. Must limit foreign money transfers to 20 percent per pay period.
9. Must be self-sufficient and not partaking in US assistance programs.

"Those foreign nationals already registered in the 10 Step to Naturalization Process to become a US Citizen remain in the current system but must comply with the above nine requirements and all other immigration laws of the United States.

"Unauthorized immigrants who apply for citizenship will enroll in a queue with all other foreign nationals who have entered the system. This queue is initially frozen for a maximum time limit of one year to ensure the new path to citizenship is equitable. Those in this queue will then enter the 10 Steps to Naturalization Program. Speaking and writing English is a primary priority.

"Unauthorized immigrants who apply for guest worker status can decide to enter the path to citizenship. They may declare that intent after one year, along with all other pertinent information. They are then placed in a queue with all other foreign nationals who entered the system. Those in this queue are then eligible to enter the 10 Steps to Naturalization Program. Speaking and writing English is a primary priority.

"Students must be accepted and enrolled in a US university or college and must state their intent to attend that specific university or college within the United States. If they decide to remain in the United States to continue their studies, they may declare that intent after one year. They must maintain and monitor an active email address weekly.

"Unauthorized immigrants who declare to depart the USA must declare their intentions and do so within 90 days. These foreign nationals must be positively identified. They are not allowed entry to the USA for one year with the exception of humanitarian reasons or purposes.

"Unauthorized immigrants currently imprisoned for convicted felonies will be processed out of prison. They will immediately be deported, transported and released from US custody and turned over to the government of their home country. The US government will file any, and all, reparation demands to that country. These released convicts will never be allowed to re-enter the United States of America."

"The 20/20 Plan spells out specific requirements and conditions to be a foreign national in the United States. This is what citizens want, and it is what immigrants want as well. Everyone desires standards and to know their expectations. People coming to the USA must respect laws and rules that are clear and fair for everyone."

"Why is speaking and writing English a condition of residence for foreign nationals?" Genie said. "Some people may not agree with that condition because they prefer their native language. They may say it is racist. Why is it so important that foreign nationals speak and write English?"

"English has become a worldwide language," Tom stated. "Numerous countries have adopted English as an official language. English is the dominant international language in science, business, aviation, entertainment, and diplomacy, and most important now, on the Internet. You convinced us to learn English in Chapter 12.

"English is the most common language spoken in the United States and its territories. However, there is no "official" language for the United States. Some individual states do list English as their official language. The 20/20 Plan revokes the federal government's current requirement to provide access to federal programs and federally assisted programs for people with limited English proficiency to a period of approximately two years. Currently those people can visit the Limited English Proficiency website. It is just not practical or economically feasible for the United States to be one nation with many languages. Limited English Speaking people will soon find they are much more comfortable living in United States when they master English. Many new and wonderful horizons are available to them as they find speaking the language of the land is a pleasant and meaningful achievement.

"In most fields of work the ability to speak English can advance the speakers career. It can also help people get the job they want to earn more money. No matter what a person's area of expertise, their skill in English will contribute immensely to success and prosperity. English classes will be available in all areas of the country.

"There are a variety of ways to learn English. Schools and books dedicated to the language are common throughout the world. English classes and textbooks help people learn vocabulary and basic grammar principles. To become truly proficient at speaking and understanding English, people have to practice with native English-speakers. They can accomplish this at work, using the internet and watching TV.

"Immigration, like everything else, is all about choices and decisions. If a foreign national wants to be a guest who lives and works in the United States, then they have made the decision to obey the laws, language and customs of the United States. If that is not acceptable to them, then they should remain in their own country or immigrate to another country. The same applies to criminal activity. If a foreign national wants to live and work in the United States, they should not make the decision to commit criminal acts in the US. People make decisions. They must live by their actions and decisions.

The team just completed the comprehensive immigration plan that is best for the nation. Even more than that, the 20/20 Plan has a schedule to detail who will implement the plan and the schedule for when it will be in place. Everyone was proud of the achievement that solved a serious national and economical problem that now makes a better life for both citizens and foreign nationals.

It was a long but a productive ride to the plant. It was hump day and everyone was charged up. After a great day at work, they would be ready to take on one of the most deadly problems the nation has ever faced. They knew the future of the nation hung on their solution to the resolve the drug problem.

CHAPTER THIRTEEN | *Immigration Summary*

1. The 20/20 Plan advances a controlled immigration process.

2. People come to America for a better life, freedom and good jobs.

3. A nation without borders is not a nation and it will surely collapse.

4. The southern border is porous and illegal entry is rampant.

5. Illegals from 75 nations are known to cross the southern border.

6. Terrorists, human traffickers and drug runners cross the border with ease.

7. Mexico has very strict immigration laws. The US does not enforce its laws.

8. The United States must lock down the southern border with Mexico.

9. The 20/20 Plan makes unauthorized entry, or stay, in the US a felony.

10. The 20/20 Plan freezes immigration for one year to sort out the circumstances.

11. The 20/20 Plan issues ICE ID Cards and options for all foreign nationals who are currently in the United States without authorization.

12. Foreign nationals have the option of applying for citizenship.

13. Foreign nationals have the option of applying for work permits.

14. Foreign nationals have the option of leaving the United States.

15. Foreign students have new requirements to reside and study in the US.

16. The 20/20 Plan reviews current quotas and sets realistic new quotas.

17. The 20/20 Plan reviews all current qualifications and requirements.

18. The 20/20 Plan sets new requirements for authorized immigration.

19. The 20/20 Plan requires registration of all authorized immigrants.

20. Foreign nations currently in the 10 Step Naturalization Process continue unimpeded in that process with some new requirements.

21. Foreign nationals who have opted to remain in the United States:

    a. Must carry, and retain, an official ICE ID Card at all times.

    b. Must report all changes of address, phone and email addresses immediately.

    c. Must maintain an active email address and monitor it for messages.

    d. Must enroll in English Classes and pass periodic proficiency tests.

Drugs and Substance Abuse

"The mentality and behavior of drug addicts and alcoholics is wholly irrational until you understand that they are completely powerless over their addiction and unless they have structured help, they have no hope." - Russell Brand

WEDNESDAY AFTERNOON. WEEK 3.

As the team walked through the parking lot to the rental car, they were thinking this had been a good hump day. Just two more days before they left for the airport and their long flights home. They knew, in the backs of their minds, this ride home would be exhausting. The next subject on the agenda for the 20/20 Plan addressed the most critical issue in America today: Drugs and Substance Abuse. This is the 'one' issue that is destroying America from within. The subject is tearing the nation apart. Challenging tough decisions must be made and solutions need to be implemented to steer America on the right course. The 20/20 Plan will be controversial and unpopular with many citizens. It will cause most citizens to open their minds to accept a new paradigm and swallow a lot of pride. Busting this paradigm is the answer to saving the nation.

As they pulled out of the parking lot, Dave spoke first. "Half the people in the United States are going to hate me, and the other half will most likely think I'm crazy, but the 20/20 Plan concerning substance abuse is the best course for America. Some background and research is necessary to understand the issues and solutions."

"Very chilling statistics are reported on the National Institute on Drug Abuse website," Tom stated. "They use a variety of sources to monitor the prevalence and trends of drug abuse in the United States. Abuse of tobacco, alcohol and illicit drugs cost the nation over $600 billion every year. Citizens should search the internet for their own information. That is the best method to urge citizens to understand the total magnitude of the substance abuse problem. The solution is to identify the problem, its costs, and then have the courage to implement the solution. The nation must show extraordinary resolve. Our citizens have the strength, but do they have the will?"

"Humans have used drugs of one sort or another for thousands of years," Dave warned.

"The following is from 'infoplease.' Wine was drunk at least from the time of the early Egyptians; narcotics used from 4000 B.C.; and medicinal use of marijuana has been dated to 2737 B.C. in China. However, not until the 19th century A.D. were the active substances in drugs extracted. There followed a time when some of these newly discovered substances—morphine, laudanum, cocaine—were completely unregulated and prescribed freely by physicians for a wide variety of ailments. They were available in patent medicines and sold by traveling tinkers, in drugstores, or through the mail.

"During the American Civil War, morphine was used freely. Wounded veterans returned home with kits of morphine and hypodermic needles. Opium dens flourished. By the early 1900s, there were an estimated 250,000 addicts in the United States.

"The problems of addiction were recognized gradually. Legal measures against drug abuse in the United States were first launched in 1875, when opium dens were outlawed in San Francisco. The first national drug law was the Pure Food and Drug Act of 1906, which required accurate labeling of patent medicines containing opium and certain other drugs. In 1914, the Harrison Narcotic Act forbade sale of substantial doses of opiates or cocaine except by licensed doctors and pharmacies. Heroin was banned.

"Subsequent Supreme Court decisions made it illegal for doctors to prescribe any narcotic to addicts. Many doctors who prescribed maintenance doses as part of an addiction treatment plan were jailed, and soon all attempts at treatment were abandoned. Use of narcotics and cocaine diminished by the 1920s. The spirit of temperance led to the prohibition of alcohol by the Eighteenth Amendment to the Constitution in 1919. Prohibition was repealed in 1933.

"In the 1930s most states required antidrug education in the schools, but fears that knowledge would lead to experimentation caused it to be abandoned in most areas. Soon after the repeal of Prohibition, the U.S. Federal Bureau of Narcotics (now the Drug Enforcement Administration) began a campaign to portray marijuana as a powerful, addicting substance that would lead users into narcotics addiction. In the 1950s, use of marijuana increased again, along with that of amphetamines and tranquilizers.

"The social upheaval of the 1960s brought with it a dramatic increase in drug use and some increased social acceptance. By the early 1970s, some states and localities had decriminalized marijuana and lowered drinking ages. The 1980s brought a decline in the use of most drugs, but cocaine and crack use soared. The military became involved in border patrols for the first time, and troops invaded Panama and brought its de facto leader, Manuel Noriega, to trial for drug trafficking. Over time, the public perception of the dangers of specific substances changed. The Surgeon General's warning label on tobacco packaging gradually made people aware of the addictive nature of nicotine. By 1995, the Food and Drug Administration was considering its regulation.

"Cigarette smoking and exposure to tobacco smoke are associated with premature death from chronic diseases, economic losses to society and a substantial burden on the United States health-care system. Smoking is the primary cause of at least 30 percent of all cancer deaths, for nearly 80 percent of deaths from chronic obstructive pulmonary disease, and for early cardiovascular disease and deaths.

"The recognition of fetal alcohol syndrome brought warning labels to alcohol products. The addictive nature of prescription drugs such as diazepam (Valium) became known and caffeine came under scrutiny as well.

"Drug laws tried to keep up with the changing perceptions and real dangers of substance abuse. By 1970 over 55 federal drug laws and countless state laws specified a variety of punitive measures, including life imprisonment and even the death penalty.

"To clarify the situation, the Comprehensive Drug Abuse Prevention and Control Act of 1970 repealed, replaced, or updated all previous federal laws concerned with narcotics and all other dangerous drugs. While possession was made illegal, the severest penalties were reserved for illicit distribution and manufacture of drugs. The act dealt with prevention and treatment of drug abuse as well as control of drug traffic.

"The Anti-Drug Abuse Acts of 1986 and 1988 increased funding for treatment and reha-bilitation. The 1988 act created the Office of National Drug Control Policy. Its director, often referred to as the drug 'czar,' is responsible for coordinating national drug control policy." (Read: drug addiction and drug abuse: History Infoplease.com)

"There is a wealth of information on the internet related to tobacco, alcohol and illicit drugs. A person could spend years trying to read it all. The statistics are extensive and confusing. Current laws and enforcement of those laws are reactive. Lives are ruined. The addictive links in the 300 million-link chain are indeed weak and very expensive to maintain. The DEA attempts to apprehend criminals, which in turn costs the country and its citizens more than $600 billion per year. Treatment is laudatory, but expensive. Drug users resort to crime to satisfy their habits. Many of our younger citizens, who should be productive and leading our nation to prosperity are becoming users, pushers, prostitutes, thieves, etc. Drug users rob and murder innocent citizens trying to satisfy their habit. The result is more links in the 300 million-link chain are damaged or destroyed. Costs grow and grow, lives are ruined, and the country continues to lose the 'War on Drugs.'

"The War on Drugs has been profoundly controversial since its outset. A poll from 2008, found that three in four Americans believed that the War on Drugs was failing. How is that working for us? Not so good. Other nations are catching on.

"In 2012, three former Presidents from Guatemala, Mexico and Colombia said that the war on drugs had failed. They proposed a discussion on alternatives, including decriminalization, at the Summit of the Americas in April of that year. Guatemalan President Otto Pérez Molina said that the war on drugs was exacting too high a price on the lives of Central Americans and that it was time to "end the taboo on discussing decriminalization." The government of Colombia pushed for the most far-reaching change to drug policy since the war on narcotics was declared by Nixon four decades prior, citing the catastrophic effects it had had in Colombia. The 'War on Drugs' is failing and the cost in lives and money is destroying the United States.

"The 20/20 Plan is a proactive approach to the problem. It is all about solutions and implementing those solutions. The 20/20 Plan on drugs, alcohol and tobacco is to tax each retail sale at a specified rate and utilize these taxes as revenue for the benefit of the economy and the American people. This is a massive benefit for the citizens and the economy. The collection of revenue becomes a financial gain that eliminates the cost of waging the war on drugs. This revenue can now help citizens cure their addiction.

"The 20/20 Plan recognizes some drug users will decide to phase out their purchase of these substances to avoid paying the tax. Some may decide to exclude these purchases from their normal routine, as they do not want the annoyance of complying with the regulations imposed on the purchase of drugs. Some may elect to choose rehabilitation as an alternative to drug use and there will be facilities available at no cost to the substance abuser for this treatment. Nonetheless, some will continue to use drugs and will purchase them from authorized retailers and pay the tax on the purchases.

"The 20/20 Plan is not so naïve to think that all illegal drug trafficking will be eliminated by this new regulation. A criminal element is sure to remain that places the priority of dealing drugs over complying with the regulation of illicit drugs. This becomes a felony tax offense and all government agencies will be mandated to exert extensive force in the collection of tax revenue to keep the country viable and solvent.

"The 20/20 Plan permits drugs to be purchased and used with restrictions. There are many drug product variations that broader classifications need review with action taken to correct and update all modifications as needed. The 20/20 Plan re-legalizes and taxes these substances and products as sourced in Chapter 5 of 20/20: A Clear Vision for America.

A summary of proposed tax rates on re-legalized drugs are enumerated below:

100% tax on marijuana and associated marijuana products.
200% tax on manufactured drugs such as methamphetamines.
300% tax on cocaine and cocaine byproducts.
500% tax on heroin and other similar addictive drugs.

Alcohol and tobacco are taxed at the following rates in every state:

50% tax for beer, wine and similar products under 20% alcoholic content.
100% tax on spirits of any type with 20% alcoholic content or higher.
100% tax on all tobacco products of all types in every state.

"Each state is responsible for tax collection and reporting of these products as well as all other products and services. Each state is also responsible and accountable for the identification of tax violations and tax violators.

"Drug, alcohol and tobacco products must be securely packaged in a precise, exact manner that displays functional bar codes, quantities, unit costs, retail prices, tax rates and total taxes charged. Taxes must be collected from consumers at the time and point of purchase, reported and remitted on all such retail sales. Retailers of these products are rigidly regulated and must register to offer these products for retail sale. Licenses are to be applied for, purchased, issued and displayed at point of sale. Timely, detailed and accurate sales records must be maintained for each purchase and are subject to regular and random audits. "Consumers of these products must carry and produce, on demand, a detailed sales receipt of these purchases when in possession of the purchased product. Failure of a consumer to produce a product sales receipt while in possession of these products is a felony and will be vigorously investigated and prosecuted.

"Retail sale, purchase, and/or use, of these products (drugs, alcohol, and tobacco) by anyone under the age of 21 years is a felony crime for all involved and is strictly prohibited. This is a zero tolerance policy. Parents are held responsible and accountable for violations of these laws by their children up to and including payment of fines.

"All tax violations and/or evasion is a felony crime as is every violation and evasion of the retail tax law. Violations of these regulations are vigorously prosecuted with convicted violators and evaders fined. Fines for not collecting taxes and/or not paying taxes on these products, or violating the business registration, display, bar coding, packaging, use and/or consumption of any or all drugs will start at $10,000 per violation. Further violations carry progressive fines of $20,000 per violation and higher. Further offenses of these tax regulations will include loss of business license and a fine of $100,000 per violation occurrence plus other penalties as they may apply. The tax rules, of the 20/20 Plan, will be rigorously investigated and enforced. The strength of the United States economy depends on revenue from the 20/20 Plan and no one is above the law, or allowed to circumvent the law, in the payment of taxes.

"The reduction of drug use in the United States will cause many links in the 300 million-link chain to become stronger and more productive. The 20/20 solution is a worthy compromise."

As the team returned to the hotel, they all knew the 20/20 Plan on drugs would be criticized and condemned by many citizens. Nonetheless, the "War on Drugs" has failed. Citizens must ask themselves, "How is this war working for us?" "It is not!"

CHAPTER FOURTEEN | *Drugs and Substance Abuse Summary*

1. Humans have used drugs of one sort or another for thousands of years.

2. Drug laws attempt to keep up with the changing perceptions and real dangers of substance abuse.

3. By 1970, 55 federal drug laws and countless state laws specified a variety of punitive measures, including life imprisonment and the death penalty.

4. Smoking causes 30 percent of all cancer deaths.

5. Smoking causes 80 percent of chronic obstructive pulmonary disease, and causes early cardiovascular disease and deaths.

6. Tobacco, alcohol and illicit drugs not only cost the nation more than $600 billion annually but these deadly substances ruin lives and harm others.

7. Current drug laws and enforcement of these laws are all reactive.

8. The 'War on Drugs' has failed.

9. The 20/20 Plan ends the "War on Drugs.'

10. The cost in lives and money is destroying the United States of America.

11. The solutions to substance abuse require extraordinary understanding, resolve and courage.

12. The 20/20 Plan permits drugs to be purchased and used with restrictions.

13. The 20/20 Plan taxes each retail sale of drugs, alcohol and tobacco.

14. The 20/20 Plan utilizes drug tax revenues for the benefit of the country.

15. Violations of these regulations will be vigorously prosecuted.

16. Convicted violators and evaders will be progressively fined.

17. Drug, alcohol and tobacco products must be securely packaged in a precise, exact manner.

18. The sale, purchase, possession, transportation, distribution and use of drugs by anyone under the age of 21 years is strictly prohibited by law.

19. Substance abuse victims can volunteer for suitable federal government funded treatment.

20. The 20/20 Plan is not so naïve to think illegal drug trafficking will be eliminated by this new regulation. It is astute enough to realize the 20/20 Plan is the best solution to this destructive problem.

CHAPTER FIFTEEN

The Judicial Process, Prisons and Parole

At his best, man is the noblest of all animals; separated from law and justice he is the worst.
- Aristotle

THURSDAY MORNING. WEEK 3.

The Thursday morning ride to work would have a different look. Ron was at the "wheel" as Dave presents the Judicial Process and its' relation to prisons and paroles. It was a subject very close to him. The original agenda for this theme took on a new light as the 20/20 Plan developed. They fully recognized this issue needed to be as comprehensive as the immigration process. Dave was well prepared with extensive research. The 20/20 Plan was ready to be unveiled.

"The 20/20 Plan addresses the Judicial System of the federal government. There is also a Judicial System, or court system, for state governments," Dave explained. "While each hears certain types of cases, neither is completely independent of the other. The two systems often interact and share the goal of fairly handling legal issues. The 20/20 Plan does not intend to make changes in the judicial process, but recognizes the need for changes to the structure of the court system to bring it in line with a population of more than 300 million people.

"The U.S. Constitution created a governmental structure known as federalism that calls for the sharing of powers between the federal and state governments. The Constitution gives certain powers to the federal government and reserves the balance for the states. The federal court system deals with legal issues expressly or implicitly granted to it by the U.S. Constitution. The state court systems deal with their respective state constitutions and the legal issues the U.S. Constitution did not give the federal government or explicitly deny the states. For example, the Constitution gives Congress sole authority to make uniform laws concerning bankruptcies. Therefore, a state court lacks jurisdiction. The Constitution does not give the federal government authority in most family law matters; therefore, a federal court would not hear a divorce case.

"Our Founding Fathers understood the need for an independent Judiciary, which was created under Article III of the United States Constitution. The Judicial Branch is one of three separate and distinct branches of the federal government. The other two are the legislative and executive branches. There are six court systems according to the United States Courts website.

They are:

The Supreme Court of the United States.
The United States Court of Appeals. (12 Regional Courts plus 1 Appeals)
The United States District Courts. (94 Judicial Courts plus Bankruptcy)
U.S. Court of International Trade
U.S. Court of Federal Claims
The United States Courts of Special Jurisdiction.
  - U.S. Court of Appeals for the Armed Forces
  - US Court of Federal Claims
  - U.S. Tax Court
  - U.S. Court of Appeals for Veterans Claims
  - Judicial Panel on Multidistrict Litigation

"The United States Supreme Court consists of the Chief Justice of the United States and eight associate justices. The Supreme Court hears a limited number of the cases it is requested to decide each year. Those cases may originate in the federal or state courts. They usually involve important questions about the Constitution or federal law.

"There are 94 federal judicial districts, including at least one district in each state, the District of Columbia and Puerto Rico. Three territories of the United States: Guam, the Virgin Islands and Northern Mariana Islands have district courts to hear federal cases, including bankruptcy cases. The 94 U.S. judicial districts are structured into 12 regional circuits, each of which has a United States Court of Appeals. The thirteen appellate courts currently have 179 judgeships. A court of appeals hears appeals from the district courts located within its circuit, as well as appeals from decisions of federal administrative agencies. In addition, the Court of Appeals for the Federal Circuit has nationwide jurisdiction to hear appeals in specialized cases, such as those involving patent laws and cases decided by the Court of International Trade and the Court of Federal Claims.

"The United States district courts are the trial courts of the federal court system. Within limits set by Congress and the Constitution, the district courts have jurisdiction to hear nearly all classes of federal cases, including both civil and criminal matters. Hundreds of people across the nation are selected for jury duty every day to help decide some of these cases.

"Bankruptcy courts are separate units of the district courts. Federal courts have exclusive jurisdiction over bankruptcy cases. A bankruptcy case cannot be filed in a state court. Each of the 94 federal judicial districts handle bankruptcy matters, and in almost all districts, bankruptcy cases are filed in the bankruptcy court. Bankruptcy laws help people who can no longer pay their creditors get a fresh start by liquidating their assets to pay debts, or to create a repayment plan.

"Bankruptcy laws also protect troubled businesses and provide for orderly distributions to business creditors through reorganization or liquidation. These procedures are covered under Title 11 of the United States Code (the Bankruptcy Code). The vast majority of cases are filed under the three main chapters of the Bankruptcy Code, which are Chapter 7, Chapter 11, and Chapter 13.

Two special trial courts have nationwide jurisdiction over certain types of cases:

1. The Court of International Trade addresses cases involving international trade and customs issues.

2. The United States Court of Federal Claims has jurisdiction over most claims for money damages against the United States, disputes over federal contracts, unlawful "takings" of private property by the federal government, and a variety of other claims against the United States.

"The Judiciary Act of 1789 established a Supreme Court with one chief justice and five associate justices. The act further defined the jurisdiction of the Supreme Court to include appellate jurisdiction in larger civil cases and cases in which state courts ruled on federal statutes. The size expanded to seven justices in 1807. In 1837, an eighth and ninth justice was added. A tenth justice was appointed in 1863. In 1866, Congress reduced the court to nine justices.

"The 20/20 Plan increases the total number of justices to fifteen (15) Supreme Court Justices, one of which will be the Chief Justice. This number correlates with an increase to 15 federal circuit courts. The purpose of this increase is to ensure that caseload backlogs are kept current in order to dispense fair and swift justice. To reorganize the Supreme Court, justices are appointed to serve a fifteen-year term instead of the current lifetime term. The justices currently on the Supreme Court will be given terms to enable the President to nominate one new justice each year to replace the justice that has reached their respective term limit. Newly appointed justices must be between the ages of 50 and 65, in order that no justice serves past the age of 80. This rotates the court and keeps the court fresh and impartial."

"This is different than what Roosevelt attempted to do in 1937," Genie stated. "He tried to pack the court with liberal justices to neutralize those hostile to the New Deal. With the 20/20 Plan the opposite is guaranteed. No single President can pack the court with nominees."

"Legal scholars have discussed whether or not to impose term limits on the Supreme Court of the United States," Dave continued. "Presently, Supreme Court Justices are appointed for life "during good behavior." An opinion has developed, among scholars, that the Supreme Court may not be accountable in a way that is most in line with the spirit of checks and balances. The justices have become activists and every decision they make is predicted as they rule along ideological lines."

"The truth is, that, even with the most secure tenure of office, during good behavior, the danger is not, that the judges will be too firm in resisting public opinion, and in defence of private rights or public liberties; but, that they will be ready to yield themselves to the passions, and politics, and prejudices of the day."
- Joseph Story Commentaries on the Constitution. Date: 1833.

"Well said and it applies today. It is imperative to restructure the Supreme Court to permit new justices to serve and to promote as much diversity of opinion and interpretation of the constitution as conceivable. This is impossible when justices remain on the court for life. The outcome is identified before they vote. There needs to be much more diversity and turnover in the Supreme Court. Justices serving into their late eighties and nineties deprive younger qualified justices from serving on the court.

"The 20/20 Plan increases the federal circuit courts to fifteen. The courts will be redistricted to represent approximately 20 million citizens each. The 94 federal judicial districts will be assessed and it will be determined if that number should be increased in order to reduce the caseload backlog. This backlog of cases refers to the situation in which a court's caseload is so burdened it is unable to hear or try cases in a timely manner. It is when the number of cases on the docket exceed the capacity of the court.

"Caseload backlogs will be monitored and determinations made to relieve the backlog to ensure that citizens receive fair and swift justice. Critical assessment of frivolous lawsuits need to be ruled on fairly and swiftly. Judicial Review Boards are established to ensure judges are held accountable to follow the law."

"He who opens a school door, closes a prison." — Victor Hugo

THE PRISON SYSTEM IN THE UNITED STATES

"An overview of the United States prison system is crucial," Dave declared. "I could present thousands of pages to document the status and conditions of the prisons in the United States, but I'll be brief as everyone should do their own research. I found a representative article in The Economist that lays the foundation for the 20/20 Plan. It should come as no surprise to anyone that the United States incarcerates a lot of men and women: almost two and a half million.

"The United States has a puzzling array of places to put prisoners. Jails are usually operated by local jurisdictions (cities or counties) and house either convicted criminals serving short sentences or people awaiting trial. States and the federal government operate prisons and penitentiaries. They house convicts serving longer sentences. There are also juvenile-detention facilities, military prisons, immigration-detention and civil-commitment centers used for court-ordered inpatient or outpatient treatment of the mentally ill; as well as jails and prisons in Indian and overseas territories, most of which are administered by different government entities. This keeps data on the overall size of America's incarcerated population, as well as information about their crimes, baffling and fragmented. The private prison industry is flourishing and corporations outsource jobs to inmates at low wages. Example: inmate call centers.

"The Prison Policy Initiative (PPI), a criminal-justice research and advocacy group, released a report and chart that draws on various data sources to present a more complete picture of specifically who is behind bars, and their reason for incarceration. PPI estimates the United States has approximately 2.4 million people imprisoned, with the majority of the prisoners, about 1.36 million in state prisons. This indicates that more than 1 million inmates are in federal prisons. These numbers fluctuate, as it does not account for turnover. Almost three-quarters of the prisoner population are in local jails. Another 23,000 are immigration detainees held in local jails under contract with Immigration and Customs Enforcement (ICE).

"Around 60.6 percent of jail inmates have been convicted; 39.4 percent, which includes the immigration detainees, have not been convicted, either because they have been recently arrested, are unable to post bail or because they are awaiting trial in clogged courts. "Local jails admitted a total of 11.6 million people between July 1, 2011 and June 30, 2012. Jails with fewer than 50 prisoners had a weekly turnover rate of 131 percent. Prisons release some 688,000 people from prisons each year. The report highlights it is credulous to think that prisons are separate from the rest of society and demonstrates how critical it is to provide services inside prisons to help inmates when released from prison. With very few exceptions, inmates are ultimately released. It is in the nation's best interest to ensure they are not imprisoned repeatedly.

"This validates that America puts too many people in prison for too many different offenses. The number of federal laws has risen from 3,000 in the early 1980s to more than 4,450 by 2008. Many of these have poor intent requirements, meaning people are being locked up not to keep the rest of society safe, but for technical violations of laws they may not have known existed.

"This overreliance on imprisonment is evident in the juvenile population, which is over 70,000 nationally. Around 11,600 are imprisoned for "technical violations" of their probation or parole terms, rather than because they committed a new crime. In 11 states, such juvenile prisoners outnumber those incarcerated for crimes against other people. Only in Massachusetts did juveniles imprisoned for crimes committed against people comprise a majority of juvenile prisoners. Roughly, 3,000 are imprisoned for offenses that are not adult crimes. Examples are running away from home, truancy and incorrigibility. Incarcerated children are less likely to graduate from high school and are more likely to spend further time in prison as adults."

"These statistics are chilling, confusing and imprecise all at the same time," Dave continued. "The cost of prisons in the United States is unknown but most estimates place the cost at over $50 billion. This is another example of a well-meaning, but costly, colossal failure. This is not a one-time expense. Prison costs are escalating every year. "Privately owned prisons and jails profit from the number of those incarcerated.

"The 20/20 Plan only imprisons felons convicted of murder, violent crimes, sexual assault, assaults on citizens, battery, rape, and crimes committed with weapons. These crimes must be prosecuted fully.

"America is interested in reducing its prison population. The 20/20 Plan releases inmates convicted of all other crimes. They are instead fined, placed on probation, given community service and/or therapy as an option when applicable. Imprisonment of fewer juveniles for minor reasons is another good place to begin.

"The 20/20 Plan for education, camping and the AmericaWorks service program will significantly reduce the amount of crime committed by young citizens because they will have new positive experiences in more favorable environments.

"The 20/20 Plan calls for a systematic release of prisoners who have committed crimes of a lesser nature including drug offenses. The release process is projected to take less than one year. These released prisoners are placed on parole, which is the temporary release of a prisoner (for a special purpose) or permanently before the completion of a sentence on the promise of good behavior. These new parolees will be assessed a fee for release plus victim reparations. Strict probation regulations and job training are conditions of release. Drug treatment and/or therapy is also an option if applicable. Crimes not included in the prison release program are murder, violent crimes, sexual assault, assaults on citizens, battery, rape, and crimes committed with weapons.

"Some recent statistics regarding parole, probation and community service are:

The number of adults under community supervision declined by about 71,300 during 2011, down to 4,814,200.

The U.S. probation population fell below 4 million; about 4.3 million adults moved onto or off probation during the year.

Nearly 853,900 adults were on parole at year-end 2011. About 1.1 million adults moved onto or off parole during the year.

"The re-incarceration rate among parolees at risk for violating their conditions of supervision continued to decline, dropping from about 12 percent in 2011 to 9 percent during 2012.

"During 2012, the state parole population fell about 0.6 percent, from an estimated 740,400, while the federal parole population grew 3.5 percent, from 106,955 to 110,739. The community supervision rate also declined at year-end 2012, down to 1,981 persons per 100,000 U.S. adult residents. The supervision rate of probationers was similar at year-end 2012, dropping to 1,633 persons per 100,000 U.S. adult residents from 1,662 per 100,000 at year-end 2011.

Community supervision and probation rates declined each year from 2007 to 2012, while parole rates fluctuated. From 2011 to 2012, the parole supervision rate declined from 357 to 353 persons per 100,000 U.S. adult residents on parole. The incarceration rate among probationers at risk for violating their conditions of supervision fell from 6 to 5.1 percent. Fifty-eight percent of parolees either completed their term of supervision or were discharged early, in 2012, up from fifty-two percent in 2011.

"These statistics prove the 20/20 Plan for the systematic release of prisoners and the granting probation to convicted persons will succeed and will generate enormous cost savings for the American taxpayer. Although the full cost of incarceration of $50 billion per year may not be realized immediately, the savings will be massive because the penalties and fines parolees and probationers pay will offset their cost of imprisonment.

"The 20/20 Plan compensates the true victims of crimes while penalizing the perpetrators and placing them in positive programs. This process is not only a huge cost reversal for taxpayers but also changes the culture in America from one of imprisonment to one of hope and self-sufficiency. This strengthens several million weak, and/or broken links in the 300 million-link chain. The 20/20 Plan is a huge success for America that keeps citizens safe and secure while providing the benefit of saving more than $50 billion annually.

As the four consultants arrived at work, they knew the majority of the republic would soon see the logic and accept the 20/20 Plan. However, it would take a lot of deep thinking and a positive outlook to forge a culture that rehabilitates citizens in need rather than housing them in prisons and forgetting about them. They knew this is a better alternative for the country but were realistic enough to know people are not perfect.

"Morality cannot be legislated but behavior can be regulated. Judicial decrees may not change the heart, but they can restrain the heartless." — Martin Luther King, Jr.

CHAPTER FIFTEEN | *Judicial Process Summary*

1. The Constitution created Federalism.

2. Federalism is the sharing of powers between national and state governments.

3. Our Founding Fathers understood the need for an independent Judiciary.

4. The 20/20 Plan increases Supreme Court Justices from nine to fifteen.

5. The 20/20 Plan sets term limits for Supreme Court Justices at 15 years.

6. The 20/20 Plan provides an opportunity to younger qualified justices to serve on the Supreme Court.

7. The 20/20 Plan increases number of Federal Circuit Courts from 12 to 15.

8. The 20/20 Plan supports reducing caseloads to provide fair and swift justice.

9. Frivolous lawsuits will be closely scrutinized and vigorously discouraged.

10. The 20/20 Plan prevents justices from being ready to yield themselves to the passions, and politics, and prejudices of the day.

CHAPTER FIFTEEN | *Prison and Parole Summary*

1. 2.5 million inmates are currently incarcerated in the United States of America.

2. 1.4 million inmates are in state or local facilities of some type.

3. $50 billion is spent annually on imprisonment that could be averted.

4. The 20/20 Plan releases all prisoners except those who committed violent crimes or crimes with weapons and enrolls them in work programs.

5. The 20/20 Plan places convicted people on probation and collects fines as penalties.

6. The 20/20 Plan places convicts in work programs and/or therapy.

7. The re-incarceration rate dropped from 12% in 2011 to 9% during 2012.

8. The 20/20 Plan changes the culture of the nation.

9. The 20/20 Plan avoids $50 billion in costs while giving people renewed hope.

10. The 20/20 Plan keeps citizens safer and more secure.

The Congress and Term Limits

"I place economy among the first and most important virtues, and public debt as the greatest of dangers to be feared. To preserve our independence, we must not let our rulers load us with perpetual debt. If we run into such debts, we must be taxed in our meat and drink, in our necessities and in our comforts, in our labor and in our amusements. If we can prevent the government from wasting the labor of the people, under the pretense of caring for them, they will be happy." — Thomas Jefferson

THURSDAY AFTERNOON. WEEK 3.

Ron pressed the open trunk button and doors button on the rental car keys and gave them to Dave. The four put their brief cases in the trunk and heard Ron say, "There is so much written about both houses of Congress, about how they operate in theory, but they are essentially a self-serving bunch who are in the process of running up $20 trillion in debt. We discussed them in earlier chapters. At this time I'll share some foundation material I found on web sites like www.britannica.com and others."

"We all took Civics in school at one time or another," Tom said. "I wonder how many citizens have studied the Constitution and really know and understand how the system is supposed to work and why it was written this way by the Founding Fathers."

"The Congress are the lawmakers of the United States of America," Ron replied somewhat sarcastically. "Many citizens, judging by the low poll numbers, now call them the 'lawbreakers of America.' Originally, they were shopkeepers, businessmen and gentleman farmers who served a term for the republic and went back to their farms and businesses. Now they are career politicians with one hand in the lobbyists' pockets and the other in the taxpayers' pockets. They would not know a budget if one were gift-wrapped for them. Does anyone remember Mark Twain's old joke, "Reader, suppose you were an idiot. And suppose you were a member of Congress. But I repeat myself."

"The Congress consists of two houses: the Senate and House of Representatives," Tom continued with a chuckle. "Two Senators represent each state, regardless of size. The House is based on the population of each state. The Congress is established under the Constitution of 1789 and is separated structurally from the Executive and Judicial branches of government. Among the express powers of Congress as defined in the Constitution are the power to lay and collect taxes, borrow money on the credit of the United States, regulate commerce, coin money, declare war, raise and support armies, and make all laws necessary for the execution of its powers.

"Although the two chambers of Congress are separate, for the most part, they have an equal role in the enactment of legislation, and there are several aspects of the business of Congress the Senate and the House of Representatives share and require common action. Congress must assemble at least once a year and agree on the date for convening and adjourning. The date for convening was set in the Constitution as the first Monday in December; however, the Twentieth Amendment to the Constitution revised the date to January 3. The House and Senate vote on the date for adjournment.

"Congress must also convene in a joint session to count the electoral votes for the President and Vice President. Although not required by the Constitution, joint sessions are also held when the President or some visiting dignitary addresses both houses.

"Both houses of Congress are also responsible for such matters as government printing, general accounting, and the Congressional budget. Congress has established individual agencies to serve these specific interests. Other agencies, which are directly responsible to Congress, include the Copyright Royalty Tribunal, the Botanical Garden, and the Library of Congress.

"The representatives in the house are elected by the people as their elected delegates for two year terms to ensure that if their actions got out of hand they could quickly be brought back home and let someone else represent the people.

"Senators were appointed by the several states to represent their needs and fill a six year term. Something went horribly wrong. Senators are now elected by popular vote. The 17th amendment changed that. It took power away from the states by not allowing the states to appoint Senators. The people, similar to electing representatives, would instead elect them. The Senate was never designed to be the people's representative body. It was intended to represent the states. The states are not regional departments of the federal government. We now have two groups in Congress that no longer fight amongst themselves, which is not beneficial to attaining the best solutions. Now two groups of elected politicians must endear themselves to the electorate by bringing home the bacon at every opportunity without regard for the common good of the republic, or our several states. Their quest for power and re-election is uncontrollable. The 17th amendment has destroyed the subtle balance given us by the Founding Fathers.

"The 20/20 Plan restores the balance the Founding Fathers gave us. The Senators must again become accountable to the state legislatures by making them report to the states at least once a year instead of squandering their time in Washington. This grants the states the opportunity to question their Senators regarding their representation.

"The term of Congress extends from each odd-numbered year to the next odd-numbered year. For its annual sessions, Congress developed the committee system to facilitate its consideration of the various items of business that arise. Each house of Congress has a number of standing (permanent) committees and select (special and temporary) committees. Together the two chambers of Congress form joint committees to consider subjects of common interest. Conference committees are formed to adjust disputed versions of legislation. No act of Congress is valid unless both houses approve an identical document.

"The President delivers an annual State of the Union Address in which the President describes in broad terms the legislative program the executive branch would like Congress to consider. An annual budget message and the report on the economy, prepared by the President's Council of Economic Advisors is submitted later. Inasmuch as Congressional committees require a period of time to prepare legislation before it is presented for general consideration, the legislative output of Congress may be small in the early weeks of a session. Legislation not enacted at the end of a session retains its status in the following session of the two-year Congress.

"In terms of legislation, the President may be considered a functioning part of the Congressional process. The President is expected to keep Congress informed of the need for new legislation and government departments and agencies are required to send Congress periodic activity reports. The President also submits certain types of treaties and nominations for the approval of the Senate. The most important legislative function of the President, however, is signing or vetoing proposed legislation.

"The President's veto may be overridden by a two-thirds vote of each chamber of Congress. The possibility of a veto gives the President influence in determining the legislation Congress should initially consider, and which amendments are acceptable. In addition to these legal and constitutional powers, the President has influence as the leader of a political party. The President may mold party policy, both in Congress, and among the electorate.

"Although the U.S. Supreme Court has no direct relations with Congress, the Supreme Court's implied power to invalidate legislation that violates the Constitution is an even stronger restriction on the powers of Congress than the Presidential veto. Supreme Court and Federal Court decisions on the constitutionality of legislation outline the constitutional framework within which Congress may act.

"Congress is also affected by representative interest groups, though they are not part of the formal structure of Congress. Lobbyists play a significant role in testifying before Congressional hearings and in mobilizing opinion on select issues.

"Many of the activities of Congress are not directly concerned with enacting laws, but the ability of Congress to enact law is often the sanction that makes its other actions effective. The general legal theory under which Congress operates is that legal authority is delegated to the President or executive departments, and agencies, and that the latter, in turn, are legally responsible for their actions. Congress may review any actions performed by a delegated authority; and in some areas of delegated legislation, such as in proposals for governmental reorganization, Congress must indicate approval of specific plans before they go into effect. Congress may also retain the right to terminate legislation by joint action of both houses.

"Congress exercises general legal control over the employment of government personnel. Political control may also be exercised, particularly through the Senate's power to advise and consent to nominations. Neither the Senate nor the House of Representatives has any direct constitutional power to nominate or otherwise select executive or judicial personnel (although in the unusual event that the electoral college fails to select a President and Vice President, the two houses, respectively, are expected to do so). Furthermore, Congress does not customarily remove officials. Congress does have the power of impeachment. The House initiates impeachment and the case is then tried before the Senate. A vote of two-thirds of the Senators present is required for conviction.

"The power to levy and collect taxes and to appropriate funds allows Congress considerable authority in fiscal matters. Although the President has the initial responsibility for determining the proposed level of appropriations, once estimates for the next fiscal year are submitted to Congress, a single budget bill is not enacted, but rather a number of appropriation bills for various departments and agencies are passed during the first six or seven months of a session.

"In its non-legislative capacity, Congress also has the power to initiate amendments to the Constitution, and it must determine whether the states should vote on a proposed amendment by state legislatures or by special state conventions. Finally, Congress has the right to investigate any subject that affects its powers. Congressional investigating committees may call witnesses and require them to produce information. These committees may also be given power to charge persons who deliberately block the legislative process with contempt of Congress and issue warrants for their arrests.

"The Budget and Accounting Act of 1921 established the framework for the modern federal budget. President Warren G. Harding approved this act to provide a national budget system and an independent audit of government accounts. The official title of this act usually referred to as "the budget act," is 'The General Accounting Act of 1921.' This was the first time the President would be required to submit to Congress an annual budget for the entire federal government. The object of the budget bill was to consolidate the spending agencies in both the executive and legislative branches of the government."

"Currently, USC 31 §1105 declares that 'on or after the first Monday in January but not later than the first Monday in February of each year, the President shall submit a budget of the United States Government for the following fiscal year.' After that, it is up to the Congress to pass budget legislation and the President to sign it into law.

"Senate Democrats passed a budget in 2009. In 2010, they marked one up in the Budget Committee, but did not bring it to the floor. They just stopped bothering with the whole budget thing altogether in 2011. Both the House and Senate pass temporary spending measures. They are called continuing resolutions (CRs). They argue that budget resolutions aren't binding and that the 2011 Budget Control Act, the legislation that resolved the debt ceiling standoff, has done the real work of the budget by setting discretionary spending levels for the coming years.

"Privately, they say they see no reason to vote on a budget House Republicans will never adopt. Republicans argue, correctly, that budgets are the vision for the country even if they do not pass. Senate Democrats, in refusing to propose or vote for a budget, are declining to give voters that information.

"The basic job of Congress is to fund the federal government. The basic question is do they really do their jobs? For example, surface transportation is another of the most fundamental jobs of federal governance. Congress sets aside money for roads, runways, bridges, subways systems, and other mainstays of our transportation infrastructure. Congress passed, and President George W. Bush signed, the Safe, Accountable, Flexible, Efficient Transportation Equity Act in 2005. That bill expired in September 2009. Congress could not agree on a replacement, so they passed 10 short-term extensions of the transportation funding. They call them 'Stopgaps.' The people do not elect Congress to pass stopgaps. That is not doing their basic job. Congress passed the Moving Ahead for Progress in the 21st Century Act in 2012. Instead of setting transportation policy for four or five years, as was the previous norm, it only set it for two years. That is not doing their job because it left most of the major problems, like how to handle the increasing inadequacy of the gas tax, for later.

"Article 1 Section 9 clause 7 states: "No Money shall be drawn from the Treasury, but in Consequence of Appropriations made by Law; and a regular Statement and Account of the Receipts and Expenditures of all public Money shall be published from time to time." This means Congress must pass laws to spend money. There really is no constitutional requirement for an annual budget. This law requires the President to submit an annual budget proposal to Congress for the federal government in its entirety.

"The country has been operating without a budget. The House of Representatives passed budgets when the Republican's regained power after the 2010 mid-term elections. The Democrat controlled Senate did not allow these bills to get to the floor for a vote. The President submitted a budget in 2012, which did not get a single vote in either the House or the Senate. It was unanimously defeated in both houses. Another example of Congress not doing their basic job.

"In order for the government to operate, Congress just keeps passing continuing resolutions (CRs) and the President keeps on signing them into law. This is not the most efficient and cost effective method to operate the government. This is especially true for a government deep in debt. Just another example of Congress not doing their basic job.

"Under the Constitution, "no money" can be drawn without Congressional appropriations. In Federalist Paper #58, James Madison argued that a "House of Representatives" was most responsible to the public, and therefore spending should be the province of the House. Madison wrote those who "hold the purse" wield a "powerful instrument" against "the overgrown prerogatives of the other branches of government."

"What is the 20/20 Plan to resolve the chaos Congress has created?" Genie asked. "Is it the balanced budget based on percentages instead of dollars?"

"That is part of the answer," Tom replied thoughtfully. "Congress squanders too much time on the wrong 'stuff.' Campaigning and fund raising are two blatant abuses. Congress being paid $174,000 per year plus other expenses demands it must to do its' basic job which is producing a budget. They need to focus on passing laws that move the country forward, and rescind laws that harm the country.

"A review and study (www.senate.gov/CRSReports/crs-publish.cfm?pid) of 'Congressional Studies and Allowances' reports the various expenses and allowances that Congress receives. Some information (usgovinfo.about.com) taken from their website along with their salaries, benefits and allowed outside income shows members of Congress receive various allowances intended to defray expenses related to carrying out their Congressional duties. According the Congressional Research Service (CRS) report, Congressional Salaries and Allowances, the allowances are provided to cover official office expenses, including staff, mail, travel between a Member's district or state and Washington, DC, and other goods and services.

"House members receive the Members' Representational Allowance (MRA). Congress cleverly votes to help themselves defray expenses resulting from three specific components of their 'representational duties;' the personal expenses component; the office expenses component; and the mailing expenses component. Members may not use their MRA allowance to pay any personal or political campaigning expenses. Conversely, members may not use campaign funds to pay for expenses related to their daily Congressional duties.

"Members of the House of Representatives may hire up to 18 permanent employees for their Congressional and district offices plus 4 interns. In the Member office, located in one of three Congressional Office Buildings, there is a distinct office hierarchy. There are six levels on the Office Organization Chart. Wow, a lot of levels. Moreover, there is this imprudent swindle.

"About 2,000 House of Representatives staffers were paid six-figure salaries in 2009, including 43 staffers who earned the maximum $172,500. This is more than three times the annual median U.S. household income we researched in Chapter 6. It is impossible to research accurate data on Congress, their staff, their pay and allowances. It is estimated more than 15,000 staffers are employed by Congress.

"Each member receives the same amount of MRA funds for personal expenses. Allowances for office expenses vary from member to member based on the distance between the member's home district and Washington, D.C., and average rent for office space in the member's home district. Allowances for mailing vary based on the number of residential mailing addresses in the member's home district as reported by the U.S. Census Bureau. The House annually sets the funding levels for the MRA as part of the federal budget process. According to the CRS report, this amount decreased from a total of $660 million for fiscal year 2010, to $573.9 million for fiscal year 2012. In 2012, individual representatives received MRA allowances ranging from $1,270,129 to $1,564,613, with an average of $1,353,205.13.

"All Senators receive the same legislative assistance allowance. Their administrative and clerical assistance allowance and the office expense allowance vary based on the population of the state the Senators represent, the distance between Washington, D.C. and their home states, and limits authorized by the Senate Committee on Rules and Administration. The Senators' administrative and clerical assistance staff size is not specified. Senators are free to structure their office staffs as they choose, as long as they do not spend more than provided to them in the administrative and clerical assistance component of their Senators' Official Personnel and Office Expense Allowance. (SOPOEA)

"Furthermore, Congress is in session eight days during a typical fall session in election years. Members earn $608 per hour during the eight days they are in session between August and November. The figures, developed by liberal activist Ralph Nader, represent a pro-rated calculation based on members' $174,000 annual salary. House Speaker John Boehner, meanwhile, will earn an estimated $781 per hour, based on his salary of $223,500. They fritter away too much time on too many elections and re-elections. Meanwhile millions of Americans are working more and more for less and less. The members of the House of Representatives seem to have no problem working less and less for more and more," Nader wrote in a letter to Boehner.

"The corrupt culture of Congress needs to be reined in. The people must bring them to justice, but for many reasons, they cannot. Term limits is the only viable answer."

TERM LIMITS

"I can see both sides of term limits, and I think, in different positions, term limits make more sense than in some others." — Caroline Kennedy

"Our elected officials have voted themselves prohibitive salaries, expense allowances and staffs," Dave interjected. "They are now the feudal lords of the kingdom. What is interesting is that Congressional Job Approval Ratings range from a low of 10-12 percent to 80 percent Disapproval Ratings. When asked, most people will say 'we need to throw the bums out.' Nevertheless, 'they then say, but my Congress person is great and needs to stay.' How does that compute? How can each one be great but all of the rest are bad?"

"Dave, for the record, there have been 102 Congressmen who have served more than 36 years in the House or Senate," Ron replied. "Eight (8) of them have served more than 50 years. That stretches the limit. A fresh approach is crucial with these dispirited disapproval ratings. Currently term limits do not exist. Term limits need to be set and rules put in place to constrain and regulate the time spent on fund raising and campaigning.

"The 20/20 Plan sets term limits for elected officials. Senators serve a six-year term. The 20/20 Plan limits Senators to 2 terms, or 12 years. The terms of the 100 Senators are staggered in order that one-third are up for election each two-year election cycle. The 20/20 Plan supports repeal of the 17th Amendment to permit state legislatures to appoint Senators.

"House members serve a two year term and are up for election each two-year election cycle. The 20/20 Plan limits them to two 4-year terms or eight total years. Half of the 435 members would be elected each two-year election cycle. The longer terms with only one-reelection shrinks the time spent on fund raising and campaigning. This allocates Congress more time to perform their basic job of building a balanced budget to make America safe and prosperous.

"The 20/20 Plan establishes a limit of one six (6) year term for the President of the United States. Most Presidents serve two four-year terms or eight years. The last two years of the second term are lame duck, or do nothing years. Therefore, a six-year term is a more productive and effective term; and it will eliminate the misused time and money spent on campaigning and fund raising. Authority must circulate frequently.

172

"The 20/20 Plan for term limits changes the culture of government from one of perpetually seeking office to one of serving the best interests of the republic and the people. "Some Americans will see this as an extreme idea," Genie declared. "This is really thinking outside the box. I can see where this will ensure accountability. This will unquestionably prevent corruption. But, can the voters accept term limits?"

"It isn't if the voters can accept term limits, can the politicians accept term limits? Term limits date back to the American Revolution, and prior to that, to the Democracies and Republics of antiquity," Ron answered. "I found this in Wikipedia. The council of 500 in ancient Athens rotated its entire membership annually, as did the Ephorate in ancient Sparta. The ancient Roman Republic featured a system of elected magistrates—tribunes of the Plebs, Aediles, Quaestors, Praetors, and Consuls—who served a single term of one year, with reelection to the same magistracy forbidden for ten years.

"According to historian Garrett Fagan, office holding in the Roman Republic was based on "limited tenure of office" which ensured that "authority circulated frequently", helping to prevent corruption. An additional benefit of the cursus honorum or Run of Offices was to bring the "most experienced" politicians to the upper echelons of power holding in the ancient republic. Many Founding Fathers were educated in the classics, and quite familiar with rotation in office during antiquity. The debates of that day reveal a desire to study and profit from the object lessons offered by ancient democracy.

"The representatives in the house would be elected by the people as their elected delegates for two year terms to ensure if their actions got out of hand they could quickly be brought back home and let someone else represent the people. The Senators would be appointed by the several states to represent their needs and would fill a six-year term. Senators would be held accountable by the state legislatures and report to them.

"In 1783, rotation experiments took place at the state level. The Pennsylvania Constitution of 1776 set maximum service in the Pennsylvania General Assembly at "four years in seven". Benjamin Franklin's influence is evident not only in that he chaired the constitutional convention that drafted the Pennsylvania Constitution, but also because it included, virtually unchanged, Franklin's earlier proposals on executive rotation. Pennsylvania's plural executive was composed of twelve citizens elected for the term of three years, followed by a mandatory four-year vacation.

"The Continental Congress appointed a committee of thirteen to examine forms of government for the impending union of the states. Among the proposals from the State of Virginia, written by Thomas Jefferson, urging a limitation of tenure, 'to prevent every danger which might arise to American freedom by continuing too long in office the members of the Continental Congress.' The committee made recommendations, which as regards Congressional term limits were incorporated unchanged into the Articles of

Confederation (1781–89). The fifth Article stated, "no person shall be capable of being a delegate [to the continental Congress] for more than three years in any term of six years." "Perhaps Jefferson meant a "limitation of terror," Dave interjected sarcastically.

Ron continued, "In contrast to the Articles of Confederation, the Constitutional Convention in Philadelphia omitted mandatory term limits from the second national frame of government, i.e. the U.S. Constitution of 1789 to the present. George Washington set the informal precedent for a two-term limit for the Presidency—a tradition that prevailed until Franklin Roosevelt's presidency, after which the 22nd Amendment to the U.S. Constitution was ratified in 1951 formally establishing in law the two-term limit."

"Congressmen can be recalled by their constituents," Tom interjected.

"However, when the states ratified the Constitution (1787–88)," Ron replied. "Several leading statesmen regarded lack of mandatory limits to tenure as a dangerous defect, especially, they thought, as regards the Presidency and the Senate. Richard Henry Lee viewed the absence of legal limits to tenure, together with certain other features of the Constitution, as 'most highly and dangerously oligarchic. Both Jefferson and George Mason advised limits on reelection to the Senate and to the Presidency, because said Mason, 'nothing is so essential to the preservation of a Republican government as a periodic rotation.' The historian Mercy Otis Warren warned that 'there is no provision for a rotation, nor anything to prevent the perpetuity of office in the same hands for life; which by a little well-timed bribery, will probably be done.'

"How right Mercy Otis Warren was. An extraordinary woman and patriot who like many other women were so important to the birth of our nation. By all accounts she was a bright young woman who was homeschooled and self-taught. One of her brothers was the noted patriot and lawyer James Otis, who is credited with the quote "taxation without representation is tyranny", the principal slogan of the American Revolution.

The team arrived back at the hotel thinking of the cultural shock politicians will have with the 20/20 Plan. The all knew something had to be resolved to shake them up.

"I have come to the conclusion that politics is too serious a matter to be left to the politicians."
— Charles de Gaulle"

CHAPTER SIXTEEN | *Congressional Summary*

1. The Constitution established the Congress in 1789.

2. The two houses of Congress are the lawmakers of the United States.

3. The Congress operates on a two-year term basis from odd year to odd year.

4. The Senate advises and consents on political nominations.

5. The Budget and Accounting Act of 1921 establishes a budget for the USA.

6. The basic job of Congress is to fund the federal government.

7. The last budget passed by the Congress was in 2009. They do not do their job.

8. Congress has perpetual low approval ratings of little more than 10 percent.

9. Congress's pay is 3.5 times more than the average citizen earns. They receive more than $1.3 million annually in Members' Representational Allowance.

10. Congress is adept at working less and less, for more and more pay and benefits.

11. The 20/20 Plan repeals the 17th Amendment for states to appoint Senators.

CHAPTER SIXTEEN | *Term Limit Summary*

1. Term limits date back to the democracy of ancient Greece.

2. Are term limits extreme? Benjamin Franklin favored term limits.

3. Thomas Jefferson urged a "limitation of tenure."

4. $20 trillion National Debt is irresponsible. Congress must began to act responsibly.

5. The 20/20 Plan sets House of Representatives terms at two 4-year terms.

6. The 20/20 Plan sets Senators terms at two 6-year terms.

7. The 20/20 Plan sets the President's term at one 6-year term.

8. The 20/20 Plan for term limits changes the culture of government and politics.

9. Authority must circulate and rotate frequently.

10. Richard Henry Lee viewed the absence of legal limits to tenure as "most highly and dangerously oligarchic."

11. Both Jefferson and George Mason advised limits on reelection to the Senate and to the Presidency.

CHAPTER SEVENTEEN

Technology and the Internet

"We refuse to turn off our computers, turn off our phone, log off Facebook, and just sit in silence, because in those moments we might actually have to face up to who we really are."
— Jefferson Bethke, Author of Jesus > Religion

FRIDAY MORNING. WEEK 3.

As the four were standing in the hotel parking lot watching Dave, the master of luggage loading, fit everything in the rental car, they were reflecting on how far they had progressed on their consulting project and the progress they had made in three short weeks in the design of the 20/20 Plan. Genie started the conversation, "did any of you ever think of what you would do without computers and the internet? Twenty years ago, I didn't have a laptop or access to the internet. Now everyone in my family calls me every time they have a computer problem. Moreover, you guys are worse. Now I know what it is like to be a doctor or lawyer. Everyone wants free advice. Well, you're going to get an earful. But I'll give you some background first."

"You're not going to quit answering all of our stupid questions and stop solving our computer problems, are you?" pleaded Tom. "Every time we get hacked or get a virus we lose time and money. And we get stressed out too." "No," Genie said," I will not do that to you. We'd never get any work done if I don't fix your problems ASAP." She thought of how the world has become dependent on electronic devices of every type, and how few people really understood how the world of technology worked.

"The Internet began with the development of electronic computers in the 1950s." Genie continued. "Initial concepts of packet networking originated in a few computer science labs in the United States, Great Britain, and France. The US Department of Defense awarded contracts in the early 1960s for packet network systems. This included the Advanced Research Projects Agency Network (ARPANET) that became the first network to use the Internet Protocol. The first message sent over the ARPANET was from computer science Professor Leonard Kleinrock's laboratory at UCLA to the second network node at Stanford Research Institute. The ARPANET in particular led to development of protocols for internetworking, in which multiple separate networks could be joined into a network of networks.

"Access to the ARPANET was expanded in 1981 when the National Science Foundation (NSF) funded the Computer Science Network. In 1982, the Internet protocol suite was introduced as the standard networking protocol on the ARPANET. In the early 1980s, the National Science Foundation (NSF) also funded the establishment for national supercomputing centers at several universities, and provided interconnectivity in 1986 with the NSFNET project, which created network access to supercomputer sites in the United States. Commercial Internet Service Providers (ISPs) began to emerge in the late 1980s. ARPANET was decommissioned in 1990. Private connections to the Internet by commercial entities quickly became widespread. The NSFNET was retired in 1995, which removed the last Internet restrictions to carry commercial traffic.

"Since the mid-1990s, the Internet has had a revolutionary impact on culture and commerce, including the rise of near-instant communication by electronic mail, instant messaging, Voice over Internet Protocol (VoIP) telephone calls, two-way interactive video calls, and the World Wide Web with its discussion forums, blogs, social networking, and online shopping sites. The research and education community continues to develop and use advanced networks such as NSF's very high speed Backbone Network Service (vBNS), Internet2, and National Lambda Rail. Increasing amounts of data are transmitted at higher and higher speeds over fiber optic networks operating at 1-Gbit/s, 10-Gbit/s, or more. In historical terms, the internet's takeover of the global communication landscape was instantaneous. Today the Internet continues to grow, driven by ever-greater amounts of online information, commerce, entertainment, and social networking.

"I read an article last night by Bruce Schneier, who is known worldwide as the foremost authority and commentator on every security issue from cyber-terrorism to airport surveillance. It was titled 'The Internet of Things Is Wildly Insecure—And Often Unpatchable.' It puts our 20/20 Plan in perspective," Genie said. "He wrote: 'We're at a crisis point with regard to the security of embedded systems, where computing is embedded into the hardware itself — as with the Internet of Things. These embedded computers are riddled with vulnerabilities, and there's no good way to patch them.'

"It's not unlike what happened in the mid-1990s, when the insecurity of personal computers was reaching crisis levels. Software and operating systems were riddled with security vulnerabilities, and there was no good way to patch them. Companies were trying to keep vulnerabilities secret, while releasing security updates quickly. When updates were released, it was difficult, if not impossible, to get users to install them. This has changed over the past twenty years, due to a combination of full disclosure by publishing vulnerabilities to force companies to issue patches quicker, and to install automatic updates: automating the process of installing updates on users' computers. The results are not perfect, but they are much better than ever before.

"This time the problem is much worse, because the world is different. All devices are connected to the Internet. The computers in our routers and modems are much more powerful than the PCs of the mid-1990s, and the 'Internet of Things' will put computers into all sorts of consumer devices. The industries producing these devices are even less capable of fixing the problem than the PC and software industries were.

"If we don't solve this soon, we're in for a security disaster as hackers figure out that it's easier to hack routers than computers. At a recent Def Con, a researcher looked at thirty home routers and broke into half of them, including some of the most popular and common brands.

"To understand the problem, we need to understand the embedded systems market. Characteristically, these systems are powered by specialized computer chips made by companies such as Broadcom, Qualcomm, and Marvell. These chips are cheap, and the profit margins slim. Aside from price, the way the manufacturers differentiate themselves from each other is by features and bandwidth. They typically put a version of the Linux operating system onto the chips, as well as a bunch of other open-source and proprietary components and drivers. They do as little engineering as possible before shipping, and there is little incentive to update their "board support package" until absolutely necessary.

"The system manufacturers — usually original device manufacturers (ODMs) don't often get their brand name on the finished product. The brand-name company on the box may add a user interface and maybe some new features, make sure everything works, and they are finished, as well. The problem with this process is that no one entity has any incentive, expertise, or even ability to patch the software once it's shipped.

"The software is old, even when the device is new. For example, one survey of common home routers found that the software components were four to five years older than the device. The minimum age of the Linux operating system is four years. The minimum age of the Samba file system software is six years. They may or may not have had all the security patches applied. No one has that job. Some of the components are so old that they are no longer being patched. This patching is especially important because security vulnerabilities are found "more easily" as systems age.

"To make matters worse, it's often impossible to patch the software or upgrade components to the latest versions. Often, the complete source code isn't available. They will have the source code to Linux and any other open-source components. However, many of the device drivers and other components are just "binary blobs." That is the most pernicious part of the problem. No one can possibly patch code that is just binary. Even when a patch is possible, it is rarely applied. Users have to manually download and install relevant patches. Since users are seldom alerted to security updates, and do not have the expertise to manually administer these devices, it does not happen.

The result is hundreds of millions of devices have been sitting on the Internet, unpatched and insecure, for the last five to ten years. Hackers are starting to notice. Malware DNS Changer attacks home routers and computers. In Brazil, 4.5 million DSL routers were compromised for financial fraud. Last month, Symantec reported a Linux worm that targets routers, cameras, and other embedded devices.

"This is only the beginning. All it will take is some easy-to-use hacker tools for the script kiddies to get into the game. And, the 'Internet of Things' will only make this problem worse. Routers and modems pose a particular problem, because they are: (1) between users and the Internet, so turning them off is not an option; (2) more powerful and more general in function than other embedded devices; (3) the only 24/7 computing device in the house, and therefore are a natural place for lots of new features.

"We were here before with personal computers, and we fixed the problem. However, disclosing vulnerabilities in an effort to force vendors to fix the problem won't work the same way as with embedded systems. The last time, the problem was computers, not connected to the Internet, and slow-spreading viruses. The scale is different today. There are more devices, more vulnerability, viruses spreading faster on the Internet, and less technical expertise on both the vendor and the user sides.

"Combine full function with lack of updates, add in a pernicious market dynamic that has inhibited updates and prevented anyone else from updating, and we have an incipient disaster in front of us. It is only a matter of when. We simply have to fix this. We have to put pressure on embedded system vendors to design their systems better. We need open-source driver software so third-party vendors and ISPs can provide security tools and software updates. We need automatic update mechanisms to ensure they are installed. "The economic incentives point to large ISPs as the driver for change. Whether they are to blame or not, the ISPs are the ones who get the service calls for crashes. They often have to send users new hardware because it's the only way to update a router or modem, and that can easily cost a year's worth of profit from that customer. This problem is only going to get worse, and more expensive."

"That's a lot of information to take in," Tom interjected. "I don't know if I have the capability to understand it, much less do anything about it."

"That's the point I'm making," Genie said. "Most of the population in America has computers and only a very small percentage understand how to diagnose and resolve computer issues. That is what the 20/20 Plan is going to do for those Americans left behind in the new age of electronic technology.

"Some of those bright kids with green hair and body piercing solve puzzles people with computer engineering backgrounds can't resolve. The young hackers are caught, and end up in the headlines. The reason they are caught is they're not professionals. They're out for the adventure, bragging rights or exploration. The professionals, the ex-KGB agents, the ex-CIA agents, those from German or Israeli intelligence – they don't get caught, and when they are detected, the people who detect them are not going to acknowledge it. The 20/20 Plan regards this activity as felonious criminal activity.

"It ranges from petty theft to state-sponsored terrorism and everything in between. There is the cyberspace mugger who will steal your personal identity, and destroy your credit by committing fraud in your name; or stalk your children, or your loved ones online. There are organized crime syndicates that are engaged in stealing massive numbers of credit cards, and selling the data, or using them for credit card fraud. This activity is global. Governments and corporate entities steal technology. They steal cutting-edge technology, biotech, high-tech, and low-tech technology. This is criminal activity and must be treated as such.

"Every time a citizen gets hacked or gets a virus they lose time and money. They get stressed out too. Their link in the 300 million-link chain is damaged. The 20/20 Plan is committed to stopping this. There is a twofold solution to this dilemma. First, there needs to be safeguards built into the entire system. As we have illustrated above, this will be very difficult. The 20/20 Plan makes this task a high priority. Second, there has to be harsh penalties on those who perpetrate technological crimes. The 20/20 Plan makes these crimes a felony and punishes them with harsh fines. People who hack into systems and/or spread viruses do so because they made the choice to do so. These exploits are not accidents; they are intentional intrusions into citizens' privacy and property. Fines for these acts of invasion, which include viruses, malware and ransomware, will be $10,000 for the first offense. The second offense will be $100,000. The third offense $1 million plus other related damages. The 20/20 Plan cannot let the lives of citizens be compromised or destroyed.

"The FBI has a website to report potential e-scams. Citizens can go the Internet Crime Complaint Center to file a report. As with any virus or malware, the way to avoid it is with safe browsing and e-mail habits. Be wary of e-mail from senders you do not know. Never open, or download, an attachment unless you are sure you know what it is and that it is safe.

"From a national security viewpoint, there are those who take the shortcut of stealing technology. They don't wait for their economies to develop and catch up with other economies. The 20/20 Plan regards these attacks as acts of war.

Examples are:

"Aum Shinri Kyo is the cult that hacked aggressively into technology companies to steal technology that they were interested in. Osama bin Laden did the same. These people have satellites, they use encryption, and they are on the Net. They gather information and they disseminate information. They gather intelligence and conduct operations. Governments do the same thing. There are reports that the US knows China is hacking into our systems. They even know the buildings they are working in. We must know what is taking place in cyberspace. Our enemies are always looking at ways to attack our digital infrastructure. Someone out there is planning his own grotesque unpleasant event that could influence the lives of thousands or millions.

"Paying the cost up front for better embedded systems is much cheaper than paying the costs of the resultant security disasters. The 20/20 Plan makes this a high priority. Hacking into the United States of America is an attack on the nation's sovereignty and is an act of war. It must be treated as such. The stakes are just too high.

NET NEUTRALITY

"I keep hearing controversial reports on something called Net Neutrality," Tom questioned. "Can you tell us what that means and what this issue is all about?"

"Politicians on both sides are giving us the worst case scenarios," Genie said. "They say we're headed for the end of the Internet, as we know it. Either we'll have state-run, censored, taxed internet or we'll have expensive, monopoly-driven, corporate internet."

"Is there the possibility of just leaving things as they are now?" Tom queried.

"Good question," Genie answered. "Leaving it the way it is means the internet is controlled by the private sector. The Internet has been perhaps the greatest example of the free market in action. With low startup costs, millions of people have had the opportunity to connect, start businesses, compete, and have their voices heard. One side wants to impose 80-year-old legislation meant for telephone lines onto the Internet. They want to put an end to this new exciting innovation."

"Isn't the Internet a luxury?" Tom asked. "Can't we trust that this time, things will be different? What could possibly go wrong?"

"The dangers of government regulation are evident. We know that government makes things worse, not better," Genie replied. " Most supporters of net neutrality are young people. That is to be expected from college students. They haven't had enough encounters with state inefficiency and overreach to be jaded. It takes filing taxes, getting driver's licenses, and observing Washington to see how unbearable the government really is. The thought of handing the federal government the greatest invention of the last fifty years is enough to send a chill up your spine. There are ample reasons to be concerned about the future of the Internet even without government interference. These problems can be solved in the private sector. As long as the federal government stays out of it, Americans can solve any problem they put their mind to. If the Internet is taken out of the hands of the private sector, the future is shrouded in dark uncertainty."

GOVERNMENT TECHNOLOGY AND HEALTH CARE TECHNOLOGY

"Twenty years ago, the federal government had better technology at work than citizens had at home," Genie said. "Now just about everyone has more powerful computers and other electronic devices than the government. The taxpayers have been spending a lot of money for the government to have the best technology. That money is not spent well. The website debacle for the ACA Plan is a perfect example.

"The government's $80 billion budget for IT spending is more than that of any organization in the world. However many workers in the public sector are sharing information that often takes archaic forms. They are using impotent hardware, and outdated software and computer systems. They often have to prowl around for critical information stuck in data silos and legacy platforms; they exchange physical hard-drives and mail CDs, etc. The American people deserve better service from their government, and a better return for their tax dollars.

"The huge technology gap between the public and private sectors results in an ineffective and inefficient government. The result is billions of dollars in waste, slow and inadequate customer service and a lack of transparency about how dollars are spent. The 20/20 Plan demands the federal government work better for the taxpayers by improving technology."

"How can doctors and hospitals benefit from improved technology?" Tom asked. "My family doctor referred me to several specialists. They were all in the same group, but I had to fill out redundant forms for each doctor. When I ask about it, they tell me 'it is what it is.' Appears to be very inefficient."

"Health care is "monstrously inefficient," writes Jim Epstein, producer at Reason TV, but the technology industry could soon change that." Genie replied.

"Theranos, a company founded in 2003, has created a device that can do a series of blood tests on a single drop of blood from a finger prick. The software provides a menu of prices (offering a cholesterol check for $2.99, or a glucose test for $8.85) from which consumers can choose. Theranos is likely to grow in popularity, as the Department of Health and Human Services issued a rule in February allowing patients to view lab results directly, rather than through a doctor.

"Curious is a technology firm that will soon begin testing a product that will take genetic information, microbiomic profiles and life events (which a user enters manually) and analyze them, showing patients what helps, or harms different ailments.

"Doctors on Demand is an online service allowing patients to chat with doctors via video chat for 15 minutes for $40, saving patients time and money. HealthTap is a similar company, offering unlimited calls with doctors for $99 per month.

"The biggest challenge are state-level and FDA regulations that limit the ability of these companies to thrive. He notes that the FDA recently pulled a personal genome test, offered by the company 23andme, off the market because it gave patients what it considered too much information about the consequences of their genetic test results.

"The 20/20 Plan promotes efficient and effective software programs to make health care less costly and more patient user friendly while being safe and secure.

"Alexander Graham Bell an early precursor to fiber-optic communications in 1880 considered the Photophone his most important invention. The device allowed the transmission of sound on a beam of light. Bell conducted the world's first wireless telephone transmission between two buildings more than two football fields apart. Due to its use of an atmospheric transmission medium, it did not prove practical. Advances in laser and optical fiber technologies now permit secure transport of light.

"Fiber-optic communication is the method of transmitting information by sending light pulses through an optical fiber. Light forms an electromagnetic carrier wave that is modulated to carry information. Fiber-optic communication systems were developed in the 1970s and they revolutionized the telecommunications industry. This technology has played a major role in the Information Age. Because of its many advantages over electrical transmission, optical fibers are replacing copper wire communications in core networks throughout the developed world.

"Optical fiber is used by many telecommunications companies to transmit telephone signals, internet communication, and cable television signals. Researchers have achieved speeds well over satellite transmission speeds. Bell Labs have reached internet speeds of over 100 petabytes per second using fiber-optic communication.

"The process of communicating using fiber-optics involves the following basic steps: Creating the optical signal involving the use of a transmitter, relaying the signal along the fiber, ensuring that the signal does not become too distorted or weak, receiving the optical signal and converting it into an electrical signal.

IDENTITY THEFT

"Identity theft is related to this issue. Much of it occurs on the internet or through technology," Tom said. "Dave, do you remember the Supervisor at the Chemical Plant we worked with? He was a victim of identity theft and as I recall his life was destroyed for all practical purposes."

"Yes I do, Tom," Dave answered. "He was an excellent supervisor and an all-around good guy. Was a real pleasure to work with and I spent a lot of time with him. I'll never forget the day he told me he couldn't meet with me because he had to attend a court session. The next day, he told me the person who stole his identity was pronounced innocent by the judge even though there was overwhelming evidence that the thief committed all of the acts the thief was charged with. The judge pronounced that this just wasn't a serious offense. No big deal. The supervisor was devastated."

"I remember that incident also, enough to make a person's blood boil" Genie stated. "The 20/20 Plan makes this criminal activity a serious felony. There must be harsh penalties on those who perpetrate identity theft crimes and punishes them with substantial fines. People who steal a person's identity do so because they made a willful choice to do so. These acts are not incidental or unfortunate accidents.

"In one infamous case of identity theft, a convicted felon, incurred more than $100,000 of credit card debt, obtained a federal home loan, and bought homes, motorcycles, and handguns in the victim's name. He then called his victim to taunt him, saying that he could continue to pose as the victim for as long as he wanted because identity theft was not a federal crime at that time. He then filed bankruptcy, also in the victim's name. The victim and his wife spent more than four years, and more than $15,000 of their own money to restore their credit and reputation. The criminal served a brief sentence for making a false statement to procure a firearm, but made no restitution to his victim for any of the harm he caused. This case, and others like it, prompted Congress in 1998 to create a new federal offense of identity theft.

"Identity theft is an intentional intrusion into a citizen's life, property and privacy. Fines for these crimes of invasion will be $100,000 for the first offense, and compensation to the victim of 20 times the amount stolen if that applies plus all court costs. The second offense will be $1,000,000, plus compensation to the victim of 20 times the amount stolen if that applies and all court costs. The third offense penalty is $10 million. The 20/20 Plan cannot let the lives of citizens be stolen, compromised or destroyed."

"That should get the attention of people who don't value the lives of others," Tom said. "I can't see how anyone would disagree with the 20/20 Plan on this. Most people will applaud it and the other measures in this chapter. Citizens have grown tired of criminals invading their lives and their computers."

"Some history will help everyone understand the 20/20 Plan better," Genie said. "Sources such as the non-profit Identity Theft Resource Center sub-divide identity theft into five categories:

1. Criminal identity theft *(posing as another person when apprehended for a crime)*
2. Financial identity theft *(using another's identity to obtain credit, goods and services)*
3. Identity cloning *(using another's information to assume his or her identity in daily life)*
4. Medical identity theft *(using another's identity to obtain medical care or drugs)*
5. Child identity theft

"Prior to 1998, crimes that would now be considered identity theft were charged under "false personation" statutes, which go back to the late 19th century. False personation is defined as "the crime of falsely assuming the identity of another to gain a benefit or avoid an expense. In 1998, Congress passed the Identity Theft and Assumption Deterrence Act. It made identity theft a federal crime. The act strengthened the criminal laws governing identity theft. It made it a federal crime to knowingly transfer, or use, without lawful authority, a means of identification of another person with the intent to commit, or to aid or abet, any unlawful activity that constitutes a violation of Federal law, or that constitutes a felony under any applicable state or local law.

"Identity theft may be used to facilitate, or fund, other crimes including illegal immigration, terrorism, phishing and espionage. There are cases of identity cloning to attack payment systems, including online credit card processing and medical insurance," Genie concluded while Dave was pulling into a parking space at the plant on a beautiful Friday morning. They completed the 20/20 Plan solution to technology and the internet. Dave knew this had to be enacted.

1. The Internet began with the development of electronic computers in the 1950s.

2. The Internet has had a revolutionary impact on culture and commerce.

3. Security disasters are imminent as hackers attack routers rather than computers.

4. Most Americans have computers, but few know how to diagnose and resolve computer issues.

5. The 20/20 Plan protects Americans left behind in the age of electronic technology.

6. The 20/20 Plan is committed to preventing hacking and espionage.

7. The FBI has a website to report potential e-scams.

8. The United States is far behind the curve in relation to high tech crime.

9. The 20/20 Plan makes foreign hacking into the USA an act of war.

10. Net Neutrality will put an end to this new exciting innovation called the Internet.

11. Twenty years ago, the federal government had better technology at work.

12. Today, citizens have computers and other electronic devices more powerful than government technology.

13. The federal government's $80 billion budget for IT spending is higher than that of any organization in the world.

14. Many workers in the public sector are sharing archaic forms of information.

15. Health care is monstrously inefficient.

16. Congress passed the Identity Theft and Assumption Deterrence Act in 1998.

17. The 20/20 Plan makes identity theft a serious felony.

18. Child identity theft is now on the rise.

19. Actions have consequences.

20. Hacking and identity theft now have severe consequences.

Political Correctness and Civility

"I got a feeling about political correctness. I hate it. It causes us to lie silently instead of saying what we think." — Hal Holbrook, American Film and Stage Actor

---

FRIDAY AFTERNOON. WEEK 3.

Another week of work was nearing an end as the team completed their reports and made plans for the next week. The project was in great shape. They felt more focused and more productive. They scheduled key meetings for the next week and they were looking forward to completing their special project: The 20/20 Plan as well. They soon left their office and headed to the blue rental car in the parking lot. Dave was anxious to get them moving so they could arrive at the airport on time. Ron started the conversation. "Remember the days before political correctness mugged the country. Most of us became fully aware of it in the 1990s. Most of what I have researched states its modern day origins with Marxism.

> ### *Political Correctness*
> po•lit•i•cal cor•rect•ness — noun — the avoidance, often considered as taken to extremes, of forms of expression or action that are perceived to exclude, marginalize, or insult groups of people who are socially disadvantaged or discriminated against.

"From "An Accuracy in Academia Address" by Bill Lind began with the question, "Where does all this stuff that you've heard about this morning – the victim feminism, the gay rights movement, the invented statistics, the rewritten history, the lies, the demands, all the rest of it – where does it come from? For the first time in our history, Americans have to be fearful of what they say, of what they write, and of what they think. They have to be afraid of using the wrong word, a word denounced as offensive or insensitive, or racist, sexist, or homophobic.

"We have seen other countries, particularly in this century, where this has been the case. We have always regarded them with a mixture of pity, and to be truthful, some amusement, because it has struck us as so strange that people would allow a situation to develop where they would be afraid of what words they used. We now have this situation in this country. We have it primarily on college campuses, but it is spreading throughout the whole society. Where does it come from? What is it?

"We call it "Political Correctness." The name originated as something of a joke, literally in a comic strip, and we tend still to think of it as only half-serious. In fact, it is deadly serious. It is the great disease of our century. It is the disease of ideology. PC is not funny. PC is deadly serious. If we look at it analytically, if we look at it historically, we quickly find out exactly what it is. Political Correctness is cultural Marxism. It is Marxism translated from economic into cultural terms. It is an effort that goes back not to the 1960s and the hippies and the peace movement, but back to World War I. If we compare the basic tenets of Political Correctness with classical Marxism the parallels are very obvious."

"That is a very strong statement," Genie interjected. "Do you think most people take political correctness that seriously?" Ron replied, "it's a very controversial subject. Some people are very emotionally involved; others are burned out over PC. The words are chilling because Americans believe in the 1st Amendment and do not want people to tell them what to say, no matter how stupid their remarks are, or if they say something insensitive.

The 20/20 Plan believes in, and wholeheartedly endorses, civility. Civility may be a bigger issue for Americans. Too many people are locked into their electronic devises and don't take the time to speak to others. The age of technology has eroded our 'people skills.' In addition, we have become more intolerant, as we tell others how tolerant they need to be. Doesn't make sense. The country needs leadership to put us on the right course. The 20/20 Plan for education and job training will put Americans back on the course to civility.

Ron said, "many people find words offensive. Others find them insensitive. Some won't agree with what is said. What is important is that everyone have the right to express an opinion. All should have the courage to speak their mind. The courage to speak is missing in an America that has become devastatingly polarized. The 20/20 Plan resolves this problem with its education and training programs. The youth of America will learn at an early age to support each other. Civility is reinforced and affirmed. It emphasizes the fact that all Americans have an important role to play in the prosperity of the republic.

"Successful people build each other up. They motivate, inspire, and push each other. They treat each other civilly and they are eager to support each other. Unsuccessful people are polarizing'" Ron continued. "They hate, blame and complain. That behavior is leading America down the wrong path. The path of destruction. A citizen who made some controversial remarks is Gene Simmons of Kiss. Read what he said in an interview with host Ricky Camilleri concerning political correctness, and why people should speak their native language as opposed to English: (Be warned that the language is colorful.)

"Why? Because he learned "goddamn English" and embraced America's melting pot instead of separatism.

"I'm actually saying the thing that needs to be said because the politically correct climate is bullsh*t," Simmons said. "You don't want to upset anybody by saying, 'Learn to speak goddamn English.' If you make the effort, then all the possibilities of this culture will open up for you and give you all the rewards that I've gotten.

"He said immigrants must "agree to one culture that we can all communicate with and then go off and speak Swahili and Farsi and whatever you want to talk."

"In America I've learned you have an inferred fiduciary duty to learn how to speak English," he said. "Get rid of your accent. I did. Be a legal immigrant. I'm a legal immigrant. Come to the country, just buckle your knees a little bit, make the effort to learn the culture, assimilate to the point that you can, you are all proud of who you are and where you come from . . . great, whatever you are proud of, just tip your hat to America, which is the melting pot that makes it all possible."

"More important than his message against political correctness, which Simmons said only prevents immigrants from succeeding, was how he did not back down from liberal host Ricky Camilleri. He even called him out on his biases and project. He successfully used Arianna Huffington's life experiences to hammer home his point to the host, who was left speechless and stumbling for words." Ron continued.

"You were correct, Ron," Genie spoke up. "Strong words to make a strong point. The 20/20 Plan encourages civility and as consultants we never use off color language. But I certainly defend his right to use whatever language he wants, and I absolutely applaud his courage." Ron jumped in, "I have another article that provides nineteen examples of political correctness. This is from an article I read by Michael Snyder in 2013. Wish he had 20 examples.

The following are 19 shocking examples of how political correctness is destroying America:

1. The Missouri State Fair has permanently banned a rodeo clown from performing just because he wore an Obama mask, and now all of the other rodeo clowns are being required to take "sensitivity training." But the state commission went further, saying it will require that before the Rodeo Cowboy Association can take part in any future state fair, "they must provide evidence to the director of the Missouri State Fair that they have proof that all officials and subcontractors of the MRCA have successfully participated in sensitivity training."

2. Government workers in Seattle have been told that they should no longer use the words "citizen" and "brown bag" because they are potentially offensive.

3. A Florida police officer recently lost his job for calling Trayvon Martin a "thug" on Facebook.

4. "Climate change deniers" are definitely not wanted at the U.S. Department of the Interior. Interior Secretary Sally Jewell was recently quoted as making the following statement: "I hope there are no climate-change deniers in the Department of Interior".

5. A professor at Ball State University was recently banned from even mentioning the concept of intelligent design because it would supposedly "violate the academic integrity" of the course that he was teaching.

6. The mayor of Washington D.C. recently asked singer Donnie McClurkin not to attend his own concert because of his views on homosexuality.

7. U.S. Senator Chuck Schumer is calling on athletes marching in the opening ceremonies at the Winter Olympics in Sochi next year to "embarrass" Russian President Vladimir Putin by protesting for gay rights.

8. Chaplains in the U.S. military are being forced to perform gay marriages, even if it goes against their personal religious beliefs. The few chaplains that have refused to follow orders know that it means the end of their careers.

9. The governor of California has signed a bill into law which will allow transgendered students to use whatever bathrooms and gym facilities that they would like. Transgendered students in California will now have the right to use whichever bathrooms they prefer and join either the boys' or girls' sports teams, thanks to landmark legislation signed by Democratic Gov. Jerry Brown on Monday. The law amends the state's education code, and stipulates that each student will have access to facilities, sports teams, and programs that are "consistent with his or her gender identity," rather than the student's actual biological composition. A male student who self-identifies as female could therefore use the girls' bathroom, even if he is anatomically male.

10. In San Francisco, authorities have installed small plastic "privacy screens" on library computers so that perverts can continue to exercise their "right" to watch pornography at the library without children being directly exposed to it.

11. In America today, there are many groups that are absolutely obsessed with eradicating every mention of God out of the public sphere. For example, an elementary school in North Carolina ordered a little six-year-old girl to remove the word "God" from a poem that she wrote to honor her two grandfathers that had served in the Vietnam War.

12. A high school track team was disqualified earlier this year because one of the runners "made a gesture thanking God" once he had crossed the finish line.

13. Earlier this year, a Florida Atlantic University student that refused to stomp on the name of Jesus was banned from class.

14. A student at Sonoma State University was ordered to take off a cross that she was wearing because someone "could be offended".

15. A teacher in New Jersey was fired for giving his own Bible to a student that did not own one.

16. Volunteer chaplains for the Charlotte-Mecklenburg Police Department have been banned from using the name of Jesus on government property.

17. According to a new Army manual, U.S. soldiers will now be instructed to avoid "any criticism of pedophilia" and to avoid criticizing "anything related to Islam." The following is from a Judicial Watch article: The draft leaked to the newspaper offers a list of "taboo conversation topics" that soldiers should avoid, including "making derogatory comments about the Taliban," "advocating women's rights," "any criticism of pedophilia," "directing any criticism towards Afghans," "mentioning homosexuality and homosexual conduct" or "anything related to Islam."

18. The Obama administration has banned all U.S. government agencies from producing any training materials that link Islam with terrorism. In fact, the FBI has gone back and purged references to Islam and terrorism from hundreds of old documents.

19. According to the Equal Employment Opportunity Commission, it is illegal for employers to discriminate against criminals as it has a "disproportionate" impact on minorities.

"It would be hard to overstate the power all this relentless "thought training" has on us. Young people are particularly susceptible to the power of suggestion," Ron continued.

"If you say the 'wrong thing' in America today, you might be penalized, fired or even taken to court. Political correctness is running rampant, and it is absolutely destroying this nation. In the novel 1984, George Orwell imagined a future world where speech was greatly restricted. He called the language the totalitarian state in his novel created 'Newspeak,' because it bears a striking resemblance to the political correctness we see in America today.

"Wikipedia calls 'Newspeak,' a reduced language created by the totalitarian state as a tool to limit free thought, and concepts that pose a threat to the regime such as freedom, self-expression, creativity, individuality, peace, etc. Any form of thought alternative to the party's construct is classified as 'thought crime.'"

"People are not usually being hauled off to prison for what they are saying just yet, but we are heading down that path. Every single day, the mainstream media in the United States bombards us with subtle messages about what we should believe and what "appropriate speech" consists of. Most of the time, most Americans quietly fall in line with this unwritten speech code. In fact, most of the time we enforce this unwritten speech code among each other. Those who dare buck the system discover the consequences can be rather severe."

"It's hard to believe these actions are taking place in America, the land of the free and the home of the brave," Tom said. "A lot of things have changed in America over the past few decades. These are not bad people. They are misguided, and misled, by their zeal to protect others. They just go too far. They actually harm people and the nation. Common sense clearly must now be called uncommon sense because it is so rare in the United States.

"People are divided, separated and polarized by politics and ideology," Ron said. "Teddy Roosevelt said it is an outrage to discriminate against any such man because of creed, or birthplace, or origin. This is predicated upon the person becoming an American, and nothing but an American in every facet of life. President Theodore Roosevelt also said in an address to the Knights of Columbus in New York City on October 12, 1915:

"There is no room in this country for hyphenated Americanism. When I refer to hyphenated Americans, I do not refer to naturalized Americans. Some of the very best Americans I have ever known were naturalized Americans, Americans born abroad. But a hyphenated American is not an American at all."

"This is just as true of the man who puts "native" before the hyphen as of the man who puts German or Irish or English or French before the hyphen. Americanism is a matter of the spirit and of the soul. Our allegiance must be purely to the United States. We must unsparingly condemn any man who holds any other allegiance."

"But if he is heartily and singly loyal to this Republic, then no matter where he was born, he is just as good an American as anyone else." — Theodore Roosevelt

---

"The one absolutely certain way of bringing this nation to ruin, of preventing all possibility of its continuing to be a nation at all, would be to permit it to become a tangle of squabbling nationalities, an intricate knot of German-Americans, Irish-Americans, English-Americans, French-Americans, Scandinavian-Americans, or Italian-Americans, each preserving its separate nationality, each at heart feeling more sympathy with Europeans of that nationality than with the other citizens of the American Republic."

"The men who do not become Americans and nothing else are hyphenated Americans; and there ought to be no room for them in this country. The man who calls himself an American citizen and who yet shows by his actions that he is primarily the citizen of a foreign land plays a thoroughly mischievous part in the life of our body politic. He has no place here; and the sooner he returns to the land, to which he feels his real heart-allegiance, the better it will be for every good American." — Theodore Roosevelt

"Those words of Teddy Roosevelt from 100 years ago ring true today," Ron said. "Hyphens divide people. In order for America to be strong, all citizens must stand together. It makes no sense for Americans to allow politicians to pit citizens against each other. Politicians have indoctrinated Americans to follow the rhetoric of the political party they think they must owe their allegiance. Americans have been conditioned to adore politicians as if they were deities. Adoration of politicians is truthfully a form of insanity. Americans must stop this ideological warfare. Why? Americans must stand together. We all really want the same thing. We all want prosperity. We all want a better life for our families. We all want a bright future for our children and grandchildren. We all want the United States be a strong country that will keep us safe.

"Citizens of both political parties go to work together. We work together. We go out to dinner together. We pray together. Americans of both political parties stand and sing the National Anthem at sporting events together. We all root for the home team no matter our political affiliation. So why do we fall for the politicians and their political persuasion. We are neighbors who live next door to each other. If one of our children is injured, do we say 'I'm not going to help that child; his parents belong to the other political party.' No, we rush to their aid.

"Then if we can do all these things together, why can't we stand together to make America strong once again. Americans have to realize the adoration of politicians is insanity. They are dividing us for their own political gain and power by training us to believe their idiotic ideology is best for us. Most politicians 'do not' believe what they themselves profess. We keep voting for them and we continue to receive the same result.

"That is the definition of insanity. We keep voting for one side or the other and both sides continue to run up the national debt at the speed of sound, while they live the life of splendor in the nations' capital pulling in 3 to 4 times the amount that average citizens are paid. Furthermore, as soon as they are elected, they start campaigning and fundraising for their re-election. "America today is in the throes of the greatest and most extreme transformation of the past 250 years. America is an ideological state. We are a country with an official state ideology enforced by the power of the state. Congress is now moving to expand this insanity ever further. Affirmative action is part of it. The terror against anyone who dissents from Political Correctness on campus is part of it. It is what we see happening in China, North Korea, Russia and the Middle East. Terrorists want to kill Americans and tolerance is mandated as they cut off the heads of our fellow citizens. We must acknowledge Political Correctness is destroying this great nation and leaving no hope for our children and grandchildren. Whom do we do this for? We do it to keep politicians in office so they can ransom our future while we lose our freedom and our culture."

Dave turned into the airport Rental Car Return lane a little early. The team was revved up. They had a very productive trip and they didn't want to be politically correct. They felt that to act with civility and treat everyone, as they would like to be treated was the best course for America.

Americans need to be Americans, not anyone else or part American and part something else. Everyone in this country has to pull together and support each other. They all felt good about their progress. The 20/20 Plan was 90 percent complete and it will bring Americans who work together back together again.

The 20/20 Vision will bring us in alignment with the vision of the Founding Fathers. The previous eighteen chapters provide the framework for the "Escape Plan for America: the 20/20 Plan."

CHAPTER EIGHTEEN | *Political Correctness and Civility Summary*

1. Political Correctness has its modern day origin with Marxism.

2. Citizens are afraid to say the wrong word; afraid of what they write; and what they think.

3. In some states, citizens are not allowed to use the word citizen.

4. PC is the great disease of our century. It is the disease of ideology.

5. All citizens should have the right to express an opinion.

6. George Orwell imagined a future world where speech was greatly restricted in his novel 1984.

7. Unsuccessful people are polarizing. They hate, blame and complain.

8. All Americans must stand together and communicate in English.

9. Examples of restricted speech, or actions, are in the news every day.

10. Politics have divided, separated and polarized the nation.

11. May people are misguided or have been misled in order to protect people.

12. There is no room in this country for hyphenated Americanism.

13. Americanism is a matter of the spirit and of the soul.

14. Hyphens divide people. We are all Americans and we are in this together.

15. Americans must resist the power of politicians to divide us.

16. We are neighbors who live next door to each other. We must stand together.

17. The 20/20 Plan endorses civility.

18. The 20/20 Plan unites the nation. It give us a common purpose.

19. The 20/20 Plan will make America strong and give us a bright future.

20. The 20/20 plan brings us in alignment with the Founding Fathers vision.

CHAPTER NINETEEN

The Operation
of the Government

"Money and corruption are ruining the land, crooked politicians betray the working man, pocketing the profits and treating us like sheep, and we're tired of hearing promises that we know they'll never keep." — Ray Davies, The Kinks, Money and Corruption

MONDAY MORNING. WEEK 4.

All four were excited and ready to go to work. Did they forget it was Monday morning? They were looking forward to the next subject in the 20/20 Plan. Their next task was to demystify the method by which the government operates.

"The federal government has a process by which it operates. Actually more than one process. How effective and efficient those processes are is up for debate, or better yet assessment." Tom stated, "It would take years to explain how the entire government operates, and that won't serve our purpose here."

"Most Americans would just say cut to the chase," Dave interjected. "The American people don't have confidence in the government at any level. Most people are afraid of the federal government. The federal government is dysfunctional, bloated, has unlimited powers, operates at a fiscal loss and is largely incompetent. Few government workers are motivated; few know what they are doing, or what anyone else in the government is doing. Nobody could possibly fix this mess no matter how hard they tried."

"Hold on there, big guy," Genie piped up. "You and most Americans are probably right, but the 20/20 Vision is more than capable of designing and implementing a solution for the taxpayers. I won't argue with your attempt to boil it down to one small paragraph, and I don't disagree with anything you said, but, and there is always a 'but,' the 20/20 Plan can put the federal government back on the right course.

We have already solved most of the glaring issues that cause the federal government to be so ineffective and inefficient. Remember the old saying about taking one bite out of the elephant at a time. Well in this case, we have a two-course meal. A healthy serving of an elephant and a donkey. Furthermore, we can eat them both at the same time, one bite at a time."

"Absolutely," Tom stated empathically. "The plan is to design an integrated, comprehensive process and then implement that process. Issues must be corrected immediately and then publish reports to the taxpayers. The first step is to trim the fat and dispose of the extra parts or byproducts. The 20/20 Plan trims the agencies and bureaus that are overreaching, or performing redundant services and activities the states are currently performing. There are agencies and bureaus that do not provide services the taxpayers require. Those agencies must be eliminated. Thus, the elephant and the donkey are now reduced down to a manageable meal.

"That makes sense Tom," Dave said. "As a team, we can typically make an assessment of a client's facility in two weeks. The federal government has a lot of agencies and facilities. How does the 20/20 Plan take that on?"

"Remember when we worked for the power generation company that had twenty power plants?" Tom said. "We had a team of two consultants assigned to each facility and we completed the assessments in two weeks. The same principal applies with the federal government. One person, or one team, is not tasked with the entire project. It must be broken down into sizable bites. The 20/20 Plan has already done most of the foundation work, or the prep work, if we keep it in food terms. Let's write the plan now, and in the next chapter, we'll map out our implementation strategy.

"The 20/20 Plan starts with the budget. Agencies and bureaus cannot function without funding. The 20/20 Plan utilizes a balanced budget based on percentages. Congress must perform this task. Currently, Congress is passing 'Continuing Resolutions.' The national debt continues to soar. The balanced budget is the first step in the process. This eliminates the opposition party from complaining about budget cuts when there never are budget cuts, just budgets that aren't as big as they want them to be. The balloon is blown up, just not puffed up as big as they prefer.

"The actual appropriations bills for the fiscal year must be enacted by both houses of Congress. The President, in accordance with the United States budget process, must then sign these bills before they are enacted. The 20/20 Plan takes the disagreements out of the process, as only a set percentage of funding can be appropriated to each line item.

"Each governmental department, agency and bureau submits their part of the budget annually. Managers at all federal agencies must conduct reviews to develop their plans for the services they perform in conjunction with the employees they need. When the federal government faces a shutdown, the laws and regulations governing shutdowns separate federal workers into "essential" and "non-essential." The preferred term is now "excepted" and "non-excepted." This was changed in 1995 because "non-essential" was politically incorrect.

"The 20/20 Plan conducts a thorough proficiency and productivity review of all federal government employees in every department, agency and bureau to determine which tasks employees are required to perform and then determine how many employees are actually required to operate the government. How do the taxpayers know if each agency/department has the exact number of employees? Every institution needs to be streamlined. We will utilize our lean management techniques to eliminate wasted or lost time, effort or money by identifying each step in the process and then revise and eliminate steps that do not create value. This is essential for the taxpayer funded federal government.

'In the government shutdown of 2013 about 800,000 federal employees were to be sent home. That left 1.3 million 'excepted' (essential) federal workers; 1.4 million active-duty military members; 500,000 Postal Service workers, and other employees in independently funded agencies who would continue to work.

"The federal government continues to hire almost 100,000 new employees ever year. Some of the new hires replace employees because of retirement, attrition or other reasons. The remainder of new hires are government growth. Federal government civilian employment had grown to 2,792,736 in 2012. The estimated annual payroll for federal government employees is more than $200 billion, not including the many contract workers the federal government hires. More than 200,000 are part time employees. The federal government does not keep employment statistics for contract workers. Incredible! Blows the mind!

"State governments employ more than five million full and part workers with an annual payroll estimated at $250 billion. Federal and state governments' total annual payroll is more than $450 Billion. Many of these employees perform valuable services the republic undeniably requires. On the other hand, does the nation require all of these services? Are all of these services effective and beneficial to the nation?

"Does every department need the total number of employees they employ? Does every federal employee have the thorough training required to perform his or her job at the highest standard? Do the departments have the latest technology to work with? Are effective work processes in place to achieve the best results? The 20/20 Implementation Plan evaluates these issues, implements corrective solutions and puts proficient work standards in place to measure performance. The taxpayers deserve no less.

"Does the government need all of these employees? Again, getting exact up to date numbers is very difficult with the government. A few examples of major departments are:

DEPARTMENT	NUMBER OF EMPLOYEES
Department of Commerce	46,420
Department of Defense	800,000
Department of Energy	13,814
Environmental Protection Agency	16,205
Department of HHS	78,198
Department of Homeland Security	231,117
Department of HUD	8,709
Department of Interior	72,562
Department of Justice	114,486
Department of Labor	16,304
NASA	18,134
Social Security Administration	62,343
Department of Treasury	112,461
Department of Transportation	55,468
Department of Veterans Affairs	332,025

U.S. Postal Service: The Postal Service is self-funded.
Supreme Court and federal courts. Not Available.
Federal Reserve Is Not a Federal Agency

"An estimated 2 million Americans work on federal contracts. In an article written by Joseph Gitter in April 2014, he asks: 'How many Americans work in government? That's a more difficult question to answer than you would think. Officially, as of 2009, the federal government employed 2.8 million individuals out of a total U.S. workforce of 236 million, or just over one percent of the workforce.'

"But that isn't the entire picture. Add in uniformed military personnel, and the figure goes up to just under 4.4 million. There are also 66,000 people who work in the legislative branch and federal courts. That makes the total figure about 2 percent of the workforce. "Even that doesn't tell the full story. Contractors— do a lot of government work from arms manufacturers to local charities, from environmental advocacy groups to university researchers. Taxpayers fund much of the work these companies and individuals perform. They should count as part of the federal government workforce as well. Unfortunately, we cannot ask the Office of Personnel Management (OPM) how many government contractors and grantees there are. Remember, they do not keep such records!"

"Perhaps we should ask the American taxpayers if they want to pay for all of those salaries, or if they can afford to pay those salaries?" Ron challenged.

"Professor Paul Light, of New York University, has estimated the size of these shadowy branches of government," Tom jumped back in. "He points out, while there are many good reasons for the government to use contractors, the use of contracts and grants also hides the true size of government. The federal government uses contracts, grants, and mandates to state and local governments to hide its true size, thereby creating the illusion that it is smaller than it actually is, and give its departments and agencies much greater flexibility in hiring labor, thereby creating the illusion that the civil-service system is somehow working effectively. OPM's failure to keep records of the number of quasi-governmental employees indicates a lack of accountability, as Professor Light says:

"Contractors and grantees do not keep count of their employees, in part because doing so would allow the federal government . . . to estimate actual labor costs."

"Nevertheless, Professor Light was able to come up with some useful estimates by using the federal government's procurement database. When he added up all the numbers, he found that the true size of the federal government was about 11 million: 1.8 million civil servants, 870,000 postal workers, 1.4 million military personnel, 4.4 million contractors, and 2.5 million grantees. However, there is more.

"State and local governments dwarf Washington in direct employment. According to the U.S. Census Bureau, there are 3.8 million full-time and 1.5 million part-time employees on state payrolls. Local governments add a further 11 million full-time and 3.2 million part-time personnel. This means state and local governments combined employ 19.5 million people. When we add up the true size of the federal workforce — civil servants, postal workers, military personnel, contractors, grantees, and bailed-out businesses — and add in state- and local-government employees — civil servants, teachers, firefighters, and police officers — we reach the astonishing figure of nearly 40 million Americans employed in some way by government. That indicates about 17 percent of the American labor pool — one in every six workers — owes its living to the taxpayer.

Dave looked back at Ron in shock. "One of six of us work for the government? How can that be?" Dave asked. "Is that right? If I walk into a restaurant, one out of every six diners works for the government. That means the other five of us are buying that person dinner. When I walk into a store, one of the shoppers is buying stuff the other five of us have to pay for. That's crazy. I can't afford that kind of largess."

"The 20/20 Vision cannot verify the above statistics. They are certainly an indicator of how large government is and how high the price of government is to the taxpayer. There is another cost government compels US citizens pay. However, it is not direct taxes paid to the various governments. It is the astronomical cost regulations add to all goods and services Americans purchase for everyday living expenses.

"In an article by Jennifer Harper in The Washington Times on Friday, May 2, 2014, she wrote: *"Yes, someone is actually tracking the hidden weight of all those pesky federal regulations. Here's the startling news: it cost Americans $1.9 trillion last year to comply with myriad rules and protocols that are issued at the rate of 3,500 a year - this according to one Clyde Wayne Crews, vice President for policy at the Competitive Enterprise Institute.' The regulations are, in essence, like a hidden tax, he says."*

"Federal agencies are churning out thousands of new regulations every year.

Does the American citizen need to be regulated to that extent?

Do all of these regulations improve the quality, and/or safety of our daily lives? Some of them are needed and some of them may be nice to have, but do the benefits justify the enormous costs in dollars and freedom?"

"Let me get this straight?" Dave asked. "Complying with government regulations adds $1.9 trillion to everything we purchase. That is more than $6,000.00 per year for each man, woman and child residing in this country. What's next? I like people but I can't afford this much charity. Does this come out of our paychecks?"

"Indirectly, yes. That is one way of putting it," Tom replied. "When you buy things with the money you bring home in your paycheck, you are buying regulations to the tune of about ten percent more for each item you purchase. It's included in all goods and services. It amounts to a small amount here, and a small amount there, and it adds up to buying $6,000.00 of regulations per year. It is similar to a value added tax on all purchases and most costly regulations need to be eliminated.

"The American people need to decide, do they want, and need, the large amount of government they are getting, or can they get along in their daily lives with less government? Do 'We the People' want to regain liberty and have freedom from reporting to the government our wages and expenses every year? Do we want to eliminate the more than 114,000 IRS Agents that have total power over our finances?"

As the team arrived at work on Monday morning, they were engrossed in a conversation about their past experiences. They recounted how many corporations had engaged the consultants to design and implement effective work management processes and systems to enable organizations to optimize their customer service, maximize their profits and reduce their operating costs. The 20/20 Plan operates a smaller, more effective limited government whose sole purpose is to serve the citizens on the United States of America.

CHAPTER NINETEEN | *The Operation of Government Summary*

1. The federal government operates at a loss causing the national debt to balloon.

2. The federal government has grown too large to serve citizens effectively.

3. Many Americans fear their government.

4. The federal government has become an unlimited entity that has lost its purpose.

5. American citizens are losing confidence in a dysfunctional federal government.

6. The 20/20 Plan assesses the operation of the federal government.

7. The 20/20 Plan designs and implements solutions to serve the people.

8. Is there true accountability in the government, or is it just number crunching?

9. 2.8 million federal government employees cost $200 billion annually.

10. 5 million state government employees cost $250 billion annually.

11. 40 million Americans are employed in some way by government at what cost?

12. One of six Americans are employed by the various government agencies.

13. Government contractors and grantees do not keep count of their employees.

14. 3,500 rules and regulations are issued every year by the government.

15. Citizens spend $1.9 trillion annually to comply with these regulations.

16. Each American purchase $6,000.00 worth of government regulations annually.

17. Regulations add an additional 10 percent purchasing tax to Americans take home pay.

18. The overburden of regulations jeopardizes freedom and liberty.

19. The 20/20 Plan operates a smaller, more effective government.

20. The sole purpose of the government is to serve and protect its citizens.

21. Can Americans afford the high price of government inefficiency?

22. Do Americans want to pay the high price of government regulations?

CHAPTER TWENTY

Implementing the 20/20 Plan

"To sit back hoping that someday, some way, someone will make things right is to go on feeding the crocodile, hoping he will eat you last - but eat you he will." — Ronald Reagan

MONDAY AFTERNOON. WEEK 4.

The morning discussions during the ride to work left the team in a somber mood. They were convinced the rapid growth and enormous size of the federal government was stifling the American economy, the daily lives, the freedom and the liberty of all Americans. It clearly was destroying ownership and entrepreneurism. America was being led down a path from which it could never recover if left unchecked. The 20/20 Vision is unmistakably the escape plan for America. The 20/20 Plan solutions are solid, sound and ready to be implemented.

The implementation time for the 20/20 Plan is now, or never. When a person is diagnosed with cancer, they don't wait until they have one day to live. They seek immediate care and cure. They do not procrastinate. The nation has a 'deep-rooted dysfunctional' cancer with only a short time to live. The cancer is diagnosed. It must be cured today before the Republic passes away.

The 20/20 Plan outlines chapter by chapter what must be achieved to give Americans a bright and booming future. The American people have the ability to implement the 20/20 Plan. They just need the federal government to get out of their way. The people have given too much authority and tax money to the government. Washington squandered the authority, money and trust of the American people. Now Americans must take that authority back and govern themselves. This is right time to take it back and they are ready, willing and able to do so.

Tom started the conversation as they pulled onto the road leading back to the hotel. "Many initiatives must be put in place immediately. Some processes will take longer to implement than others. All are equally important, just as every citizen is equally important. Some initiatives may require more analysis than others.

"Implementation does not occur in a vacuum, nor does it happen because it is articulated, or written, in eloquent prose. Implementation is hard work accomplished by the participation of all. The voters must elect a President who is unconditionally committed to the 20/20 Vision. The voters must elect Senators and Representatives to Congress and then send them to Washington with the message that they want the entire 20/20 Plan implemented immediately. Each citizen must challenge themselves and their fellow citizens to participate in and cooperate with the principles and techniques of the 20/20 Plan to change the pervasive path our beautiful America is on to a new path of prosperity leading our children to a bright future.

"Remember those 27 bullet points we listed in Chapter Three to design the 20/20 Plan? Those issues provided the guidance needed to chart the implementation course. The implementation plan specifies the 'what' and the 'how' of the 20/20 Plan. An implementation schedule to specify the 'who' and the 'when' will be determined when the 20/20 Plan is activated by the voters. Let's review our notes and meet in the hotel tonight. Pizza and soft drinks are on me."

"I'm all in for that," Dave said enthusiastically. Everyone agreed this was a good plan. As the team sat around the small conference room table of the hotel lobby, littered with pizza boxes, soft drinks and napkins, they started the difficult task of writing down the major implementation points of the 20/20 Plan:

1. Enact a Balanced Budget to achieve a robust growing US economy based on Free Market Capitalism. (Chapter 5)

i. Free Market Capitalism is an economic system that minimizes governmental intervention and maximizes market performance. The Free Market is based on the most efficient use of rational economic actors to deal with goods and services. Government regulations, trade barriers and labor laws block the free market. The free market creates market and price competition for consumers as it creates successful businesses and jobs.

ii. A vibrant, growing American economy achieves the goals and common purpose of the republic to self-govern, explore and create.

a. Each federal department and agency will be instructed to submit a budget to operate their entity for the next fiscal year. Each instruction will include the anticipated funding based on the balanced budget allocation to serve as a guideline for the entity. The budget process will consider the services the department offers and the activities the department, or agency, is engaged in. Each entities' budget is then submitted to the executive branch for review and compilation in the overall federal budget.

b. The Executive Branch compiles all budgets plus the executive budget and submits it to Congress for review, input, adjustment and presentation. The budget must not exceed the forecasted annual revenue and must conform to the guidelines established by the predetermined budget percentages not to exceed 100 percent of revenues.

c. Both houses of Congress must then detail out the line item budget and vote to approve the budget before sending it to the President to sign into law.

d. Issue a directive to abolish Capital Gains Taxes in order to stimulate new investments, both domestic and foreign; and to create confidence in the American economy, which in turn will generate robust tax revenues.

e. Issue a directive to abolish corporate taxes to eliminate the oppressive burden of tax preparation and reporting; and provide the stimulus for economic growth thus ensuring new vibrant employment in all sectors.

2. Funding the federal, state and county governments. (Chapter 5)

a. An executive directive is issued to all government agencies to abolish all taxes, currently in effect, and being collected at all levels of federal, state, county and local governments.

b. Issue an executive directive to all state governments instructing them to collect the Twenty Percent Retail Tax on all transactions of goods and services that occur in their states in lieu of the current state sales taxes. Food, rent, banking charges, prescription medicine, educational expenses, school vouchers and medical expenses are exempt from this Retail Tax. Tax alcohol, tobacco, drugs and other illicit services at the rates prescribed in Chapter 5. Tax internet sales at the prescribed rate.

c. The IRS will continue to process and collect tax returns from the previous year. The IRS will cease to collect corporate and personal income and other taxes from that point on. The Department of the Treasury will be instructed to collect the revenues generated from the Retail Tax from each state as prescribed above.

d. The Department of the Treasury will send monthly appropriations to each state in accordance with the taxes collected from that state. The states will disburse 50 percent of the federal funds to the appropriate counties and maintain 50 percent for the state budget. Internet sales will be credited to the county and state of the purchaser.

e. Each state makes provisions for all business entities and employers located in their respective states to register with the state and declare the employment status of each person they compensate. Each business entity and employer, including contractors and self-employed workers register with their state in compliance with the directives applying to conducting business and commerce.

f. Each employer calculates the 20/20 Plan wage for each employee in accordance with the instructions in Chapter 5. This will eliminate all previous deductions and adjust each employees take home pay by adding all previous labor costs to the employee. Most employees will receive a 40%-50% take-home pay increase.

g. A directive instructing all states and counties to cease the method of assessing and collecting Real Estate Taxes and to conform with the 20/20 Plan of Real Estate assessments and tax collection.

h. Explorers and extractors of petroleum, ores, etc. will be instructed to pay the 20 percent Extraction Tax in accordance with the 20/20 Plan.

i. An executive directive will be issued to the Bureau of Land Management to expedite all applications involving domestic energy resources and mining ores. Multiagency reviews will be streamlined and eliminated where applicable.

j. Each state will be directed to operate a business registration site to facilitate registration. Businesses that sell alcohol, tobacco, firearms, drugs and prostitution register in separate categories.

3. Service and Employment Training. (Chapter 6)

a. Instruct the Armed Forces to review and assess their missions and staffing requirements.

b. Review the Selective Service System procedures and install necessary adjustments or changes to ensure all male and female citizens register when they reach 18 years of age.

c. Enact a bill to increase pay to all Armed Forces personnel by 20 percent.

d. Enact a bill to increase services and allowances for military personnel including health care, commissaries, etc.

e. Conduct a thorough review of military entrance processing qualifications.

f. Review the Basic Training programs with all Armed Services to discover the best programs for each service to ensure all military personnel are prepared to serve the USA. Establish the two medical academies.

g. Enact the AmericaWorks Career Program into law to grant permission for employers to employ interns in accordance with the 20/20 Plan.

h. Enact the Federal Minimum Wage Rate of $10.00 per hour be paid to all employees including all in the armed forces and the AmericaWorks Career Program.

i. Instruct all banks to create 'Employee Individual Bank Accounts.'

j. Design a Basic Training Program for the AmericaWorks Career Program patterned after the military basic training program with emphasis on job skills.

k. Design the Training Program for the Intermediate Phase of the AmericaWorks Career Program with emphasis on job specific skills.

4. The Department of Defense and the Veterans Administration. (Chapter 7)

a. Conduct a comprehensive review of mission statements, objectives and procedures with all branches of the Armed Forces.

b. Bring all military branches up to full Table of Operations staffing.

c. Streamline the Armed Forces with state of the art equipment and technology.

d. Utilize the Armed Forces to assist the employment training of all citizens.

e. Fold the VA into the Department of Defense.

f. Eliminate the bloated bureaucracy of the Veterans Administration.

g. Review and consolidate all veterans' services to provide exceptional care.

h. Bring all base facilities to state of the art condition.

i. Design the Training Program for the Advanced Phase of the AmericaWorks Career Program with emphasis on job placement and job specific skills.

5. Social Security and Medicare. (Chapter 8)

a. Increase the Social Security Pay to all senior citizens by 20 percent.

b. Pay all Social Security recipients $100.00 per month for Medicare Supplemental Part B.

c. Pay all Social Security recipients $50.00 per month for Medicare Supplemental Part D.

d. Enact law to exempt senior citizens over 85 years of age from Real Estate Tax assessments on primary residences.

e. Enact law to permit citizens to opt out of Social Security.

f. Initiate refund payments to all citizens who opt out of Social Security.

6. Health Care and Science. (Chapter 9)

a. Issue permission for Health Care Insurance policies to be sold across state lines.

b. Instruct Health Insurance providers to streamline and customize health Insurance policies to meet individual purchaser's requirements.

c. Enact price transparency initiatives on Health Insurance Policies.

d. Enact initiatives for hospitals and medical centers to streamline procedures.

e. Place a cap on malpractice insurance claims to reduce medical costs.

f. Review missions and objectives for NASA, NIH and NOAA to bring them in alignment with current and future requirements.

g. Initiate a thorough review of the ISS and determine America's future in space.

h. Energize America by launching a new Space Program.

i. Initiate a thorough review of NIH and implement safety protocols for America's health future.

j. Initiate a thorough review of the NOAA and implement a new program for America's oceanic exploration.

7. Energy, Oil, Gas, Mining and Minerals. (Chapter 10)

a. Initiate resolutions to make exploration, drilling and mining a top priority in America to reduce foreign dependence on these valuable resources.

b. Roll back regulations 20 years to produce oil, gas and ore exploration in America.

c. Streamline and expedite energy and mining permitting in America.

d. Turn over to the states the regulatory authority of the EPA, OSHA and MSHA.

e. Enact initiatives to mine rare earth minerals for use in America and to reduce foreign dependence on theses minerals.

8. International Relations. (Chapter 11)

a. Cancel the membership of the United States in the United Nations.

b. Organize and found a new global organization for the US and other nations with similar governments and moral values.

c. Review and reduce foreign aid to an absolute minimum.

d. Institute new "Peace Corps" to help nations that are in alignment with new US philosophy.

e. Review and implement a new strategy to combat global and domestic terrorism.

9. Education and Poverty. (Chapter 12)

a. Eliminate the Department of Education.

b. Eliminate the Secretary of Education cabinet post.

c. Enact a law that privatizes all education from grades 1 through 12.

d. Instruct the Department of the Treasury to fund education to the states based on education requirements and/or enrolled students.

e. Enact a law that specifies federal funding to the states to provide a voucher program for all students from grades 1 through 12.

f. Enact a law that specifies federal funding to the states to provide a voucher program for all pre-school students attending Day Care.

g. Enact a law that specifies federal funding to the states to provide a voucher program for all students to attend Summer Camp Programs.

h. Enact a law to initiate a work program for college graduates to gain employment that leads to student loan payment.

i. Enact a law to initiate a work program for unemployed adults to gain training and employment that leads to career employment.

j. Enact a law to train all young secondary school graduates for two years at the wage of $10.00 per hour with no tax obligations.

10. Immigration. (Chapter 13)

a. Lock down the southern border of the United States.

b. Issue an Executive Order to initiate a controlled immigration process.

c. Instruct the various federal agencies to enforce all immigration laws.

d. Enact a law to make it a felony to make an unauthorized entry into, or stay, in the US unlawfully.

e. Freeze immigration for one year to sort out the immigration problem.

f. Issue ICE ID Cards and options for all foreign nationals who are currently in the United States without authorization.

g. Give foreign nationals the option to apply for citizenship status.

h. Give foreign nationals the option to apply for work permits.

i. Give foreign nationals the option to depart from the United States.

j. Issue foreign students new requirements to study, and reside, in the US.

k. Review current quotas and institute new realistic immigration quotas.

l. Review current immigration qualifications and requirements.

m. Institute new qualifications and requirements for authorized immigration.

n. Instruct ICE to register all foreign nationals within the United States.

o. Permit foreign nationals currently in the 10 Step naturalization process to continue unimpeded in that process with some new requirements.

p. Instruct foreign nationals who have opted to remain in the United States:

   i. Must carry, and retain, an official ICE ID Card at all times.

   ii. Must report all changes of address, phone and email addresses.

   iii. Must maintain an active email address and monitor it for messages.

   iv. Must enroll in English Classes and pass periodic proficiency tests.

11. Drugs and Substance Abuse. (Chapter 14)

a. Repeal the Comprehensive Drug Abuse Prevention and Control Act of 1970.

b. Repeal, replace, and/or update all previous federal laws concerned with narcotics and all other dangerous drugs.

c. Review current Drug Enforcement Agency missions and objectives and focus the DEA on treatment of victims of substance abuse and the collection of tax revenue from the sale of all drugs.

d. Implement the collection of taxes on drugs at the various rates in the 20/20 Plan.

e. Instruct all law enforcement agencies to strictly enforce the collection of taxes on the sale and purchase of drugs.

f. Provide drug rehabilitation programs for all citizens who volunteer for treatment.

12. The Judicial Process, Prisons and Parole (Chapter 15)

a. Increase Supreme Court Justices to 15 from nine.

b. Set term limits for Supreme Court Justices at 15 years.

c. Increase the number of Federal Circuit Courts to 15 from twelve.

d. Instruct the Justice department to emphasize reducing caseloads to provide fair and swift justice.

e. Instruct the Justice department to refuse to hear frivolous lawsuits including those that have no merit that will further reduce caseloads.

f. Instruct an orderly release of all prisoners except for those who committed violent crimes, or crimes with weapons.

g. Institute training and work programs for parolees.

h. Institute a process to monetarily fine those convicted of crimes and place them in probation programs and/or therapy.

i. Institute programs to educate citizens to change the culture of the nation to one that makes the citizens safe and secure.

13. The Congress and Term Limits (Chapter 16)

a. Repeal the 17th Amendment to enable the states to appoint Senators as representatives of the states.

b. Enact a law that sets House of Representatives terms at two 4-year terms.

c. Enact a law that sets Senators terms at two 6-year terms.

d. Enact a law that sets the President's term at one 6-year term.

e. Mandate Congress to submit annual balanced budgets.

14. Technology and the Internet (Chapter 17)

a. Enact a law that makes foreign hacking into the United States of America an attack on the nation's sovereignty, and an act of war.

b. Enact laws to make hacking into federal government programs and websites a felony.

c. Enact laws to make espionage hacking into federal government programs and websites an act of treason.

d. Enact laws to make hacking into banking and financial institutions programs and websites a felony.

e. Enact laws to make hacking and spreading computer viruses to citizens and private companies and organizations programs and websites a felony.

f. Instruct the FBI to make its' website available to report potential e-scams, hacking, spreading viruses, malware, ransomware, and other devices.

g. Instruct the FBI to vigorously investigate and prosecute all occurrences of hacking, spreading viruses, malware, ransomware, etc.

h. Bring the US governments hardware and software technology up to state of the art conditions with powerful computers and software.

i. Institute software technology to make health care operations efficient.

j. Enact a federal law that makes identity theft a felony with a high priority.

15. Political Correctness and Civility (Chapter 18)

a. Enact a federal law to make English the official language of the USA.

b. Institute language education courses to teach English to all citizens.

c. Change the culture of America to prohibit restricted speech, or actions.

d. Enact laws that prohibit institutions from making regulations based on political correctness.

e. Change the American culture to prohibit political correctness.

f. Change the American culture to prohibit restrictions of speech, or actions.

g. Change the culture of America to help citizens understand that political correctness is used to mislead people.

h. Change all references in the federal government to eliminate hyphenated Americanism.

i. Endorse a culture that sanctions and promotes civility among citizens.

j. Institute an American culture that unites the nation and gives Americans a common purpose that brings us in alignment with the vision of the Founding Fathers to give Americans a bright, viable future.

a. Conduct a joint review of the entire federal government and all of its agencies to determine the feasibility of operating those agencies.

b. Design and implement solutions to serve the citizens based on the joint review.

c. Operate the federal government with a balanced budget to decrease the national debt.

d. Reduce the federal government to a size whereby it can effectively, and efficiently, function to serve the citizens with a unified mission and common purpose.

e. Institute true accountability in the government, not just number crunching.

f. Examine the rules and protocols that are issued every year by the government.

g. Mandate the unique purpose of the government is to serve and protect its citizens.

Things do not happen. Things are made to happen. — John F. Kennedy

---

The team completed charting the major implementation points knowing they had a good comprehensive outline of what needed to happen to put America on the right course. "We haven't put the implementation to a schedule," Tom said. "Any thoughts?" Genie was the first to speak, "All of the major implementation points can begin during the same initial time period. Our country can multitask.

"Some will take more resources than others, and some will take longer than others to implement. When the American people make the decision they want the government to commit to the 20/20 Plan, they will demand it. It will take the leadership of a newly inaugurated President who not only has made the commitment to the 20/20 Plan, but has the experience and the skills to implement complex processes." The other three nodded in agreement, as they were ready to call it a night.

"We need to have our wits about us if we are going to change our country for the better. A highly technological society will not last without a highly responsible citizenry, who are honest and trustworthy, who are sharp and aware of what is going on around them."

— Duke Lakeland, Divided We Are Falling But United We Can Stand!

The Afterword

"There are no easy answers, but there are simple answers. We must have the courage to do what we know is morally right." — Ronald Reagan

TUESDAY MORNING. WEEK 4.

As Dave started the car and everyone fastened seat belts, Tom said, "It took us three full weeks to develop and design the 20/20 Plan. I am proud of everyone, and proud of the good work we accomplished. We were not looking to write watered down weak solutions. That's what politicians do when they compromise. They merge two bad ideas into one worse idea. We were not looking to write solutions that are ineffective, indecisive, indistinct, or inept. The nation has had enough of that foolhardiness with Congress and the current state of affairs caused by an inept federal government.

"We should write an Afterword. I've been giving this some thought throughout the three weeks and want to submit my thoughts for your approval."

"A society grows great when old men plant trees whose shade they know they will never sit in." — Greek proverb

References are deliberately omitted. Everyone needs to do his or her own research. The data and information found on government sites is inconsistent at best. Much of the information in this book is from federal government sites that are mostly incomplete, inconsistent and lagging. No complete list of the numerous agencies and bureaus in the federal government exists.

Government agencies do not use the same programs/software. Some are in WordPerfect, pdf, others in Word or some dinosaur from the past. I must, however, confess to copying and pasting some phrases and passages that expressed my thoughts much better than I ever could. If used, most were paraphrased. Most are in the common domain. If they are not, please accept my regrets. I am not an author. I am a problem solver.

The book is not political in nature. No political parties or ideologies are mentioned. Just the issues Americans face today and the solutions to make America exceptional once more. I wrote and sent many of the solutions in the 20/20 Plan to Congress and both national political party organizations. The only replies I ever received were form letter requests for donations and then more requests for more donations.

I have written and edited more than 300 work process manuals to support my career work. Some say it is a strength, others a weakness. Whatever it was, the successful implementation of processes to change the culture, habits and methods of various organizations was the result. The principles and techniques I learned and applied in business are the same principles and techniques required by all organizations including the federal government.

The 20/20 Vision is based on analytical thinking, using history, background, statistical data analysis, cost-benefit analysis, root cause analysis and the many management and leadership tenets I employed over my career to arrive at common sense solutions to make America safe and prosperous. Most recently I started to put the vision into book form. I completed years of research and then wrote the 20/20 Vision.

"20/20: A Clear Vision for America" is a vision that dates back to the 1980s. I wrote it for 320 million reasons. I wrote it for Americans, not politicians. But especially for our young citizens to sustain our exceptionalism. There are 20 major solutions designed for all Americans with emphasis on the youth of America.

"America grew great two hundred and thirty-nine years ago when our forefathers planted the mighty shade trees of the Constitution, ownership, freedom and liberty for their children's children to enjoy." — Bill Muckler

---

Over the past one hundred years, greedy, corrupt politicians have cut down those mighty shade trees of the Constitution, ownership, freedom and liberty. They have stripped away the branches of the Constitution. They have devalued our currency and placed us in crushing debt. They have stripped away our freedom and independence. Our borders might as well be drawn with a stick in soft dust. The "20/20 Vision" is my blueprint to present the issues and most importantly the solutions to a better life and a brighter future for everyone in the country.

I shared the 20/20 Plan with family, friends and associates. Many times at Saturday Night Dinners at home with family and friends, or as I rode to work in rental cars as an alternative to talking sports and entertainment. While a few of my thoughts were accepted, most were met with something like, "it is what it is" or "you can't fight City Hall."

The author developed every concept in this book. No ideas were copied or pasted. Some concepts are just now being explored and discussed by politicians or in the media. However, no comprehensive solutions exist. It's good to know that some are finally catching up. No matter who gets the credit, it is time to "take back America."

Acknowledgements

"Prosperity does not happen. It is the result of a skilled implementer." — Bill Muckler

The author wishes to acknowledge the following people who contributed to the creation of this book. My late wife Jane sat and listened to my many weekend rants about the federal government and my solutions for over 25 years. She was always gracious and exhibited greater patience than I ever had.

My son Christian has been instrumental in helping me with the mechanics of producing and publishing this book. His varied experiences and insights proved immensely valuable as he also shared with me the thoughts and feelings of those much younger.

My heartfelt thanks go to the twenty patriots who volunteered to read, edit and facilitate the production the 20/20 Vision book, and/or contributed in countless ways, especially my brother Carl Muckler who graciously agreed to write the Preface.

Their dedication and effort are much appreciated. They demonstrated what the 20/20 Vision is all about. People recognizing something special and then doing their best to help make the project successful.

The remarkable twenty are: Sandra Anderson, of Rockledge, Florida; Lorena Backus, of Rockledge, Florida; Matt Deddens of Conroe, Texas; Dr. David Ross Jones of Austin, Texas; Christa Leone of St. Charles, Missouri; Tom Lutz of Bowie, Maryland; Michael Morrison of Los Angeles, California; John Moure of Hilton Head, South Carolina; Carl Muckler of Buckeye, Arizona; Christian Muckler of Jacksonville, Florida; Dick Reynolds of Santa Fe, New Mexico; Diana Roach Rojek of Oxford, New York; Amber Rodrigues of Jacksonville, Florida; Don Smith of Cocoa, Florida; Marc Starcke of Pembrooke Pines, Florida; Don Spann of Greenville, South Carolina; Gary Volosin of Youngstown, Ohio; Dee and Roland Wetzel of St. Charles, Missouri; and Elaine Wichmann of Cocoa, Florida.

Special thanks to Steven Wroczynski of Element One Design, Jacksonville, Florida for his patience, expert graphic design and formatting of "20/20: A Clear Vision for America."

About The Author

Bill Muckler was born and raised in St. Louis, Missouri. He attended the same parochial school for 9 years and graduated from Christian Brothers College High School (an Army Junior ROTC School) in St. Louis. Bill graduated from the University of Missouri-Columbia with a B.A. in Psychology (Personnel Management) with 2 years Air Force ROTC. After graduation, Bill dodged both the draft and jury duty to enter the USMC Officer Candidate Course in Quantico, VA. He was commissioned a Second Lieutenant and spent four and one-half years on active duty and eleven years as a Ready Reservist. He holds the permanent rank of Captain and held a Top Secret Security Clearance.

As an entrepreneur, Bill founded Muckler Typographic Corporation in St. Louis, MO. He was the owner and operator of that small business which provided typography services for Ad Agencies, Art Studios Printers and Lithographers for 10 years.

Bill has been a Work Process Management Consultant for 40 years and eventually an owner and director of a consultancy. His firm assessed business operations, conducted management and leadership training, and implemented process solutions as a problem solver in energy, mining, manufacturing, construction, fabrication, assembly, technology, food processing, health care and communications at more than 300 locations.

Bill has three children: Angela, Christa and Christian; five grandchildren and one great granddaughter. He has lived in St. Louis, Columbia, Ferguson and St. Charles in Missouri; Quantico, Virginia; Kaneohe, Oahu, Hawaii; Panama City, Marco Island, St. Augustine and Cocoa, Florida. He has worked in, visited or travelled to 45 states, eleven countries and numerous islands in many seas.

He is the author of "20/20: A Clear Vision for America" released on 12/18/2014."

THIS BOOK WAS TYPESET IN ADOBE GARAMOND PRO

Chapter Headings have been set to 30pt Regular
Subect Headings have been set to 12pt Bold
Body Copy & Page Headers have been set to 10pt Regular
Call Outs & Quotes have been set to 10pt Bold Italic
Chapter List & Summmaries have been set to 9 point regular